STATE OF WASHINGTON

2016
Washington State
Juvenile Disposition
Guidelines Manual

Washington State
Caseload Forecast Council

State of Washington

Caseload Forecast Council

Derek Stanford, Chair
Washington State Representative

John Braun
Washington State Senator

Jeannie Darneille
Washington State Senator

David Schumacher, Vice Chair
Director, Office of Financial Management

Bruce Chandler
Washington State Representative

Bill Moss
Acting Secretary
Department of Social and Health Services

Council Staff

Elaine Deschamps
Executive Director

Kathleen Turnbow
Confidential Secretary

Jennifer Jones
Research Analyst

Duc Luu
Database and Sentencing
Administration Manager

Erik Cornellier
Deputy Director

Gongwei Chen
Senior Caseload Forecaster

Thuy Le
Research Analyst

Ed Vukich
Senior Caseload Forecaster

Shidong Zhang
Senior Caseload Forecaster

ACKNOWLEDGMENTS

The Caseload Forecast Council acknowledges the work of Ed Vukich, Duc Luu, Thuy Le and Elaine Deschamps in updating, reviewing, proofing, and offering language and formatting suggestions for revisions in the current manual.

The Caseload Forecast Council would like to express a special acknowledgement for the contributions of Todd Dowell, Kitsap County Senior Deputy Prosecutor. Mr. Dowell provided numerous suggestions for improvements to the manual, and drafted a comprehensive revision and expansion of Section I: Juvenile Disposition Guidelines.

The Council acknowledges Judge Ronald Kessler, of the King County Superior Court, for providing the 2016 update for the juvenile portion of the *Criminal Caselaw Notebook©*.

The Council also appreciates the suggestions for improvements and additions to the manual received from users.

We always welcome suggestions for making the manual easier to use.

The Caseload Forecast Council is not liable for errors or omissions in the manual, for sentences that may be inappropriately calculated as a result of a practitioner's or court's reliance on the manual, or for any other written or verbal information related to adult or juvenile sentencing. The scoring sheets are intended to provide assistance in most cases but does not cover all permutations of the scoring rules. If you find any errors or omissions, we encourage you to report them to the Caseload Forecast Council.

FORWARD

The purpose of this manual is to provide a reference for those interested in Washington State's Juvenile Disposition Guidelines. It is not intended to provide legal advice.

The Caseload Forecast Council and its staff are not liable for errors or omissions in the manual, for sentences that may be inappropriately calculated as a result of a practitioner's or court's reliance on the manual, or for any other written or verbal information related to adult or juvenile sentencing. The scoring instructions are intended to provide assistance in most cases but do not cover all permutations of the scoring rules. If you find any errors or omissions, we encourage you to report them to the Caseload Forecast Council.

Copies of the 1996 through 2006 and 2012 through 2016 Juvenile Disposition Guidelines Manuals are available electronically on the Council's website.

> http://www.cfc.wa.gov

Bound copies of the 2012 through 2016 Juvenile Disposition Guidelines Manuals are available for purchase through the web site as well.

Comments or suggestions related to this manual should be directed to:

Ed Vukich
Senior Caseload Forecaster
Washington State Caseload Forecast Council
P.O. Box 40962
Olympia, WA 98504-0962

Telephone: (360) 664-9374
E-mail: Ed.Vukich@cfc.wa.gov

TABLE OF CONTENTS

Contents

The Caseload Forecast Council is not liable for errors or omissions in the manual, for sentences that may be inappropriately calculated as a result of a practitioner's or court's reliance on the manual, or for any other written or verbal information related to adult or juvenile sentencing. The scoring sheets are intended to provide assistance in most cases but does not cover all permutations of the scoring rules. If you find any errors or omissions, we encourage you to report them to the Caseload Forecast Council.

SECTION 1

2016 LAW CHANGES AFFECTING JUVENILE JUSTICE

RCW	RCW Title	Effective Date	Summary	Session Law	Section	Bill Number
RCW 13.50.010	Definitions—Conditions when filing petition or information—Duties to maintain accurate records and access—Confidential child welfare records.	6/9/2016	Specifies that AOC shall maintain an electronic research copy of all records in JIS related to juveniles for research purposes as authorized by the Supreme Court or by state statute. Expands research possibilities by allowing AOC to share the research copy with other governmental agencies under the proper conditions.	Ch. 72	§109	4SHB 1541
RCW 13.50.010	Definitions—Conditions when filing petition or information—Duties to maintain accurate records and access—Confidential child welfare records.	6/9/2016	Specifies that, concerning youth in foster care, DSHS may disclose only those confidential child welfare records that pertain to or may assist with meeting the educational needs of foster youth to another state agency or contracted provider, and that those records retain their confidentiality.	Ch. 71	§2	4SHB 1999
RCW 13.50.010	Definitions—Conditions when filing petition or information—Duties to maintain accurate records and access—Confidential child welfare records.	6/9/2016	Expands the definition of official juvenile court file.	Ch. 93	§2	SHB 2405
RCW 9.41.330	Felony firearm offenders—Determination of registration.	6/9/2019	Establishes provisions under which an offender must be required to register as a felony firearm offender.	Ch. 94	§1	SSB 2410
RCW 13.40.020	Definitions.	6/9/2016	Amends the definition of assessment. Expands the definition of community supervision by including residential treatment.	Ch. 106	§1	ESHB 2746

The Caseload Forecast Council is not liable for errors or omissions in the manual, for sentences that may be inappropriately calculated as a result of a practitioner's or court's reliance on the manual, or for any other written or verbal information related to adult or juvenile sentencing. The scoring sheets are intended to provide assistance in most cases but does not cover all permutations of the scoring rules. If you find any errors or omissions, we encourage you to report them to the Caseload Forecast Council.

RCW	RCW Title	Effective Date	Summary	Session Law	Section	Bill Number
RCW 13.40.0357	Juvenile offender sentencing standards.	6/9/2016	Makes two technical corrections. Adds mental health to the title of chemical dependency disposition alternative.	Ch. 106	§2	ESHB 2746
RCW 13.40.165	Chemical dependency disposition alternative.	6/9/2016	Incorporates the mental health disposition alternative into the chemical dependency disposition alternative.	Ch. 106	§3	ESHB 2746
RCW 13.40.167	Mental health disposition alternative.	6/9/2016	Repeals the mental health disposition alternative.	Ch. 106	§4	ESHB 2746
RCW 13.40.010	Short title—Intent—Purpose.	6/9/2016	Expands the intent/purpose of the Juvenile Justice Act of 1977.	Ch. 136	§1	ESHB 2906
RCW 13.40.020	Definitions.	6/9/2016	Amends the definition of assessment. Amends the definition of community-based rehabilitation.	Ch. 136	§2	ESHB 2906
RCW 13.40.127	Deferred disposition.	6/9/2016	Amends deferred disposition provisions to make deferred disposition presumptive for those who are eligible.	Ch. 136	§3	ESHB 2906
RCW 13.40.308	Juvenile offender adjudicated of taking motor vehicle without permission in the first degree, theft of motor vehicle, possession of a stolen vehicle, taking motor vehicle without permission in the second degree—Minimum sentences.	6/9/2016	Amends provisions concerning taking a motor vehicle without permission in the first degree by: • Removing the minimum $200 fine where the juvenile's prior criminal history score is 0 to ½ points; • Removing the minimum $400 fine where the juvenile's prior criminal history score is ¾ to 1½ points; and • Removing the minimum $400 fine where the juvenile's prior criminal history score is 2 or more points. Amends provisions concerning theft of a motor vehicle by: • Removing the minimum $200 fine where the juvenile's prior criminal history score is 0 to ½ points;	Ch. 136	§4	ESHB 2906

RCW	RCW Title	Effective Date	Summary	Session Law	Section	Bill Number
			• Replacing the minimum 45 hours of community restitution with a minimum combination of 3 days of home confinement and 40 hours of community restitution where the juvenile's prior criminal history score is 0 to ½ points; • Removing the minimum $400 fine where the juvenile's prior criminal history score is ¾ to 1½ points; and • Removing the minimum $400 fine where the juvenile's prior criminal history score is 2 or more points. Amends provisions concerning taking a motor vehicle without permission in the second degree by: • Removing the minimum $150 fine where the juvenile's prior criminal history score is ¾ to 1½ points; and • Removing the minimum $150 fine where the juvenile's prior criminal history score is 2 or more points.			
RCW 10.99.030	Law enforcement officers—Training, powers, duties—Domestic violence reports.	6/9/2016	Establishes that, upon receiving an offense report concerning domestic violence, the prosecuting attorney has the discretion to not file the information as a domestic violence offense if the offense was committed against a sibling, parent, stepparent or grandparent.	Ch. 136	§5	ESHB 2906
RCW 13.40.265	Firearm, alcohol, and drug violations.	6/9/2016	Amends provisions concerning notifying DOL about juveniles who are found to have	Ch. 136	§6	ESHB 2906

The Caseload Forecast Council is not liable for errors or omissions in the manual, for sentences that may be inappropriately calculated as a result of a practitioner's or court's reliance on the manual, or for any other written or verbal information related to adult or juvenile sentencing. The scoring sheets are intended to provide assistance in most cases but does not cover all permutations of the scoring rules. If you find any errors or omissions, we encourage you to report them to the Caseload Forecast Council.

RCW	RCW Title	Effective Date	Summary	Session Law	Section	Bill Number
			committed firearm-, alcohol- and/or drug-related offenses by excluding first offenses from notification. Makes technical corrections. Removes reinstatement provisions for first offenses. Removes provisions concerning diversions.			
RCW 9.41.040	Unlawful possession of firearms—Ownership, possession by certain persons—Restoration of right to possess—Penalties.	6/9/2016	Amends provisions concerning notifying DOL about juveniles who are found to have committed firearm-, alcohol- and/or drug-related offenses by excluding first offenses from notification.	Ch. 136	§7	ESHB 2906
RCW 46.20.265	Juvenile driving privileges—Revocation for alcohol or drug violations.	6/9/2016	Makes a technical correction. Removes diversion provisions concerning the revocation of juvenile driving privileges.	Ch. 136	§8	ESHB 2906
RCW 66.44.365	Juvenile driving privileges—Alcohol or drug violations.	6/9/2016	Amends provisions concerning notifying DOL about juveniles who are found to have committed firearm-, alcohol- and/or drug-related offenses by excluding first offenses from notification.	Ch. 136	§9	ESHB 2906
RCW 69.41.065	Violations—Juvenile driving privileges.	6/9/2016	Amends provisions concerning notifying DOL about juveniles who are found to have committed firearm-, alcohol- and/or drug-related offenses by excluding first offenses from notification.	Ch. 136	§10	ESHB 2906
RCW 69.50.420	Violations—Juvenile driving privileges.	6/9/2016	Amends provisions concerning notifying DOL about juveniles who are found to have committed firearm-, alcohol- and/or drug-related offenses by excluding first offenses from notification.	Ch. 136	§11	ESHB 2906

RCW	RCW Title	Effective Date	Summary	Session Law	Section	Bill Number
RCW 69.52.070	Violations—Juvenile driving privileges.	6/9/2016	Amends provisions concerning notifying DOL about juveniles who are found to have committed firearm-, alcohol- and/or drug-related offenses by excluding first offenses from notification.	Ch. 136	§12	ESHB 2906
RCW 10.31.100	Arrest without warrant.	6/9/2016	Raises the age, from 16- to 18-years-old, concerning the age for which a law enforcement officer may arrest a domestic violence suspect without a warrant under certain circumstances. Establishes new arrest provisions for 16-year-old and 17-year-old domestic violence suspects. Mandates that juvenile detention facilities must book juveniles arrested for domestic violence.	Ch.113	§1	SB 5605

SECTION 2

RECENT CASE LAW AFFECTING JUVENILE JUSTICE

Introduction

The following reviews of juvenile case law were provided by Judge Ronald Kessler, King County Superior Court. It is copyrighted by Judge Kessler and is used with permission.

JUVENILES
Dispositions

State v. Houston-Sconiers, 191 Wn.App. 436 (2015)

Automatic decline statute, RCW 13.04.030(1)(e)(v)(C) (2009), is not cruel and unusual, distinguishing *Roper v. Simmons,* 543 U.S. 551, 568, 161 L.Ed.2d 1 (2005), *Graham v. Florida,* 560 U.S. 48, 76, 176 L.Ed.2d 825 (2010), *Miller v. Alabama,* ___ U.S. ___, 183 L.Wed.2d 407 (2012); 2-1, III.

State v. K.H.-H., 185 Wn.2d 745 (2016)

Requiring a respondent to write a letter of apology following adjudication of assault with sexual motivation doesn't violate the First Amendment or CONST. Art I, § 5; affirms *State v. K.H.-H.,* 188 Wn.App. 413 (2015); 5-4.

State v. Flores, 194 Wn.App. 29 (2016)

Disrupting school activities, RCW 28A.635.030 (1984), which states that the charge is "a misdemeanor, the penalty for which shall be a fine…not more than fifty dollars" authorizes only a fine and cannot be construed to authorize general misdemeanor penalties such as detention or community supervision; III.

SECTION 3

JUVENILE DISPOSITION GUIDELINES

Introduction

Juveniles who commit criminal offenses in Washington are subject to the provisions of Chapter 13.40 RCW, the Juvenile Justice Act of 1977, as amended.

The Act contains guidelines and procedures for the imposition of a presumptive standard range of sanctions commensurate with the offender's age, seriousness of the current offense and prior criminal history.

The Act also specifies a number of sentencing alternatives to the standard range which the court may select if deemed appropriate.

We offer a special note of caution to those practitioners who are familiar with the state's adult felony sentencing guidelines. Washington is perhaps unique in that both adult felony sentencing and juvenile court dispositions are structured by statutorily defined sentencing guidelines. However, while similar in many ways to its adult felony guidelines, the juvenile sentencing guidelines in Washington State differ in significant ways. For example:

- Juveniles sentenced to more than 30 days of confinement are sentenced to a range of confinement, with the actual release date set within the range at the discretion of the state Juvenile Rehabilitation Administration (JRA)[1]; adults are sentenced to a specific sentence within a specified standard range, but may be released early as a result of "earned release time."
- The "seriousness" of juvenile offense, while generally following the state's adult felony classification, is more differentiated and includes adjustments reflecting recognition of the differences between juvenile and adult social development.
- With the exception of supervision time across dispositions, terms of juvenile dispositions are served consecutively; adult sentences are typically run concurrently.

---

[1] In 2013, the Department of Social and Health Service (DSHS) Juvenile Rehabilitation Administration (JRA) was reorganized as the Juvenile Justice and Rehabilitation Administration (JJRA), and then later renamed Juvenile Rehabilitation (JR). In this publication, we will continue to reference the Juvenile Rehabilitation Administration (JRA) consistent with current statutory references.

Determining the Appropriate Court of Jurisdiction

The sentencing guidelines in this manual only apply to cases properly before a juvenile court. Juvenile courts are not separate constitutional courts; rather, they are a statutory division of the superior courts in Washington State.[2]

A juvenile court's constitutional jurisdiction to act derives from the superior court's general jurisdiction set out in Art. IV, §6 of the Washington State Constitution. Terminology such as "juvenile court jurisdiction" and "jurisdiction of the juvenile court" do not refer to a juvenile court's constitutional jurisdiction. Instead, terms related to a juvenile court's jurisdiction refer to the statutory procedures and protections provided in cases before the juvenile court.[3]

Those statutory provisions exclusive to juveniles include a set of sentencing guidelines discussed in this manual. Failure to substantively abide by these statutory provisions violates a juvenile's right to due process, but never deprives the juvenile court of its constitutional authority to act as a division of superior court.[4]

In Washington State, any *juvenile* alleged or found to have committed a criminal offense is subject to the jurisdiction of the juvenile court.[5] With few exceptions, only a *juvenile* is entitled to the statutory sentencing guidelines exclusive to juveniles. Thus, the initial inquiry for sentencing will focus on determining whether the person is a *juvenile* or otherwise remains subject to the jurisdiction of the juvenile court on a residual basis.

What is a *Juvenile* for Purposes of Juvenile Court Jurisdiction?

While commonly thought to encompass anyone under 18 years of age, for purposes of juvenile jurisdiction, the term *juvenile* is more complex. The Act defines the term *juvenile*.[6] That legal definition contains two primary components, both of which are required for a person to be a *juvenile* for purposes of juvenile court jurisdiction:

1. **The person must be under the age of 18; and,**

2. **The person must not be subject to adult court proceedings.**

Unless both components are present, the person is not a *juvenile* for purposes of juvenile court jurisdiction, and, with the exception of residual juvenile jurisdiction, may not remain in juvenile court. However, a person who is either a *juvenile* or is subject to the residual jurisdiction of the

---

[2] RCW 13.04.021(1).
[3] *Dillenburg v. Maxwell*, 70 Wn.2d 331, 353, 422 P.2d 783 (1967).
[4] *State v. Posey*, 174 Wn.2d 131, 139-40, 272 P.3d 840 (2012).
[5] RCW 13.04.030(1)
[6] RCW 13.40.020(15).

juvenile court is deemed a "*juvenile offender*.[7] A *juvenile offender* must be given a juvenile disposition.

Less Than 18 Years Old

Being less than 18 years of age requires the person remain under age 18 *up to and through adjudication* of a case in juvenile court.[8] A person loses their status as a *juvenile* anytime they turn 18 years old regardless of their age at the time they commit an offense. There are however three exceptions that continue juvenile court jurisdiction past age 18 despite the loss of juvenile status.

The first exception requires the juvenile court to issue a written order extending juvenile court jurisdiction past the person's 18th birthday pre-adjudication.[9]

The second exception extends juvenile court jurisdiction automatically past age 18 for purposes of imposing or supervising a juvenile court disposition.[10]

The third exception extends juvenile court jurisdiction past age 18 for purposes of disposition after failed "exclusive adult jurisdiction", a term discussed later in this manual.[11]

All three exceptions must be in effect prior to the person turning 18, which is why they create residual jurisdiction in the juvenile court even after a juvenile offender turns age 18.

Not Subject to Adult Court Proceedings

Even if a person is under the age of 18, they may not qualify as a *juvenile* if they are subject to proceedings in adult court either by statutory mandate or judicial decision. There are functionally three ways a person under the age of 18 can be subject to adult court:

1. **Certain "License" Offenses if 16 or 17 Years Old**

   For those who are 16 or 17 years old, there are certain "license" type offenses which require prosecution in adult courts of limited jurisdiction (district and municipal courts). These violations involve any "traffic, fish, boating, or game offense, or traffic or civil infraction" that would, if committed by an adult, be heard in a court of limited jurisdiction.[12] They are referred to as "license" offenses because they involve activities which require licensing or adult status, and, therefore, anyone violating them should be

---

[7] RCW 13.40.020(16).
[8] See, RCW 13.40.300; *State v. Calderon*, 102 Wn.2d 348, 351-52. 684 P.2d 1293 (1984).
[9] RCW 13.40.300(1)(a).
[10] RCW 13.40.300(1)(b)&(c).
[11] RCW 13.40.300(1)(d).
[12] RCW 13.04.030(1)(e)(iii).

held to the same standard as any adult properly licensed or otherwise authorized to perform the activity.[13]

The person must be 16 or 17 years old when the offense is committed, and, there is an exception made if the license offense is committed in the same incident as another offense which would properly be before the juvenile court (i.e., Driving while License Suspended and Possession of Marijuana for instance). In that case, both the license offense and the juvenile offense may proceed in juvenile court.

2. **Exclusive Adult Jurisdiction if 16 or 17 Years Old ("Automatic Adult")**

For those who are 16 or 17 years old, there are certain offenses considered so serious they require prosecution in adult court. Generally, they include any serious violent offense, or, any violent offense along with certain criminal history or use of firearms.

The conditions for exclusive adult jurisdiction are contained in RCW 13.04.030(1)(e)(v), and require the person to be 16 or 17 years of age at the time the offense is committed. Exclusive adult jurisdiction requires one or more enumerated offenses and/or conditions, so it is necessary to examine and be aware of the particular offenses and conditions in the statute.[14]

Because adult court jurisdiction is primarily based on the offense charged, any alteration of the crime outside of one of the statutorily enumerated offenses, either pre or post adjudication, may subject the person charged to the jurisdiction of the juvenile court for further proceedings, including disposition.[15] This is referred to as failed exclusive adult jurisdiction.

As discussed earlier, there is an exception allowing for residual juvenile jurisdiction for failed exclusive adult jurisdiction where the person turns 18 while pending adult

---

[13] *State v. Kravchuk*, 86 Wn. App. 276, 280, 936 P.2d 1161 (1997).
[14] Exclusive Adult Jurisdiction: The juvenile must be 16 or 17 at the time of the offense and the offense must be:
   (1) A serious violent offense as defined in RCW 9.94A.030;
   (2) A violent offense as defined in RCW 9.94A.030 and the juvenile has a criminal history consisting of: (I) One or more prior serious violent offenses; (II) two or more prior violent offenses; or (III) three or more of any combination of the following offenses: Any class A felony, any class B felony, vehicular assault, or manslaughter in the second degree, all of which must have been committed after the juvenile's thirteenth birthday and prosecuted separately;
   (3) Robbery in the first degree, rape of a child in the first degree, or drive-by shooting, committed on or after July 1, 1997;
   (4) Burglary in the first degree committed on or after July 1, 1997, and the juvenile has a criminal history consisting of one or more prior felony or misdemeanor offenses; or
   (5) Any violent offense as defined in RCW 9.94A.030 committed on or after July 1, 1997, and the juvenile is alleged to have been armed with a firearm.
   See, RCW 13.04.030(1)(v)(A-E)

[15] RCW 13.04.030(1)(e)(v)(E)(II); *State v. Mora*, 138 Wn.2d 43, 54, 977 P.2d 564 (1999).

proceedings.[16] For example: A person age 17 pending adult court for Robbery in the First Degree turns 18 years old prior to trial, but is later found guilty in adult court of the lesser included offense of Robbery in the Second Degree, a non-exclusive adult offense. In this example, the case must return to juvenile court for disposition, and, despite the person being over 18, residual juvenile jurisdiction remains to sentence the matter in juvenile court. Once returned, the juvenile court must sentence the individual to the juvenile sentencing guidelines unless a judicial decline hearing determines the case can return to adult court for sentencing.[17]

There is another exception to exclusive adult jurisdiction which allows the parties and the court to agree to send an exclusive adult case from adult court to juvenile court for further proceedings.[18]

3. **Judicial Decline Hearings for Any Age**

Under certain circumstances, a juvenile court may decide to waive its jurisdiction over a juvenile and have the juvenile remanded to the jurisdiction of the adult superior court for further proceedings. This is commonly referred to as a judicial "decline hearing" authorized by statute.[19] Decline hearings are done in juvenile court while a person is pending juvenile court proceedings. Judicial decline hearings can be done for any juvenile regardless of age. In certain cases where the juvenile is 16 or 17 years old and charged with certain offenses, a decline hearing is mandatory unless waived by all parties, including the juvenile court.[20]

During the decline hearing, the parties present testimony and evidence to the juvenile court. At the end of the hearing the juvenile court decides to either retain juvenile court jurisdiction, or, to remand the individual to adult court for further proceedings, in which case the person is no longer subject to juvenile court jurisdiction. The court decides the case based on a specific set of factors, often referred to as the eight *Kent* factors.[21]

If the juvenile court decides to remand an individual under age 18 to adult court, the individual loses his or her *juvenile* status for any and all cases brought thereafter unless the charge remanded to adult court is later reduced or dismissed in adult court.[22] This is sometimes referred to as "*once declined, always declined.*"

Judicial decline hearings may be held either pre-adjudication, or in the case of failed exclusive adult jurisdiction, post-adjudication for purposes of adult sentencing.

---

[16] RCW 13.40.300(1)(d) and RCW 13.04.030(1)(e)(v)(E)(II).
[17] RCW 13.04.030(1)(e)(v)(E)(II).
[18] RCW 13.04.030(1)(e)(v)(E)(III).
[19] See, RCW 13.40.110.
[20] RCW 13.40.110(2).
[21] *Kent v. United States*, 383 U.S. 541, 566-67, 86 Sup.Ct. 1045, 16 L.Ed. 2d 84 (1966).
[22] RCW 13.40.020(15); *State v. Sharon*, 33 Wn. App. 491, 496, 655 P.2d 1193 (1982).

When Does Juvenile Court Jurisdiction End?

Once it is determined the juvenile court has jurisdiction to impose disposition on a juvenile offender, that jurisdiction will not remain indefinitely. A juvenile court's jurisdiction to impose a disposition order ends when a juvenile offender turns 21 years of age.[23] However, even in rare instances where the juvenile court loses jurisdiction to impose disposition past age 21, the adult superior courts always maintains constitutional jurisdiction to impose a juvenile disposition.[24]

Once disposition is imposed, there are additional time limits on how long the juvenile court maintains procedural jurisdiction to enforce the disposition order. That depends on both the disposition condition as well as the age of the individual subject to the disposition.

With some exceptions, a juvenile court's procedural jurisdiction to enforce a disposition order against a juvenile offender terminates when the supervision period in the disposition order ends.[25] In no case may the juvenile court extend supervision past the offender's 21st birthday.[26] For purposes of enforcing financial obligations such as payment of restitution, a juvenile court maintains jurisdiction for a period of ten years past disposition, or up to the offender's 28th birthday, whichever is less.[27] That period may be extended for an additional 10 years by written order.[28]

---

[23] RCW 13.40.300(3).
[24] *State v. Posey*, 174 Wn.2d at 142.
[25] *State v. May*, 80 Wn. App. 711, 716-17, 911 P.2d 399 (1996).
[26] RCW 13.40.300(3).
[27] RCW 13.40.190(1)(d); *In Re Brady*, 154 Wn. App. 189, 198, 224 P.3d 842 (2010).
[28] RCW 13.40.190(1)(d).

Washington State Juvenile Disposition Guidelines

Title 13 RCW is the Exclusive Authority for Juvenile Dispositions

Chapter 13.04 RCW and Chapter 13.40 RCW are the exclusive authority for the adjudication and sentencing of juveniles unless specifically provided in other statutes.[29] This means juvenile courts are not allowed to utilize other disposition options or sentences that don't specifically include juveniles. For instance, the ability to compromise a misdemeanor under Chapter 10.22 RCW does not apply to juvenile proceedings.[30] Similarly, unless otherwise stated, enhancements and penalties imposed outside of Title 13 RCW do not apply to juvenile dispositions. Examples include: Mandatory minimum jail sentences, school zone enhancements, gang enhancements, and, most fines and fees.

Rarely, a particular consequence outside of Title 13 RCW will specifically state its application to juvenile cases. For example, the Crime Victim's Compensation (CVC) fine contained in Chapter 7.68 RCW applies to juveniles by specific reference.[31]

More often, application of a particular consequence outside of Title 13 RCW depends on whether or not the juvenile is deemed "convicted" of an offense. Like adult convictions, typically juvenile adjudications involve a finding by the juvenile court that a juvenile has committed an offense.[32] However, unless otherwise stated, juvenile adjudications are not "convictions" for purposes of sentencing a juvenile outside Title 13 RCW.[33]

Consequences: Local Sanctions vs. Confinement to JRA

In Title 13 RCW there are two general types of consequences for juveniles adjudicated of offenses. The first involves "local Sanctions" or "LS" for short.[34] Local sanctions are community based consequences wherein the juvenile remains in the community, or, is released after a short stay in the local juvenile detention facility. Local sanctions can include up to 30 days of confinement in detention, up to 12 months of community supervision, up to 150 hours of community restitution, and/or up to a $500 fine.

The second involves confinement to a Juvenile Rehabilitation Administration facility or "JRA" for short. In this case the juvenile is confined to the custody of the Dept. of Social and Health Services to serve more than 30 days of confinement in a facility operated by JRA.[35] Confinement in JRA is typically done for a number of weeks within a range ordered by the

---

[29] RCW 13.04.450.
[30] Id.
[31] See, RCW 7.68.035(1)(b) and 9A.88.120(2).
[32] RCW 13.40.020(16); RCW 13.40.150(3).
[33] RCW 13.04.011(1).
[34] RCW 13.40.020(18).
[35] RCW 13.40.020(6) and RCW 13.40.185.

juvenile court.[36] In most instances, JRA will determine the amount of weeks within the range ordered and may provide parole services to the juvenile after release.

Multiple Juvenile Offenses

As stated earlier, the juvenile sentencing structure differs significantly from the adult system. One primary difference is how sentences for multiple offenses within a single disposition order, as well as across multiple disposition orders are served. There are also rules which limit the total amount of time that may be served among multiple offenses.

If a juvenile is sentenced for two or more offenses in a single disposition order, the disposition terms for each offense run consecutive to one another.[37] That includes community supervision, community restitution, and, any confinement imposed. For example: A juvenile sentenced for two assault counts is ordered to serve 6 months of supervision, 16 hours of community restitution, and 1 day of detention on each count. Those terms run consecutive to one another so the juvenile will have a total of 12 months supervision (6 x 2 = 12 months), 32 hours of community service (16 x 2 = 32 hours), and, 2 days of detention (1 x 2 = 2 days) total. Likewise, a juvenile facing two counts, each of which involves commitment to JRA, will serve those consecutively as well. For example, two counts each of which involves a standard range of 15 to 36 weeks at JRA will total a minimum of 30 weeks to a maximum of 72 weeks commitment.

In addition, where multiple offenses each impose less than 30 days of detention, but the aggregate total of all counts exceeds 30 days, the detention may be served at JRA at the discretion of the juvenile court.[38]

There are limitations however. First, the aggregate of all consecutive terms in a single disposition may not exceed three hundred percent (300%) of the term imposed for the most serious offense.[39] This is often referred to as the "300% rule". Keep in mind the rule does not allow for 300% of the maximum which the court *could* presumptively impose; rather, it presumes a total no greater than three times the term *actually imposed* by the court on the most serious offense. Logically, the 300% rule will only be relevant for those dispositions where there are four or more counts sentenced in a single disposition order. Sentencing three or less offenses will avoid application of the rule altogether.

Second, the aggregate of all consecutive terms of community supervision shall not exceed two years in length, or require payment of more than two hundred dollars in fines or the performance of more than two hundred hours of community restitution.[40]

---

[36] RCW 13.40.0357.
[37] RCW 13.40.180(1).
[38] RCW 13.40.185(1).
[39] RCW 13.40.180(1)(b).
[40] RCW 13.40.180(1)(c).

Third, in very rare cases where multiple offenses are closely related to the same action, the aggregate disposition must not exceed one hundred fifty percent of the total imposed for the most serious offense.[41] This is often referred to as the "150% rule". In order for the 150% rule to apply, the offenses must either be committed through a single act or omission, or, through an act or omission which in itself constitutes one of the offenses and is also an element of the other. Because the 150% rule requires the offenses be similar, the fact patterns for application of the 150% rule are rare, but there are a few cases which discuss the rule's application should one encounter a potential issue.[42]

Finally, there is one exception to concurrent sentencing where a juvenile is sentenced across multiple disposition orders. Amongst multiple disposition orders, all terms will remain consecutive with the exception of supervision, which runs concurrent between separate disposition orders.[43]

Disposition Options for Juvenile Adjudications

There are several statutory options for sentencing a juvenile adjudicated of an offense in Title 13. Some cases may be excluded from a particular option based on the type of case, the juvenile's age, or the potential sentence. The juvenile disposition options are:

1. **Standard Range (RCW 13.40.0357 Option A)**

2. **Deferred Disposition (RCW 13.40.127)**

3. **Manifest Injustice (RCW 13.40.0357 Option D)**

4. **Suspended Disposition (three alternatives):**
   a. Suspended Disposition Alternative (RCW 13.40.0357 Option B)
   b. Chemical Dependency/Mental Health Disposition Alternative (RCW 13.40.0357 Option C)
   c. Special Sexual Offender Disposition Alternative (RCW 13.40.162)

Each option is explained below beginning with the standard range which should always be calculated first before considering other options.

Standard Range (RCW 13.40.0357 Option A)

The standard range, or "Option A" in RCW 13.40.0357, is the most common disposition option in juvenile court. This is considered the presumptive sentence based on a juvenile's age and type of offense committed. Every juvenile offender is subject to imposition of the standard range, which the court must consider before determining a final disposition.[44] Therefore, the standard

---

[41] RCW 13.40.180(1)(a).
[42] See, *State v. Contreras*, 124 P.2d 741, 880 P.2d 1000 (1994); and, *State v. S.S.Y.*, 150 Wn. App. 325, 207 P.3d 1273 (2009), affirmed and remanded, 170 Wn.2d 322, 241 P.3d 781 (2010).
[43] RCW 13.40.180(2).
[44] See, RCW 13.40.150.

range should be calculated in every juvenile case regardless of what other disposition options may be available to a juvenile offender. A standard range sentence may not be appealed.[45]

In most cases, calculation of the standard range is done using a statutory grid in RCW 13.40.0357. The grid takes into account three variables: Type of offense, prior criminal history, and, age of the juvenile offender. An example of the grid found in RCW 13.40.0357 is shown below.

OPTION A **JUVENILE OFFENDER SENTENCING GRID** **STANDARD RANGE**						
CURRENT OFFENSE CATAGORY	**A+**	180 weeks to age 21 for all category A+ offenses				
	A	103-129 weeks for all category A offenses				
	A-	15 - 36 WEEKS EXCEPT 30 - 40 WEEKS FOR 15 TO 17 YEAR OLDS	52 – 65 WEEKS	80 – 100 WEEKS	103 – 129 WEEKS	103 – 129 WEEKS
	B+	15 - 36 WEEKS	15 - 36 WEEKS	52 - 65 WEEKS	80 - 100 WEEKS	103 - 129 WEEKS
	B	LS	LS	15 – 36 WEEKS	15 – 36 WEEKS	52 – 65 WEEKS
	C+	LS	LS	LS	15 – 36 WEEKS	15 – 36 WEEKS
	C	LS	LS	LS	LS	15 – 36 WEEKS
	D+	LS	LS	LS	LS	LS
	D	LS	LS	LS	LS	LS
	E	LS	LS	LS	LS	LS
		0	**1**	**2**	**3**	**4 or more**
		PRIOR ADJUDICATIONS				

NOTE: References in the grid to days or weeks mean periods of confinement. "LS" means "local sanctions" as defined in RCW 13.40.020.

The vertical axis of the grid is the "current offense category" which is determined using a list of offenses also found in RCW 13.40.0357. The horizontal axis of the grid is the "prior adjudications" which is determined using the juvenile offender's criminal history. The standard range is found where the vertical and horizontal axes converge for a particular juvenile offender. Depending on where the axes converge, the standard range will consist of one of the two general consequences previously discussed: Either local sanctions ("LS") or a range of weeks confined to JRA.

Current Offense Category

The vertical axis of the grid sets the juvenile disposition category which is based on each current offense for which the juvenile offender is adjudicated. A short example of the list of current offense categories in RCW 13.40.0357 appears below:

---

[45] RCW 13.40.160(2).

DESCRIPTION AND OFFENSE CATEGORY

JUVENILE DISPOSITION OFFENSE CATEGORY	DESCRIPTION (RCW CITATION)	JUVENILE DISPOSITION CATEGORY FOR ATTEMPT, BAILJUMP, CONSPIRACY, OR SOLICITATION
	Arson and Malicious Mischief	
A	Arson 1 (9A.48.020)	B+
B	Arson 2 (9A.48.030)	C
C	Reckless Burning 1 (9A.48.040)	D
D	Reckless Burning 2 (9A.48.050)	E
B	Malicious Mischief 1 (9A.48.070)	C
C	Malicious Mischief 2 (9A.48.080)	D
D	Malicious Mischief 3 (9A.48.090)	E
E	Tampering with Fire Alarm Apparatus (9.40.100)	E
E	Tampering with Fire Alarm Apparatus with Intent to Commit Arson (9.40.105)	E
A	Possession of Incendiary Device (9.40.120)	B+

The above example shows only a small number of offenses but many more are listed specifically by name in RCW 13.40.0357. In the event the current offense is not listed by name, there is an "other offense" category to include any offense not otherwise listed.

In many cases the disposition category parallels the standard severity of the offense; but not always. For example, while Assault in the Second Degree is a class B felony, for purposes of juvenile disposition it is a B+ current offense category. Likewise, Vehicular Homicide is a class A felony, but a B+ current offense category. Therefore, the current offense category must always be determined using the list of offenses in RCW 13.40.0357.

The list in RCW 13.40.0357 contains two different categories for any offense. The first column to the left of the offense is the category for the principal offense. The second column to the right of the offense lists the category for any anticipatory version (attempt, conspiracy, or solicitation) or calculating bail jump from the same. For example, Arson 1 is a class A felony for disposition, but an attempt of the same crime, or a bail jump from that crime, would be a class B+ felony for disposition.

Prior Adjudications

The horizontal axis of the grid is determined using the juvenile offender's criminal history to calculate the number of prior adjudications. Prior adjudications are those alleged offenses found correct by a court prior to commission of the current offense being calculated.[46] In other words, any previous offense for which the juvenile offender was adjudicated before he or she committed the current offense. Prior diversions do not count as prior adjudications because diversions do not involve a finding of guilt by a court. Offenses committed but not adjudicated prior to commission of the current offense do not count as prior adjudications.

---

[46] See, RCW 13.40.020(8).

Each prior adjudication is given a numbered "point" score depending on whether or not it involved a felony. Each prior felony adjudication counts as 1whole point. However, if the prior adjudication involved a gross misdemeanor or misdemeanor offense, the adjudication only counts as a ¼ of a point (or .25 points). Points are added together and rounded down to the nearest full number to obtain the final score for all prior adjudications. So, for example, a person with one prior felony and three prior misdemeanors will have a prior adjudication score of 1 (not 1.75). A person with four prior felony adjudications will have a prior adjudication score of 4.

Prior adjudications do not affect the standard range for any current offense that is not a felony. Any current offense that is a misdemeanor or gross misdemeanor will always involve local sanctions regardless of the offender's prior adjudication score.

Finally, prior adjudications are never counted for purposes of determining standard range for a current offense of either Escape in the First Degree, or, Escape in the Second Degree. For each of those offenses the disposition offense category is a C, and, instead of the grid, the standard range is calculated using footnote 1 at the end of the offenses listed in RCW 13.40.0357. The calculation is based on the number of previous escapes or attempted escapes and ranges between 4 weeks and 12 weeks of confinement.

Firearm Enhancement

There are two special juvenile enhancements for firearm crimes. The first involves a disposition for Unlawful Possession of a Firearm where the offender is under 18 years old per RCW 9.41.040(2)(a)(iv). Disposition for that offense requires a minimum of 10 days confinement.[47] The second involves disposition for any current felony offense where there is a special allegation under RCW 13.40.196 alleging the juvenile offender is "armed with a firearm" during commission (except certain offenses where possession of a firearm is an element).[48] In that case there is an additional commitment time period to be served at JRA in addition to other sanctions. The additional commitment period is based on the level of offense: 6 months for class A offenses, 4 months for class B offenses, and, 2 months for class C offenses.

Motor Vehicle Minimums

There are minimum sentencing requirements for certain crimes involving motor vehicle theft (Theft of a Motor Vehicle, Possession of a Stolen Motor Vehicle, and, Taking a Motor Vehicle Without Owner's Permission). The minimum requirements for disposition of those offenses are set forth in RCW 13.40.308.

---

[47] RCW 13.40.193(1).
[48] RCW 13.40.193(3)

The Caseload Forecast Council is not liable for errors or omissions in the manual, for sentences that may be inappropriately calculated as a result of a practitioner's or court's reliance on the manual, or for any other written or verbal information related to adult or juvenile sentencing. The scoring sheets are intended to provide assistance in most cases but does not cover all permutations of the scoring rules. If you find any errors or omissions, we encourage you to report them to the Caseload Forecast Council.

Deferred Disposition (RCW 13.40.127)

Deferred Disposition is an option available to many juveniles. This disposition option in RCW 13.40.127 allows an adjudicated juvenile to defer imposition of sentence and instead be placed on conditions of supervision for up to 12 months. The conditions of supervision can include up to 150 hours of community service and up to a $500 fine, but cannot include detention or commitment to JRA.[49] Because deferred disposition is not considered a final juvenile offense disposition or sentence, certain mandatory fines like crime victim's compensation, do not apply.[50] Likewise, because no detention or commitment time is allowed, the mandatory minimum sentences for vehicle crimes and firearms won't apply to deferred dispositions either.

First, the juvenile offender must qualify in order to request a deferred disposition. There are a few limitations in the statute requiring the juvenile:

1. Is not charged with a sex or violent offense;
2. Has no prior felony history;
3. Has no prior deferred disposition; and
4. Has no more than one prior adjudication.

Second, the juvenile must move for imposition of the deferred disposition at least 14 days prior to trial unless that time period is shortened for good cause. This limits use of the deferred disposition to cases where the juvenile has not yet been adjudicated guilty by means of a trial. In addition, the court may not impose a deferred disposition unless the juvenile agrees to it.[51] In all cases where a juvenile is eligible for a deferred disposition, there shall be a strong presumption that the deferred disposition will be granted.

Third, the juvenile must either stipulate to admission of the law enforcement reports or plead guilty to the offenses. The adjudication is limited to a finding of guilt based on either stipulation to the reports or the plea of guilt.

Fourth, should the juvenile offender fail to comply with the terms of the deferred disposition, the court may either treat the violation as a probation violation, or, in the alternative, may revoke the deferred disposition and impose another disposition option.

Finally, full payment of restitution is generally required in order for the court to dismiss and vacate the case later on. There is one exception, however, where the court finds the juvenile made a "good faith" effort to pay restitution, in which case the court may dismiss, vacate the conviction, and impose a new restitution order for any unpaid amount which remains enforceable the same as any other restitution order issued under RCW 13.40.190.

---

[49] *State v. I.K.C.*, 160 Wn. App. 660, 669, 248 P.3d 145 (2011).
[50] *State v. M.C.*, 148 Wn. App. 968, 972, 201 P.3d 413 (2009).
[51] *State v. Mohamoud*, 159 Wn.App. 753, 765, 246 P.3d 849 (2011).

Upon completion of the deferred disposition conditions, the conviction is vacated and the case is dismissed (except for a charge of Animal Cruelty 1°, which cannot be vacated). If the conditions are not satisfied by the end of supervision, the court can continue the case an additional 12 months for good cause; however, at any time the court finds the conditions have not been satisfied, the court can revoke the deferred disposition and impose a disposition order under one of the other sentencing options.

In addition to the benefit of having the case dismissed and vacated, so long as restitution is paid or not otherwise required, the dismissed deferred disposition will be subject to sealing at the time the juvenile is 18 years or older. This makes deferred disposition an attractive option for many juveniles.

Manifest Injustice (RCW 13.40.0357 Option D)

Manifest Injustice is a disposition outside of the standard range. In order to impose a manifest injustice disposition, the court must first find the standard range would be *manifestly unjust* either because a standard range sentence would be too excessive, or, too lenient in light of various factors.[52]

A manifest injustice sentence can only be imposed where the court finds by *clear and convincing evidence*[53] the standard range manifestly unjust[54]. In this case "clear and convincing evidence" is equivalent to "beyond a reasonable doubt."[55] The court must support the finding with circumstances applicable to the juvenile.

There is a list of statutory aggravating and mitigating circumstances set out in RCW 13.40.150(3). In addition to the statutory factors, a manifest injustice can be based on any additional "non-statutory" factors peculiar to the juvenile and any pre-sentence report.[56] Because the court must provide adequate findings, a manifest injustice sentence may be appealed.[57]

A manifest injustice sentence must be determinate, meaning the court sets forth the terms of the sentence. Where a manifest injustice disposition involves local sanctions, the court sets the terms of confinement less than 30 days as well as any terms of community supervision. Likewise, where the manifest injustice would impose a term of confinement greater than 30 days on any offense, the court may set a determinate range of confinement to JRA, the minimum limited only by the security guidelines set out in RCW 13.40.030 (which limits the court to a minimum based on the percentage of the maximum time).[58]

---

[52] RCW 13.40.160(2); and, *State v. M.L.*, 134 Wn.2d 657, 660, 952 P.2d 187 (1998).
[53] *Id.*
[54] *Id.*
[55] *State v. Meade*, 129 Wn. App. 918, 922, 120 P.3d 975 (2005), citing, *State v. Rhoades*, 92 Wn.2d 755, 760, 600 P.2d 1264 (1979).
[56] *Rhoads*, 92 Wn.2d at 759, citing, *In Re Luft*, 21 Wn. App. 841, 589 P.2d 314 (1979).
[57] RCW 13.40.160(2).
[58] RCW 13.40.160(2).

This means a judge may sentence a juvenile to a range where both the maximum and minimum are the same.[59] Where the maximum and minimum are not the same, then the minimum can be any number of weeks so long as the minimum is not lower than that allowed by computation under the security guidelines in RCW 13.40.030.[60]

A manifest injustice can provide authority for a court to supervise, detain, or commit a juvenile up to age 21.[61] However, regardless of that authority, the juvenile may not be detained or committed for a period that is longer than that which an adult would receive for the same offense.[62]

Suspended Disposition Alternatives

There are three "alternative" dispositions which allow a court to impose a sentence, and then suspend that sentence in favor of a community based local sanctions disposition. These three alternatives are based on compliance with appropriate treatment goals. Provided the juvenile maintains compliance, the suspended sentence is not served. However, should the offender violate the community based disposition, the court has the option of revoking the suspended disposition in which case the original sentence goes into effect. Other than the three alternatives mentioned, the court has no authority to suspend imposition of a juvenile sentence.[63]

1. Suspended Disposition Alternative (Option B)

The Suspended Disposition Alternative is a treatment based suspended sentence set forth under "Option B" of RCW 13.40.0357. The offender must be subject to a standard range disposition involving confinement by JRA and the court must find the offender and community would benefit from the use of a suspended disposition. In this case the court may impose the standard range and suspend execution of the disposition on condition the offender comply with one or more local sanctions and any educational or treatment requirement. The treatment programs provided to the offender must be research-based best practice programs.

These programs must qualify as either: a) Programs approved by the Washington State Institute for Public Policy or the Joint Legislative Audit and Review Committee; or, b) In the case of chemical dependency treatment, evidence based or research based best practice programs. Note: These programs will not be available in every county.

---

[59] *State v. Beaver*, 148 Wn.2d 338, 350, 60 P.3d 586 (2002).
[60] *Id.*
[61] See, RCW 13.40.300.
[62] RCW 13.40.160(11).
[63] RCW 13.40.160(10).

If the offender fails to comply with the suspended disposition condition(s), the court may impose sanctions pursuant to RCW 13.40.200 or may revoke the suspended disposition and order the disposition's execution.

An offender is ineligible for the Suspended Disposition Alternative if the offender:

1) Committed a category A+ offense; or,
2) Is fourteen years or older and committed any of the following offenses:
    a) a category A offense (completed and anticipatory) r
    b) Manslaughter in the first degree
    c) Assault in the second degree
    d) Extortion in the first degree
    e) Robbery in the second degree
    f) Residential Burglary
    g) Burglary in the second degree
    h) Drive-by Shooting
    i) Vehicle Homicide (RCW 46.61.520)
    j) Hit and Run Death (RCW 46.52.020(4)(a))
    k) Intimidating a Witness (RCW 9A.72.110)
    l) Violation of the Uniform Controlled Substance Act
    m) Manslaughter 2, when the offense includes infliction of bodily harm upon another or when during the commission or immediate withdrawal from the offense the respondent was armed with a deadly weapon
3) Is ordered to serve a disposition for a firearm violation under RCW 13.40.193
4) Committed a sex offense as defined in RCW 9.94A.030.

2. Chemical Dependency/Mental Health Disposition Alternative (Option C)

The 2016 Legislature repealed the Mental Health Disposition Alternative (formerly RCW 13.40.167) and incorporated a somewhat less restrictive (in terms of eligibility) version into the Chemical Dependency Disposition Alternative.[64]

The Chemical Dependency Disposition Alternative, a.k.a. "CDDA", and the Mental Health Disposition Alternative, a.k.a. "MHDA", are a substance abuse, mental health and co-occurring disorder treatment-based suspended sentence set forth under "Option C" of RCW 13.40.0357, as well as RCW 13.40.165, which contains most of the requirements for this suspended disposition alternative.

---

[64] ESHB 2746 – Chapter 106, Laws of 2016.

The court must consider eligibility for CDMHDA whenever the offender is subject to a standard range disposition of either local sanctions, or, 15 to 36 weeks of confinement, and, has not committed a category A- or B+ offense. Provided the court finds the offender is chemically dependent, has mental health issues or has a co-occurring disorder, and is amenable to treatment, the court may either impose a disposition within the standard range, or, where appropriate, impose a manifest injustice sentence (up to 52 weeks or as otherwise limited by that which an adult could receive), and, thereafter suspend that disposition, and, impose a community based disposition including up to 12 months of community supervision, up to 150 hours of community service, up to 30 days of detention, and, payment of restitution. As a condition of supervision, the court must require the offender undergo available inpatient/outpatient treatment. The court shall only order inpatient treatment if a funded bed is available.

If the inpatient treatment exceeds 90 days, the court shall hold a review hearing every thirty days beyond the initial 90 days. The treatment provider must submit monthly progress reports and the court may schedule treatment review hearings. The suspension may be revoked and the disposition executed (with credit for confinement time served on the same offense) for violating conditions or failing to make satisfactory progress in treatment.

A CDMHDA disposition is not appealable.[65]

Legislation passed in the 2014 session (HB 1724; C 110 L 14) clarified the degree to which statements made during the course of a mental health or chemical dependency screening or assessment when ordered by a court is not be admissible into evidence against the juvenile (RCW 13.40.020, RCW 13.40.140).

3. **Special Sex Offender Disposition Alternative (RCW 13.40.162 SSODA)**

The Special Sex Offender Disposition Alternative, a.k.a. "SSODA", is primarily a sexual deviancy treatment based suspended sentence set forth in RCW 13.40.162.

The offender must have committed a sex offense, other than a sex offense that is also a serious violent offense as defined in RCW 9.94A.030, and must have no history of sex offense(s). The court may order an examination to determine whether the offender is amenable to treatment. If, following such an examination, the court determines the offender and the community would benefit from the use of the SSODA, the court may either impose a determinate

---

[65] RCW 13.40.165(11).

disposition within the standard range,[66] or, in the alternative, impose a manifest injustice and, thereafter, suspend execution of the disposition and place the offender on community supervision for at least two years. The court may impose conditions of community supervision and other conditions, including up to thirty days of confinement and requirements that the offender:

- Devote time to specific education, employment, or occupation;
- Undergo available outpatient sex offender treatment for up to two years, or inpatient treatment sex offender treatment not to exceed the standard range of confinement for that offense;
- Remain within prescribed geographical boundaries and notify the court or the probation counselor prior to any change of address, educational program or employment;
- Report to the prosecutor and the probation counselor prior to any change in a sex offender treatment provider (Prior approval by the court is required for any change);
- Report as directed to the court and a probation counselor;
- Pay all court-ordered legal financial obligations, perform community service, or any combination thereof;
- Make restitution to the victim for counseling costs reasonably related to the offense;
- Comply with the conditions of any court-ordered probation bond; or
- The court shall order that the offender may not attend the public or approved private elementary, middle or high school attended by the victim or the victim's siblings.

A disposition entered under the SSODA option may not be appealed.[67]

---

[66] Imposition of the standard range in a SSODA must be a determinate number within the range; not the range itself. *State v. Linssen*, 131 Wn. App. 292, 296, 126 P.3 1287 (2006).
[67] RCW 13.40.162(10).

The Caseload Forecast Council is not liable for errors or omissions in the manual, for sentences that may be inappropriately calculated as a result of a practitioner's or court's reliance on the manual, or for any other written or verbal information related to adult or juvenile sentencing. The scoring sheets are intended to provide assistance in most cases but does not cover all permutations of the scoring rules. If you find any errors or omissions, we encourage you to report them to the Caseload Forecast Council.

SECTION 4

Chapter 13.40 RCW: JUVENILE JUSTICE ACT OF 1977, AS AMENDED

13.40.010
Short title—Intent—Purpose.

(1) This chapter shall be known and cited as the Juvenile Justice Act of 1977.

(2) It is the intent of the legislature that a system capable of having primary responsibility for, being accountable for, and responding to the needs of youthful offenders and their victims, as defined by this chapter, be established. It is the further intent of the legislature that youth, in turn, be held accountable for their offenses and that communities, families, and the juvenile courts carry out their functions consistent with this intent. To effectuate these policies, the legislature declares the following to be equally important purposes of this chapter:

(a) Protect the citizenry from criminal behavior;

(b) Provide for determining whether accused juveniles have committed offenses as defined by this chapter;

(c) Make the juvenile offender accountable for his or her criminal behavior;

(d) Provide for punishment commensurate with the age, crime, and criminal history of the juvenile offender;

(e) Provide due process for juveniles alleged to have committed an offense;

(f) Provide for the rehabilitation and reintegration of juvenile offenders;

(g) Provide necessary treatment, supervision, and custody for juvenile offenders;

(h) Provide for the handling of juvenile offenders by communities whenever consistent with public safety;

(i) Provide for restitution to victims of crime;

(j) Develop effective standards and goals for the operation, funding, and evaluation of all components of the juvenile justice system and related services at the state and local levels;

(k) Provide for a clear policy to determine what types of offenders shall receive punishment, treatment, or both, and to determine the jurisdictional limitations of the courts, institutions, and community services;

(l) Provide opportunities for victim participation in juvenile justice process, including court hearings on juvenile offender matters, and ensure that Article I, section 35 of the Washington state Constitution, the victim bill of rights, is fully observed; and

(m) Encourage the parents, guardian, or custodian of the juvenile to actively participate in the juvenile justice process.

[2016 c 136 § 1; 2004 c 120 § 1; 1997 c 338 § 8; 1992 c 205 § 101; 1977 ex.s. c 291 § 55.]

NOTES:
> **Effective date—2004 c 120:** "This act takes effect July 1, 2004." [2004 c 120 § 11.]
> **Finding—Evaluation—Report—1997 c 338:** See note following RCW 13.40.0357.
> **Severability—Effective dates—1997 c 338:** See notes following RCW 5.60.060.
> **Part headings not law—1992 c 205:** "Part headings as used in this act do not constitute any part of the law." [1992 c 205 § 405.]
> **Severability—1992 c 205:** "If any provision of this act or its application to any person or circumstance is held invalid, the remainder of the act or the application of the provision to other persons or circumstances is not affected." [1992 c 205 § 406.]
> **Effective dates—Severability—1977 ex.s. c 291:** See notes following RCW 13.04.005.

13.40.020
Definitions.

For the purposes of this chapter:

(1) "Assessment" means an individualized examination of a child to determine the child's psychosocial needs and problems, including the type and extent of any mental health, substance abuse, or co-occurring mental health and substance abuse disorders, and recommendations for treatment. "Assessment" includes, but is not limited to, drug and alcohol evaluations, psychological and psychiatric evaluations, records review, clinical interview, and administration of a formal test or instrument;

(2) "Community-based rehabilitation" means one or more of the following: Employment; attendance of information classes; literacy classes; counseling, outpatient substance abuse treatment programs, outpatient mental health programs, anger management classes, education or outpatient treatment programs to prevent animal cruelty, or other services including, when appropriate, restorative justice programs; or attendance at school or other educational programs appropriate for the juvenile as determined by the school district. Placement in community-based rehabilitation programs is subject to available funds;

(3) "Community-based sanctions" may include one or more of the following:

(a) A fine, not to exceed five hundred dollars;

(b) Community restitution not to exceed one hundred fifty hours of community restitution;

(4) "Community restitution" means compulsory service, without compensation, performed for the benefit of the community by the offender as punishment for committing an offense. Community restitution may be performed through public or private organizations or through work crews;

(5) "Community supervision" means an order of disposition by the court of an adjudicated youth not committed to the department or an order granting a deferred disposition. A community supervision order for a single offense may be for a period of up to two years for a sex offense as defined by RCW 9.94A.030 and up to one year for other offenses. As a mandatory condition of any term of community supervision, the court shall order the juvenile to refrain from committing new offenses. As a mandatory condition of community supervision, the court shall order the

juvenile to comply with the mandatory school attendance provisions of chapter 28A.225 RCW and to inform the school of the existence of this requirement. Community supervision is an individualized program comprised of one or more of the following:

(a) Community-based sanctions;

(b) Community-based rehabilitation;

(c) Monitoring and reporting requirements;

(d) Posting of a probation bond;

(e) Residential treatment, where substance abuse, mental health, and/or co-occurring disorders have been identified in an assessment by a qualified mental health professional, psychologist, psychiatrist, or chemical dependency professional and a funded bed is available. If a child agrees to voluntary placement in a state-funded long-term evaluation and treatment facility, the case must follow the existing placement procedure including consideration of less restrictive treatment options and medical necessity.

(i) A court may order residential treatment after consideration and findings regarding whether:

(A) The referral is necessary to rehabilitate the child;

(B) The referral is necessary to protect the public or the child;

(C) The referral is in the child's best interest;

(D) The child has been given the opportunity to engage in less restrictive treatment and has been unable or unwilling to comply; and

(E) Inpatient treatment is the least restrictive action consistent with the child's needs and circumstances.

(ii) In any case where a court orders a child to inpatient treatment under this section, the court must hold a review hearing no later than sixty days after the youth begins inpatient treatment, and every thirty days thereafter, as long as the youth is in inpatient treatment;

(6) "Confinement" means physical custody by the department of social and health services in a facility operated by or pursuant to a contract with the state, or physical custody in a detention facility operated by or pursuant to a contract with any county. The county may operate or contract with vendors to operate county detention facilities. The department may operate or contract to operate detention facilities for juveniles committed to the department. Pretrial confinement or confinement of less than thirty-one days imposed as part of a disposition or modification order may be served consecutively or intermittently, in the discretion of the court;

(7) "Court," when used without further qualification, means the juvenile court judge(s) or commissioner(s);

(8) "Criminal history" includes all criminal complaints against the respondent for which, prior to the commission of a current offense:

(a) The allegations were found correct by a court. If a respondent is convicted of two or more charges arising out of the same course of conduct, only the highest charge from among these shall count as an offense for the purposes of this chapter; or

(b) The criminal complaint was diverted by a prosecutor pursuant to the provisions of this chapter on agreement of the respondent and after an advisement to the respondent that the criminal complaint would be considered as part of the respondent's criminal history. A successfully completed deferred adjudication that was entered before July 1, 1998, or a deferred disposition shall not be considered part of the respondent's criminal history;

(9) "Department" means the department of social and health services;

(10) "Detention facility" means a county facility, paid for by the county, for the physical confinement of a juvenile alleged to have committed an offense or an adjudicated offender subject to a disposition or modification order. "Detention facility" includes county group homes, inpatient substance abuse programs, juvenile basic training camps, and electronic monitoring;

(11) "Diversion unit" means any probation counselor who enters into a diversion agreement with an alleged youthful offender, or any other person, community accountability board, youth court under the supervision of the juvenile court, or other entity except a law enforcement official or entity, with whom the juvenile court administrator has contracted to arrange and supervise such agreements pursuant to RCW 13.40.080, or any person, community accountability board, or other entity specially funded by the legislature to arrange and supervise diversion agreements in accordance with the requirements of this chapter. For purposes of this subsection, "community accountability board" means a board comprised of members of the local community in which the juvenile offender resides. The superior court shall appoint the members. The boards shall consist of at least three and not more than seven members. If possible, the board should include a variety of representatives from the community, such as a law enforcement officer, teacher or school administrator, high school student, parent, and business owner, and should represent the cultural diversity of the local community;

(12) "Foster care" means temporary physical care in a foster family home or group care facility as defined in RCW 74.15.020 and licensed by the department, or other legally authorized care;

(13) "Institution" means a juvenile facility established pursuant to chapters 72.05 and 72.16 through 72.20 RCW;

(14) "Intensive supervision program" means a parole program that requires intensive supervision and monitoring, offers an array of individualized treatment and transitional services, and emphasizes community involvement and support in order to reduce the likelihood a juvenile offender will commit further offenses;

(15) "Juvenile," "youth," and "child" mean any individual who is under the chronological age of eighteen years and who has not been previously transferred to adult court pursuant to RCW 13.40.110, unless the individual was convicted of a lesser charge or acquitted of the charge for which he or she was previously transferred pursuant to RCW 13.40.110 or who is not otherwise under adult court jurisdiction;

(16) "Juvenile offender" means any juvenile who has been found by the juvenile court to have committed an offense, including a person eighteen years of age or older over whom jurisdiction has been extended under RCW 13.40.300;

(17) "Labor" means the period of time before a birth during which contractions are of sufficient frequency, intensity, and duration to bring about effacement and progressive dilation of the cervix;

(18) "Local sanctions" means one or more of the following: (a) 0-30 days of confinement; (b) 0-12 months of community supervision; (c) 0-150 hours of community restitution; or (d) $0-$500 fine;

(19) "Manifest injustice" means a disposition that would either impose an excessive penalty on the juvenile or would impose a serious, and clear danger to society in light of the purposes of this chapter;

(20) "Monitoring and reporting requirements" means one or more of the following: Curfews; requirements to remain at home, school, work, or court-ordered treatment programs during specified hours; restrictions from leaving or entering specified geographical areas; requirements to report to the probation officer as directed and to remain under the probation officer's supervision; and other conditions or limitations as the court may require which may not include confinement;

(21) "Offense" means an act designated a violation or a crime if committed by an adult under the law of this state, under any ordinance of any city or county of this state, under any federal law, or under the law of another state if the act occurred in that state;

(22) "Physical restraint" means the use of any bodily force or physical intervention to control a juvenile offender or limit a juvenile offender's freedom of movement in a way that does not involve a mechanical restraint. Physical restraint does not include momentary periods of minimal physical restriction by direct person-to-person contact, without the aid of mechanical restraint, accomplished with limited force and designed to:

(a) Prevent a juvenile offender from completing an act that would result in potential bodily harm to self or others or damage property;

(b) Remove a disruptive juvenile offender who is unwilling to leave the area voluntarily; or

(c) Guide a juvenile offender from one location to another;

(23) "Postpartum recovery" means (a) the entire period a woman or youth is in the hospital, birthing center, or clinic after giving birth and (b) an additional time period, if any, a treating physician determines is necessary for healing after the youth leaves the hospital, birthing center, or clinic;

(24) "Probation bond" means a bond, posted with sufficient security by a surety justified and approved by the court, to secure the offender's appearance at required court proceedings and compliance with court-ordered community supervision or conditions of release ordered pursuant to RCW 13.40.040 or 13.40.050. It also means a deposit of cash or posting of other collateral in lieu of a bond if approved by the court;

(25) "Respondent" means a juvenile who is alleged or proven to have committed an offense;

(26) "Restitution" means financial reimbursement by the offender to the victim, and shall be limited to easily ascertainable damages for injury to or loss of property, actual expenses incurred for medical treatment for physical injury to persons, lost wages resulting from physical injury, and costs of the victim's counseling reasonably related to the offense. Restitution shall not include reimbursement for damages for mental anguish, pain and suffering, or other intangible losses. Nothing in this chapter shall limit or replace civil remedies or defenses available to the victim or offender;

(27) "Restorative justice" means practices, policies, and programs informed by and sensitive to the needs of crime victims that are designed to encourage offenders to accept responsibility for repairing the harm caused by their offense by providing safe and supportive opportunities for voluntary participation and communication between the victim, the offender, their families, and relevant community members;

(28) "Restraints" means anything used to control the movement of a person's body or limbs and includes:

(a) Physical restraint; or

(b) Mechanical device including but not limited to: Metal handcuffs, plastic ties, ankle restraints, leather cuffs, other hospital-type restraints, tasers, or batons;

(29) "Screening" means a process that is designed to identify a child who is at risk of having mental health, substance abuse, or co-occurring mental health and substance abuse disorders that warrant immediate attention, intervention, or more comprehensive assessment. A screening may be undertaken with or without the administration of a formal instrument;

(30) "Secretary" means the secretary of the department of social and health services. "Assistant secretary" means the assistant secretary for juvenile rehabilitation for the department;

(31) "Services" means services which provide alternatives to incarceration for those juveniles who have pleaded or been adjudicated guilty of an offense or have signed a diversion agreement pursuant to this chapter;

(32) "Sex offense" means an offense defined as a sex offense in RCW 9.94A.030;

(33) "Sexual motivation" means that one of the purposes for which the respondent committed the offense was for the purpose of his or her sexual gratification;

(34) "Surety" means an entity licensed under state insurance laws or by the state department of licensing, to write corporate, property, or probation bonds within the state, and justified and approved by the superior court of the county having jurisdiction of the case;

(35) "Transportation" means the conveying, by any means, of an incarcerated pregnant youth from the institution or detention facility to another location from the moment she leaves the institution or detention facility to the time of arrival at the other location, and includes the escorting of the pregnant incarcerated youth from the institution or detention facility to a transport vehicle and from the vehicle to the other location;

(36) "Violation" means an act or omission, which if committed by an adult, must be proven beyond a reasonable doubt, and is punishable by sanctions which do not include incarceration;

(37) "Violent offense" means a violent offense as defined in RCW 9.94A.030;

(38) "Youth court" means a diversion unit under the supervision of the juvenile court.
[2016 c 136 § 2; 2016 c 106 § 1; 2014 c 110 § 1; 2012 c 201 § 1; 2010 c 181 § 10; 2009 c 454 § 2; 2004 c 120 § 2. Prior: 2002 c 237 § 7; 2002 c 175 § 19; 1997 c 338 § 10; (1997 c 338 § 9 expired July 1, 1998); prior: 1995 c 395 § 2; 1995 c 134 § 1; prior: 1994 sp.s. c 7 § 520; 1994 c 271 § 803; 1994 c 261 § 18; 1993 c 373 § 1; 1990 1st ex.s. c 12 § 1; 1990 c 3 § 301; 1989 c 407 § 1; 1988 c 145 § 17; 1983 c 191 § 7; 1981 c 299 § 2; 1979 c 155 § 54; 1977 ex.s. c 291 § 56.]
NOTES:

Reviser's note: This section was amended by 2016 c 106 § 1 and by 2016 c 136 § 2, each without reference to the other. Both amendments are incorporated in the publication of this section under RCW 1.12.025(2). For rule of construction, see RCW 1.12.025(1).

Effective date—2004 c 120: See note following RCW 13.40.010.

Effective date—2002 c 175: See note following RCW 7.80.130.

Alphabetization of definitions—1997 c 338: "The code reviser shall alphabetize the definitions in RCW 13.40.020 and correct any references." [1997 c 338 § 71.]

Finding—Evaluation—Report—1997 c 338: See note following RCW 13.40.0357.

Severability—Effective dates—1997 c 338: See notes following RCW 5.60.060.

Finding—Intent—Severability—1994 sp.s. c 7: See notes following RCW 43.70.540.

Purpose—Severability—1994 c 271: See notes following RCW 9A.28.020.

Finding—Intent—1994 c 261: See note following RCW 16.52.011.

The Caseload Forecast Council is not liable for errors or omissions in the manual, for sentences that may be inappropriately calculated as a result of a practitioner's or court's reliance on the manual, or for any other written or verbal information related to adult or juvenile sentencing. The scoring sheets are intended to provide assistance in most cases but does not cover all permutations of the scoring rules. If you find any errors or omissions, we encourage you to report them to the Caseload Forecast Council.

Severability—1993 c 373: "If any provision of this act or its application to any person or circumstance is held invalid, the remainder of the act or the application of the provision to other persons or circumstances is not affected." [1993 c 373 § 3.]

Effective date—1990 1st ex.s. c 12: "This act shall take effect July 1, 1990." [1990 1st ex.s. c 12 § 5.]

Index, part headings not law—Severability—Effective dates—Application—1990 c 3: See RCW 18.155.900 through 18.155.902.

Effective date—Savings—Application—1988 c 145: See notes following RCW 9A.44.010.

Effective date—Severability—1979 c 155: See notes following RCW 13.04.011.

Effective dates—Severability—1977 ex.s. c 291: See notes following RCW 13.04.005.

13.40.030
Security guidelines—Legislative review—Limitations on permissible ranges of confinement.

(1) The secretary shall submit guidelines pertaining to the nature of the security to be imposed on youth placed in his or her custody based on the age, offense(s), and criminal history of the juvenile offender. Such guidelines shall be submitted to the legislature for its review no later than November 1st of each year. The department shall include security status definitions in the security guidelines it submits to the legislature pursuant to this section.

(2) The permissible ranges of confinement resulting from a finding of manifest injustice under RCW 13.40.0357 are subject to the following limitations:

(a) Where the maximum term in the range is ninety days or less, the minimum term in the range may be no less than fifty percent of the maximum term in the range;

(b) Where the maximum term in the range is greater than ninety days but not greater than one year, the minimum term in the range may be no less than seventy-five percent of the maximum term in the range; and

(c) Where the maximum term in the range is more than one year, the minimum term in the range may be no less than eighty percent of the maximum term in the range.
[2003 c 207 § 5; 1996 c 232 § 5; 1989 c 407 § 3; 1985 c 73 § 1; 1983 c 191 § 6; 1981 c 299 § 5; 1979 c 155 § 55; 1977 ex.s. c 291 § 57.]

NOTES:

Effective dates—1996 c 232: "(1) Sections 1 through 8 of this act are necessary for the immediate preservation of the public peace, health, or safety, or support of the state government and its existing public institutions, and take effect immediately [March 28, 1996].

(2) Section 9 of this act takes effect July 1, 1996." [1996 c 232 § 12.]

Legislative ratification—1989 c 271: "The legislature ratifies the juvenile disposition standards commission guidelines submitted to the 1989 legislature and endorses the action to increase penalties for juvenile drug offenders." [1989 c 271 § 602.]

Effective date—1985 c 73: "This act is necessary for the immediate preservation of the public peace, health, and safety, the support of the state government and its existing public institutions, and shall take effect June 30, 1985." [1985 c 73 § 3.]

Effective date—Severability—1979 c 155: See notes following RCW 13.04.011.

Effective dates—Severability—1977 ex.s. c 291: See notes following RCW 13.04.005.

13.40.0351
Equal application of guidelines and standards.

The sentencing guidelines and prosecuting standards apply equally to juvenile offenders in all parts of the state, without discrimination as to any element that does not relate to the crime or the previous record of the offender.

[1989 c 407 § 5.]

13.40.0357
Juvenile offender sentencing standards.

DESCRIPTION AND OFFENSE CATEGORY

JUVENILE DISPOSITION OFFENSE CATEGORY	DESCRIPTION (RCW CITATION)	JUVENILE DISPOSITION CATEGORY FOR ATTEMPT, BAILJUMP, CONSPIRACY, OR SOLICITATION
	Arson and Malicious Mischief	
A	Arson 1 (9A.48.020)	B+
B	Arson 2 (9A.48.030)	C
C	Reckless Burning 1 (9A.48.040)	D
D	Reckless Burning 2 (9A.48.050)	E
B	Malicious Mischief 1 (9A.48.070)	C
C	Malicious Mischief 2 (9A.48.080)	D
D	Malicious Mischief 3 (9A.48.090)	E
E	Tampering with Fire Alarm Apparatus (9.40.100)	E

E	Tampering with Fire Alarm Apparatus with Intent to Commit Arson (9.40.105)	E
A	Possession of Incendiary Device (9.40.120)	B+

Assault and Other Crimes Involving Physical Harm

A	Assault 1 (9A.36.011)	B+
B+	Assault 2 (9A.36.021)	C+
C+	Assault 3 (9A.36.031)	D+
D+	Assault 4 (9A.36.041)	E
B+	Drive-By Shooting (9A.36.045)	C+
D+	Reckless Endangerment (9A.36.050)	E
C+	Promoting Suicide Attempt (9A.36.060)	D+
D+	Coercion (9A.36.070)	E
C+	Custodial Assault (9A.36.100)	D+

Burglary and Trespass

B+	Burglary 1 (9A.52.020)	C+
B	Residential Burglary (9A.52.025)	C
B	Burglary 2 (9A.52.030)	C
D	Burglary Tools (Possession of) (9A.52.060)	E
D	Criminal Trespass 1 (9A.52.070)	E
E	Criminal Trespass 2 (9A.52.080)	E
C	Mineral Trespass (78.44.330)	C
C	Vehicle Prowling 1 (9A.52.095)	D
D	Vehicle Prowling 2 (9A.52.100)	E

Drugs

E	Possession/Consumption of Alcohol (66.44.270)	E
C	Illegally Obtaining Legend Drug (69.41.020)	D
C+	Sale, Delivery, Possession of Legend Drug with Intent to Sell (69.41.030(2)(a))	D+
E	Possession of Legend Drug (69.41.030(2)(b))	E
B+	Violation of Uniform Controlled Substances Act - Narcotic, Methamphetamine, or Flunitrazepam Sale (69.50.401(2) (a) or (b))	B+
C	Violation of Uniform Controlled Substances Act - Nonnarcotic Sale (69.50.401(2)(c))	C
E	Possession of Marihuana <40 grams (69.50.4014)	E
C	Fraudulently Obtaining Controlled Substance (69.50.403)	C
C+	Sale of Controlled Substance for Profit (69.50.410)	C+

The Caseload Forecast Council is not liable for errors or omissions in the manual, for sentences that may be inappropriately calculated as a result of a practitioner's or court's reliance on the manual, or for any other written or verbal information related to adult or juvenile sentencing. The scoring sheets are intended to provide assistance in most cases but does not cover all permutations of the scoring rules. If you find any errors or omissions, we encourage you to report them to the Caseload Forecast Council.

E	Unlawful Inhalation (9.47A.020)	E
B	Violation of Uniform Controlled Substances Act - Narcotic, Methamphetamine, or Flunitrazepam Counterfeit Substances (69.50.4011(2) (a) or (b))	B
C	Violation of Uniform Controlled Substances Act - Nonnarcotic Counterfeit Substances (69.50.4011(2) (c), (d), or (e))	C
C	Violation of Uniform Controlled Substances Act - Possession of a Controlled Substance (69.50.4013)	C
C	Violation of Uniform Controlled Substances Act - Possession of a Controlled Substance (69.50.4012)	C

Firearms and Weapons

B	Theft of Firearm (9A.56.300)	C
B	Possession of Stolen Firearm (9A.56.310)	C
E	Carrying Loaded Pistol Without Permit (9.41.050)	E
C	Possession of Firearms by Minor (<18) (9.41.040(2)(a) (iv))	C
D+	Possession of Dangerous Weapon (9.41.250)	E
D	Intimidating Another Person by use of Weapon (9.41.270)	E

Homicide

A+	Murder 1 (9A.32.030)	A
A+	Murder 2 (9A.32.050)	B+
B+	Manslaughter 1 (9A.32.060)	C+
C+	Manslaughter 2 (9A.32.070)	D+
B+	Vehicular Homicide (46.61.520)	C+

Kidnapping

A	Kidnap 1 (9A.40.020)	B+
B+	Kidnap 2 (9A.40.030)	C+
C+	Unlawful Imprisonment (9A.40.040)	D+

Obstructing Governmental Operation

D	Obstructing a Law Enforcement Officer (9A.76.020)	E
E	Resisting Arrest (9A.76.040)	E
B	Introducing Contraband 1 (9A.76.140)	C
C	Introducing Contraband 2 (9A.76.150)	D
E	Introducing Contraband 3 (9A.76.160)	E
B+	Intimidating a Public Servant (9A.76.180)	C+
B+	Intimidating a Witness (9A.72.110)	C+

Public Disturbance

C+	Criminal Mischief with Weapon (9A.84.010(2)(b))	D+
D+	Criminal Mischief Without Weapon (9A.84.010(2)(a))	E
E	Failure to Disperse (9A.84.020)	E
E	Disorderly Conduct (9A.84.030)	E

Sex Crimes

A	Rape 1 (9A.44.040)	B+
A-	Rape 2 (9A.44.050)	B+
C+	Rape 3 (9A.44.060)	D+
A-	Rape of a Child 1 (9A.44.073)	B+
B+	Rape of a Child 2 (9A.44.076)	C+
B	Incest 1 (9A.64.020(1))	C
C	Incest 2 (9A.64.020(2))	D
D+	Indecent Exposure (Victim <14) (9A.88.010)	E
E	Indecent Exposure (Victim 14 or over) (9A.88.010)	E
B+	Promoting Prostitution 1 (9A.88.070)	C+
C+	Promoting Prostitution 2 (9A.88.080)	D+
E	O & A (Prostitution) (9A.88.030)	E
B+	Indecent Liberties (9A.44.100)	C+
A-	Child Molestation 1 (9A.44.083)	B+
B	Child Molestation 2 (9A.44.086)	C+
C	Failure to Register as a Sex Offender (9A.44.132)	D

Theft, Robbery, Extortion, and Forgery

B	Theft 1 (9A.56.030)	C
C	Theft 2 (9A.56.040)	D
D	Theft 3 (9A.56.050)	E
B	Theft of Livestock 1 and 2 (9A.56.080 and 9A.56.083)	C
C	Forgery (9A.60.020)	D
A	Robbery 1 (9A.56.200)	B+
B+	Robbery 2 (9A.56.210)	C+
B+	Extortion 1 (9A.56.120)	C+
C+	Extortion 2 (9A.56.130)	D+
C	Identity Theft 1 (9.35.020(2))	D
D	Identity Theft 2 (9.35.020(3))	E
D	Improperly Obtaining Financial Information (9.35.010)	E
B	Possession of a Stolen Vehicle (9A.56.068)	C

B	Possession of Stolen Property 1 (9A.56.150)	C
C	Possession of Stolen Property 2 (9A.56.160)	D
D	Possession of Stolen Property 3 (9A.56.170)	E
B	Taking Motor Vehicle Without Permission 1 (9A.56.070)	C
C	Taking Motor Vehicle Without Permission 2 (9A.56.075)	D
B	Theft of a Motor Vehicle (9A.56.065)	C

Motor Vehicle Related Crimes

E	Driving Without a License (46.20.005)	E
B+	Hit and Run - Death (46.52.020(4)(a))	C+
C	Hit and Run - Injury (46.52.020(4)(b))	D
D	Hit and Run-Attended (46.52.020(5))	E
E	Hit and Run-Unattended (46.52.010)	E
C	Vehicular Assault (46.61.522)	D
C	Attempting to Elude Pursuing Police Vehicle (46.61.024)	D
E	Reckless Driving (46.61.500)	E
D	Driving While Under the Influence (46.61.502 and 46.61.504)	E
B+	Felony Driving While Under the Influence (46.61.502(6))	B
B+	Felony Physical Control of a Vehicle While Under the Influence (46.61.504(6))	B

Other

B	Animal Cruelty 1 (16.52.205)	C
B	Bomb Threat (9.61.160)	C
C	Escape 1₁ (9A.76.110)	C
C	Escape 2₁ (9A.76.120)	C
D	Escape 3 (9A.76.130)	E
E	Obscene, Harassing, Etc., Phone Calls (9.61.230)	E
A	Other Offense Equivalent to an Adult Class A Felony	B+
B	Other Offense Equivalent to an Adult Class B Felony	C
C	Other Offense Equivalent to an Adult Class C Felony	D
D	Other Offense Equivalent to an Adult Gross Misdemeanor	E
E	Other Offense Equivalent to an Adult Misdemeanor	E
V	Violation of Order of Restitution, Community Supervision, or Confinement (13.40.200)₂	V

[1]Escape 1 and 2 and Attempted Escape 1 and 2 are classed as C offenses and the standard range is established as follows:

   1st escape or attempted escape during 12-month period - 4 weeks confinement

---

2nd escape or attempted escape during 12-month period - 8 weeks confinement

3rd and subsequent escape or attempted escape during 12-month period - 12 weeks confinement

[2]If the court finds that a respondent has violated terms of an order, it may impose a penalty of up to 30 days of confinement.

JUVENILE SENTENCING STANDARDS

This schedule must be used for juvenile offenders. The court may select sentencing option A, B, C, or D.

OPTION A
JUVENILE OFFENDER SENTENCING GRID

STANDARD RANGE

CURRENT OFFENSE CATEGORY	0	1	2	3	4 or More
A+	180 Weeks to Age 21 for All Category A+ Offenses				
A	103 - 129 Weeks for All Category A Offenses				
A-	15 - 36 Weeks Except 30 - 40 Weeks for 15 to 17 Year Olds	52 - 65 Weeks	80 - 100 Weeks	103 - 129 Weeks	103 - 129 Weeks
B+	15 - 36 Weeks	15 - 36 Weeks	52 - 65 Weeks	80 - 100 Weeks	103 - 129 Weeks
B	LS	LS	15 - 36 Weeks	15 - 36 Weeks	52 - 65 Weeks
C+	LS	LS	LS	15 - 36 Weeks	15 - 36 Weeks
C	LS	LS	LS	LS	15 - 36 Weeks
D+	LS	LS	LS	LS	LS
D	LS	LS	LS	LS	LS
E	LS	LS	LS	LS	LS

PRIOR ADJUDICATIONS

NOTE: References in the grid to days or weeks mean periods of confinement. "LS" means "local sanctions" as defined in RCW 13.40.020.

(1) The vertical axis of the grid is the current offense category. The current offense category is determined by the offense of adjudication.

(2) The horizontal axis of the grid is the number of prior adjudications included in the juvenile's criminal history. Each prior felony adjudication shall count as one point. Each prior violation, misdemeanor, and gross misdemeanor adjudication shall count as 1/4 point. Fractional points shall be rounded down.

(3) The standard range disposition for each offense is determined by the intersection of the column defined by the prior adjudications and the row defined by the current offense category.

(4) RCW 13.40.180 applies if the offender is being sentenced for more than one offense.

(5) A current offense that is a violation is equivalent to an offense category of E. However, a disposition for a violation shall not include confinement.

OR

**OPTION B
SUSPENDED DISPOSITION ALTERNATIVE**

(1) If the offender is subject to a standard range disposition involving confinement by the department, the court may impose the standard range and suspend the disposition on condition that the offender comply with one or more local sanctions and any educational or treatment requirement. The treatment programs provided to the offender must be either research-based best practice programs as identified by the Washington state institute for public policy or the joint legislative audit and review committee, or for chemical dependency treatment programs or services, they must be evidence-based or research-based best practice programs. For the purposes of this subsection:

(a) "Evidence-based" means a program or practice that has had multiple site random controlled trials across heterogeneous populations demonstrating that the program or practice is effective for the population; and

(b) "Research-based" means a program or practice that has some research demonstrating effectiveness, but that does not yet meet the standard of evidence-based practices.

(2) If the offender fails to comply with the suspended disposition, the court may impose sanctions pursuant to RCW 13.40.200 or may revoke the suspended disposition and order the disposition's execution.

(3) An offender is ineligible for the suspended disposition option under this section if the offender is:

(a) Adjudicated of an A+ offense;

(b) Fourteen years of age or older and is adjudicated of one or more of the following offenses:

(i) A class A offense, or an attempt, conspiracy, or solicitation to commit a class A offense;

(ii) Manslaughter in the first degree (RCW 9A.32.060); or

(iii) Assault in the second degree (RCW 9A.36.021), extortion in the first degree (RCW 9A.56.120), kidnapping in the second degree (RCW 9A.40.030), robbery in the second degree (RCW 9A.56.210), residential burglary (RCW 9A.52.025), burglary in the second degree (RCW 9A.52.030), drive-by shooting (RCW 9A.36.045), vehicular homicide (RCW 46.61.520), hit and run death (RCW 46.52.020(4)(a)), intimidating a witness (RCW 9A.72.110), violation of the uniform controlled substances act (RCW 69.50.401 (2)(a) and (b)), or manslaughter 2 (RCW 9A.32.070), when the offense includes infliction of bodily harm upon another or when during the commission or immediate withdrawal from the offense the respondent was armed with a deadly weapon;

(c) Ordered to serve a disposition for a firearm violation under RCW 13.40.193; or

(d) Adjudicated of a sex offense as defined in RCW 9.94A.030.

OR

OPTION C
CHEMICAL DEPENDENCY/MENTAL HEALTH DISPOSITION ALTERNATIVE

If the juvenile offender is subject to a standard range disposition of local sanctions or 15 to 36 weeks of confinement and has not committed an A- or B+ offense, the court may impose a disposition under RCW 13.40.160(4) and 13.40.165.

OR

OPTION D
MANIFEST INJUSTICE

If the court determines that a disposition under option A, B, or C would effectuate a manifest injustice, the court shall impose a disposition outside the standard range under RCW 13.40.160(2).

[2016 c 106 § 2; 2013 c 20 § 2; 2012 c 177 § 4. Prior: 2008 c 230 § 3; 2008 c 158 § 1; 2007 c 199 § 11; 2006 c 73 § 14; 2004 c 117 § 1; prior: 2003 c 378 § 2; 2003 c 335 § 6; 2003 c 53 § 97; prior: 2002 c 324 § 3; 2002 c 175 § 20; 2001 c 217 § 13; 2000 c 66 § 3; 1998 c 290 § 5; prior: 1997 c 338 § 12; (1997 c 338 § 11 expired July 1, 1998); 1997 c 66 § 6; 1996 c 205 § 6; 1995 c 395 § 3; 1994 sp.s. c 7 § 522; 1989 c 407 § 7.]

NOTES:

> **Effective date—2013 c 20:** See note following RCW 9A.84.010.
> **Delayed effective date—2008 c 230 §§ 1-3:** See note following RCW 9A.44.130.
> **Findings—Intent—Short title—2007 c 199:** See notes following RCW 9A.56.065.
> **Effective date—2006 c 73:** See note following RCW 46.61.502.
> **Effective date—2004 c 117:** "This act takes effect July 1, 2004." [2004 c 117 § 3.]
> **Intent—Effective date—2003 c 53:** See notes following RCW 2.48.180.
> **Study and report—2002 c 324:** See note following RCW 9A.56.070.
> **Effective date—2002 c 175:** See note following RCW 7.80.130.
> **Captions not law—2001 c 217:** See note following RCW 9.35.005.
> **Application—Effective date—Severability—1998 c 290:** See notes following RCW

69.50.401.

> **Severability—Effective dates—1997 c 338:** See notes following RCW 5.60.060.
> **Finding—Evaluation—Report—1997 c 338:** "The legislature finds it critical to

evaluate the effectiveness of the revisions made in this act to juvenile sentencing for purposes of measuring improvements in public safety and reduction of recidivism.

To accomplish this evaluation, the Washington state institute for public policy shall conduct a study of the sentencing revisions. The study shall: (1) Be conducted starting January 1, 2001; (2) examine whether the revisions have affected the rate of initial offense commission and recidivism; (3) determine the impacts of the revisions by age, race, and gender impacts of the revisions; (4) compare the utilization and effectiveness of sentencing alternatives and manifest injustice determinations before and after the revisions; and (5) examine the impact and effectiveness of changes made in the exclusive original jurisdiction of juvenile court over juvenile offenders.

The institute shall report the results of the study to the governor and legislature not later than July 1, 2002." [1997 c 338 § 59.]

Finding—Intent—Severability—1994 sp.s. c 7: See notes following RCW 43.70.540.

13.40.038
County juvenile detention facilities—Policy—Detention and risk assessment standards.

(1) It is the policy of this state that all county juvenile detention facilities provide a humane, safe, and rehabilitative environment and that unadjudicated youth remain in the community whenever possible, consistent with public safety and the provisions of chapter 13.40 RCW.

(2) The counties shall develop and implement detention intake standards and risk assessment standards to determine whether detention is warranted, whether the juvenile is developmentally disabled, and if detention is warranted, whether the juvenile should be placed in secure, nonsecure, or home detention to implement the goals of this section.

(3) Inability to pay for a less restrictive detention placement shall not be a basis for denying a respondent a less restrictive placement in the community.

(4) The assessment standards to determine whether a juvenile entering detention is developmentally disabled must be developed and implemented no later than December 31, 2012. [2012 c 120 § 1; 1992 c 205 § 105; 1986 c 288 § 7.]

NOTES:

Part headings not law—Severability—1992 c 205: See notes following RCW 13.40.010.

Severability—1986 c 288: See note following RCW 43.185C.260.

13.40.040
Taking juvenile into custody, grounds—Detention of, grounds—Detention pending disposition—Release on bond, conditions—Bail jumping.

(1) A juvenile may be taken into custody:

(a) Pursuant to a court order if a complaint is filed with the court alleging, and the court finds probable cause to believe, that the juvenile has committed an offense or has violated terms of a disposition order or release order; or

(b) Without a court order, by a law enforcement officer if grounds exist for the arrest of an adult in identical circumstances. Admission to, and continued custody in, a court detention facility shall be governed by subsection (2) of this section; or

(c) Pursuant to a court order that the juvenile be held as a material witness; or

(d) Where the secretary or the secretary's designee has suspended the parole of a juvenile offender.

(2) A juvenile may not be held in detention unless there is probable cause to believe that:

(a) The juvenile has committed an offense or has violated the terms of a disposition order; and

(i) The juvenile will likely fail to appear for further proceedings; or

(ii) Detention is required to protect the juvenile from himself or herself; or

(iii) The juvenile is a threat to community safety; or

(iv) The juvenile will intimidate witnesses or otherwise unlawfully interfere with the administration of justice; or

(v) The juvenile has committed a crime while another case was pending; or

(b) The juvenile is a fugitive from justice; or

(c) The juvenile's parole has been suspended or modified; or

(d) The juvenile is a material witness.

(3) Notwithstanding subsection (2) of this section, and within available funds, a juvenile who has been found guilty of one of the following offenses shall be detained pending disposition: Rape in the first or second degree (RCW 9A.44.040 and 9A.44.050); or rape of a child in the first degree (RCW 9A.44.073).

(4) Upon a finding that members of the community have threatened the health of a juvenile taken into custody, at the juvenile's request the court may order continued detention pending further order of the court.

(5) Except as provided in RCW 9.41.280, a juvenile detained under this section may be released upon posting a probation bond set by the court. The juvenile's parent or guardian may sign for the probation bond. A court authorizing such a release shall issue an order containing a statement of conditions imposed upon the juvenile and shall set the date of his or her next court appearance. The court shall advise the juvenile of any conditions specified in the order and may at any time amend such an order in order to impose additional or different conditions of release upon the juvenile or to return the juvenile to custody for failing to conform to the conditions imposed. In addition to requiring the juvenile to appear at the next court date, the court may condition the probation bond on the juvenile's compliance with conditions of release. The juvenile's parent or guardian may notify the court that the juvenile has failed to conform to the conditions of release or the provisions in the probation bond. If the parent notifies the court of the juvenile's failure to comply with the probation bond, the court shall notify the surety. As provided in the terms of the bond, the surety shall provide notice to the court of the offender's noncompliance. A juvenile may be released only to a responsible adult or the department of social and health services. Failure to appear on the date scheduled by the court pursuant to this section shall constitute the crime of bail jumping.
[2002 c 171 § 2; 1999 c 167 § 2; 1997 c 338 § 13; 1995 c 395 § 4; 1979 c 155 § 57; 1977 ex.s. c 291 § 58.]

NOTES:

Effective date—2002 c 171: See note following RCW 72.01.410.
Finding—Evaluation—Report—1997 c 338: See note following RCW 13.40.0357.
Severability—Effective dates—1997 c 338: See notes following RCW 5.60.060.
Effective date—Severability—1979 c 155: See notes following RCW 13.04.011.
Effective dates—Severability—1977 ex.s. c 291: See notes following RCW 13.04.005.

13.40.042
Detention of juvenile suffering from mental disorder or chemical dependency.

(1) When a police officer has reasonable cause to believe that a juvenile has committed acts constituting a nonfelony crime that is not a serious offense as identified in RCW 10.77.092, and the officer believes that the juvenile suffers from a mental disorder, and the local prosecutor has entered into an agreement with law enforcement regarding the detention of juveniles who may have a mental disorder or may be suffering from chemical dependency, the arresting officer, instead of taking the juvenile to the local juvenile detention facility, may take the juvenile to:

(a) An evaluation and treatment facility as defined in RCW 71.34.020 if the juvenile suffers from a mental disorder and the facility has been identified as an alternative location by agreement of the prosecutor, law enforcement, and the mental health provider;

(b) A facility or program identified by agreement of the prosecutor and law enforcement; or

(c) A location already identified and in use by law enforcement for the purpose of a behavioral health diversion.

(2) For the purposes of this section, an "alternative location" means a facility or program that has the capacity to evaluate a youth and, if determined to be appropriate, develop a behavioral health intervention plan and initiate treatment.

(3) If a juvenile is taken to any location described in subsection (1)(a) or (b) of this section, the juvenile may be held for up to twelve hours and must be examined by a mental health or chemical dependency professional within three hours of arrival.

(4) The authority provided pursuant to this section is in addition to existing authority under RCW 10.31.110 and 10.31.120.
[2014 c 128 § 4; 2013 c 179 § 2.]

NOTES:

Finding—2014 c 128: See note following RCW 10.31.120.
Finding—2013 c 179: "The legislature finds that the large number of youth involved in the juvenile justice system with mental health challenges is of significant concern. Access to effective treatment is critical to the successful treatment of youth in the early stages of their contact with the juvenile justice system. Such access may prevent further involvement in the system after an initial contact or assist a youth in avoiding any further contact with the juvenile justice system altogether. There is growing evidence that mental health diversion strategies, in particular, are effective in connecting youth with needed treatment and preventing additional offending behaviors. These strategies allow a continuum of opportunities for connecting youth

who may be facing a mental illness or disorder to community mental health services at multiple decision points, such as law enforcement diversion, prosecutor diversion, court-based diversion, and court disposition. The effective use of these strategies can result not only in significant cost savings for the juvenile justice system, but can create the benefit of improved lives of the youth who face mental health challenges and barriers." [2013 c 179 § 1.]

13.40.045
Escapees—Arrest warrants.

The secretary, assistant secretary, or the secretary's designee shall issue arrest warrants for juveniles who escape from department residential custody. The secretary, assistant secretary, or the secretary's designee may issue arrest warrants for juveniles who abscond from parole supervision or fail to meet conditions of parole. These arrest warrants shall authorize any law enforcement, probation and parole, or peace officer of this state, or any other state where the juvenile is located, to arrest the juvenile and to place the juvenile in physical custody pending the juvenile's return to confinement in a state juvenile rehabilitation facility.
[1997 c 338 § 14; 1994 sp.s. c 7 § 518.]
NOTES:
> **Finding—Evaluation—Report—1997 c 338:** See note following RCW 13.40.0357.
> **Severability—Effective dates—1997 c 338:** See notes following RCW 5.60.060.
> **Finding—Intent—Severability—1994 sp.s. c 7:** See notes following RCW 43.70.540.

13.40.050
Detention procedures—Notice of hearing—Conditions of release—Consultation with parent, guardian, or custodian.

(1) When a juvenile taken into custody is held in detention:
(a) An information, a community supervision modification or termination of diversion petition, or a parole modification petition shall be filed within seventy-two hours, Saturdays, Sundays, and holidays excluded, or the juvenile shall be released; and
(b) A detention hearing, a community supervision modification or termination of diversion petition, or a parole modification petition shall be held within seventy-two hours, Saturdays, Sundays, and holidays excluded, from the time of filing the information or petition, to determine whether continued detention is necessary under RCW 13.40.040.
(2) Notice of the detention hearing, stating the time, place, and purpose of the hearing, stating the right to counsel, and requiring attendance shall be given to the parent, guardian, or custodian if such person can be found and shall also be given to the juvenile if over twelve years of age.

(3) At the commencement of the detention hearing, the court shall advise the parties of their rights under this chapter and shall appoint counsel as specified in this chapter.

(4) The court shall, based upon the allegations in the information, determine whether the case is properly before it or whether the case should be treated as a diversion case under RCW 13.40.080. If the case is not properly before the court the juvenile shall be ordered released.

(5) Notwithstanding a determination that the case is properly before the court and that probable cause exists, a juvenile shall at the detention hearing be ordered released on the juvenile's personal recognizance pending further hearing unless the court finds detention is necessary under RCW 13.40.040.

(6) If detention is not necessary under RCW 13.40.040, the court shall impose the most appropriate of the following conditions or, if necessary, any combination of the following conditions:

(a) Place the juvenile in the custody of a designated person agreeing to supervise such juvenile;

(b) Place restrictions on the travel of the juvenile during the period of release;

(c) Require the juvenile to report regularly to and remain under the supervision of the juvenile court;

(d) Impose any condition other than detention deemed reasonably necessary to assure appearance as required;

(e) Require that the juvenile return to detention during specified hours; or

(f) Require the juvenile to post a probation bond set by the court under terms and conditions as provided in *RCW 13.40.040(4).

(7) A juvenile may be released only to a responsible adult or the department.

(8) If the parent, guardian, or custodian of the juvenile in detention is available, the court shall consult with them prior to a determination to further detain or release the juvenile or treat the case as a diversion case under RCW 13.40.080.

(9) A person notified under this section who fails without reasonable cause to appear and abide by the order of the court may be proceeded against as for contempt of court. In determining whether a parent, guardian, or custodian had reasonable cause not to appear, the court may consider all factors relevant to the person's ability to appear as summoned.

[1997 c 338 § 15; 1995 c 395 § 5; 1992 c 205 § 106; 1979 c 155 § 58; 1977 ex.s. c 291 § 59.]

NOTES:

*Reviser's note: RCW 13.40.040 was amended by 2002 c 171 § 2, changing subsection (4) to subsection (5).

Finding—Evaluation—Report—1997 c 338: See note following RCW 13.40.0357.

Severability—Effective dates—1997 c 338: See notes following RCW 5.60.060.

Part headings not law—Severability—1992 c 205: See notes following RCW 13.40.010.

Effective date—Severability—1979 c 155: See notes following RCW 13.04.011.

Effective dates—Severability—1977 ex.s. c 291: See notes following RCW 13.04.005.

13.40.054
Probation bond or collateral—Modification or revocation of probation bond.

(1) As provided in this chapter, the court may order a juvenile to post a probation bond as defined in RCW 13.40.020 or to deposit cash or post other collateral in lieu of a probation bond, to enhance public safety, increase the likelihood that a respondent will appear as required to respond to charges, and increase compliance with community supervision imposed under various alternative disposition options. The parents or guardians of the juvenile may sign for a probation bond on behalf of the juvenile or deposit cash or other collateral in lieu of a bond if approved by the court.

(2) A parent or guardian who has signed for a probation bond, deposited cash, or posted other collateral on behalf of a juvenile has the right to notify the court if the juvenile violates any of the terms and conditions of the bond. The parent or guardian who signed for a probation bond may move the court to modify the terms of the bond or revoke the bond without penalty to the surety or parent. The court shall notify the surety if a parent or guardian notifies the court that the juvenile has violated conditions of the probation bond and has requested modification or revocation of the bond. At a hearing on the motion, the court may consider the nature and seriousness of the violation or violations and may either keep the bond in effect, modify the terms of the bond with the consent of the parent or guardian and surety, or revoke the bond. If the court revokes the bond the court may require full payment of the face amount of the bond. In the alternative, the court may revoke the bond and impose a partial payment for less than the full amount of the bond or may revoke the bond without imposing any penalty. In reaching its decision, the court may consider the timeliness of the parent's or guardian's notification to the court and the efforts of the parent and surety to monitor the offender's compliance with conditions of the bond and release. A surety shall have the same obligations and rights as provided sureties in adult criminal cases. Rules of forfeiture and revocation of bonds issued in adult criminal cases shall apply to forfeiture and revocation of probation bonds issued under this chapter except as specifically provided in this subsection.
[1995 c 395 § 1.]

13.40.056
Nonrefundable bail fee.

When a juvenile charged with an offense posts a probation bond or deposits cash or posts other collateral in lieu of a bond, ten dollars of the total amount required to be posted as bail shall be paid in cash as a nonrefundable bail fee. The bail fee shall be distributed to the county for costs associated with implementing chapter 395, Laws of 1995.
[1995 c 395 § 9.]

13.40.060
Jurisdiction of actions—Transfer of case and records, when—Change in venue, grounds.

(1) All actions under this chapter shall be commenced and tried in the county where any element of the offense was committed except as otherwise specially provided by statute. In cases in which diversion is provided by statute, venue is in the county in which the juvenile resides or in the county in which any element of the offense was committed.

(2)(a) The court upon motion of any party or upon its own motion may, at any time, transfer a proceeding to another juvenile court when there is reason to believe that an impartial proceeding cannot be held in the county in which the proceeding was begun; and

(b) A court may transfer a proceeding to another juvenile court following disposition for the purposes of supervision and enforcement of the disposition order.

(3) If the court orders a transfer of the proceeding pursuant to subsection (2)(b) of this section:

(a) The case and copies of only those legal and social documents pertaining thereto shall be transferred to the county in which the juvenile resides, without regard to whether or not his or her custodial parent resides there, for supervision and enforcement of the disposition order.

(b) If any restitution is yet to be determined, the originating court shall transfer the case to the new county with the exception of the restitution. Venue over restitution shall be retained by the originating court for purposes of establishing a restitution order. Once restitution is determined, the originating county shall then transfer venue over modification and enforcement of the restitution to the new county.

(c) The court of the receiving county may modify and enforce the disposition order, including restitution.

(d) The clerk of the originating county shall maintain the account receivable in the judicial information system and all payments shall be made to the clerk of the originating county.

(e) Any collection of the offender legal financial obligation shall be managed by the juvenile probation department of the new county while the offender is under juvenile probation supervision, or by the clerk of the original county at the conclusion of supervision by juvenile probation. The probation department of the new county shall notify the clerk of the originating county when they end supervision of the offender.

(f) In cases where a civil judgment has already been established, venue may not be transferred to another county.

[2005 c 165 § 1; 1997 c 338 § 16; 1989 c 71 § 1; 1981 c 299 § 6; 1979 c 155 § 59; 1977 ex.s. c 291 § 60.]

NOTES:

Finding—Evaluation—Report—1997 c 338: See note following RCW 13.40.0357.

Severability—Effective dates—1997 c 338: See notes following RCW 5.60.060.

Effective date—1989 c 71: "This act shall take effect September 1, 1989." [1989 c 71 § 2.]

Effective date—Severability—1979 c 155: See notes following RCW 13.04.011.

Effective dates—Severability—1977 ex.s. c 291: See notes following RCW 13.04.005.

13.40.070

Complaints—Screening—Filing information—Diversion—Modification of community supervision—Notice to parent or guardian—Probation counselor acting for prosecutor—Referral to mediation or reconciliation programs.

(1) Complaints referred to the juvenile court alleging the commission of an offense shall be referred directly to the prosecutor. The prosecutor, upon receipt of a complaint, shall screen the complaint to determine whether:

(a) The alleged facts bring the case within the jurisdiction of the court; and

(b) On a basis of available evidence there is probable cause to believe that the juvenile did commit the offense.

(2) If the identical alleged acts constitute an offense under both the law of this state and an ordinance of any city or county of this state, state law shall govern the prosecutor's screening and charging decision for both filed and diverted cases.

(3) If the requirements of subsections (1)(a) and (b) of this section are met, the prosecutor shall either file an information in juvenile court or divert the case, as set forth in subsections (5), (6), and (8) of this section. If the prosecutor finds that the requirements of subsection (1)(a) and (b) of this section are not met, the prosecutor shall maintain a record, for one year, of such decision and the reasons therefor. In lieu of filing an information or diverting an offense a prosecutor may file a motion to modify community supervision where such offense constitutes a violation of community supervision.

(4) An information shall be a plain, concise, and definite written statement of the essential facts constituting the offense charged. It shall be signed by the prosecuting attorney and conform to chapter 10.37 RCW.

(5) Except as provided in RCW 13.40.213 and subsection (7) of this section, where a case is legally sufficient, the prosecutor shall file an information with the juvenile court if:

(a) An alleged offender is accused of a class A felony, a class B felony, an attempt to commit a class B felony, a class C felony listed in RCW 9.94A.411(2) as a crime against persons or listed in RCW 9A.46.060 as a crime of harassment, or a class C felony that is a violation of RCW 9.41.080 or * 9.41.040(2)(a)(iii); or

(b) An alleged offender is accused of a felony and has a criminal history of any felony, or at least two gross misdemeanors, or at least two misdemeanors; or

(c) An alleged offender has previously been committed to the department; or

(d) An alleged offender has been referred by a diversion unit for prosecution or desires prosecution instead of diversion; or

(e) An alleged offender has three or more diversion agreements on the alleged offender's criminal history; or

(f) A special allegation has been filed that the offender or an accomplice was armed with a firearm when the offense was committed.

(6) Where a case is legally sufficient the prosecutor shall divert the case if the alleged offense is a misdemeanor or gross misdemeanor or violation and the alleged offense is the offender's first

offense or violation. If the alleged offender is charged with a related offense that must or may be filed under subsections (5) and (8) of this section, a case under this subsection may also be filed.

(7) Where a case is legally sufficient to charge an alleged offender with either prostitution or prostitution loitering and the alleged offense is the offender's first prostitution or prostitution loitering offense, the prosecutor shall divert the case.

(8) Where a case is legally sufficient and falls into neither subsection (5) nor (6) of this section, it may be filed or diverted. In deciding whether to file or divert an offense under this section the prosecutor shall be guided only by the length, seriousness, and recency of the alleged offender's criminal history and the circumstances surrounding the commission of the alleged offense.

(9) Whenever a juvenile is placed in custody or, where not placed in custody, referred to a diversion interview, the parent or legal guardian of the juvenile shall be notified as soon as possible concerning the allegation made against the juvenile and the current status of the juvenile. Where a case involves victims of crimes against persons or victims whose property has not been recovered at the time a juvenile is referred to a diversion unit, the victim shall be notified of the referral and informed how to contact the unit.

(10) The responsibilities of the prosecutor under subsections (1) through (9) of this section may be performed by a juvenile court probation counselor for any complaint referred to the court alleging the commission of an offense which would not be a felony if committed by an adult, if the prosecutor has given sufficient written notice to the juvenile court that the prosecutor will not review such complaints.

(11) The prosecutor, juvenile court probation counselor, or diversion unit may, in exercising their authority under this section or RCW 13.40.080, refer juveniles to mediation or victim offender reconciliation programs. Such mediation or victim offender reconciliation programs shall be voluntary for victims.

[2013 c 179 § 3; 2010 c 289 § 7; 2009 c 252 § 3; 2003 c 53 § 98; 2001 c 175 § 2; 1997 c 338 § 17; 1994 sp.s. c 7 § 543; 1992 c 205 § 107; 1989 c 407 § 9; 1983 c 191 § 18; 1981 c 299 § 7; 1979 c 155 § 60; 1977 ex.s. c 291 § 61.]

NOTES:

*Reviser's note: RCW 9.41.040 was amended by 2014 c 111 § 1, changing subsection (2)(a)(iii) to subsection (2)(a)(iv).

Finding—2013 c 179: See note following RCW 13.40.042.

Findings—2009 c 252: See note following RCW 13.40.213.

Intent—Effective date—2003 c 53: See notes following RCW 2.48.180.

Finding—Evaluation—Report—1997 c 338: See note following RCW 13.40.0357.

Severability—Effective dates—1997 c 338: See notes following RCW 5.60.060.

Finding—Intent—Severability—1994 sp.s. c 7: See notes following RCW 43.70.540.

Application—1994 sp.s. c 7 §§ 540-545: See note following RCW 13.50.010.

Part headings not law—Severability—1992 c 205: See notes following RCW 13.40.010.

Effective date—Severability—1979 c 155: See notes following RCW 13.04.011.

Effective dates—Severability—1977 ex.s. c 291: See notes following RCW 13.04.005.

13.40.077
Recommended prosecuting standards for charging and plea dispositions.

RECOMMENDED PROSECUTING STANDARDS
FOR CHARGING AND PLEA DISPOSITIONS

INTRODUCTION: These standards are intended solely for the guidance of prosecutors in the state of Washington. They are not intended to, do not, and may not be relied upon to create a right or benefit, substantive or procedural, enforceable at law by a party in litigation with the state.

Evidentiary sufficiency.

(1) Decision not to prosecute.

STANDARD: A prosecuting attorney may decline to prosecute, even though technically sufficient evidence to prosecute exists, in situations where prosecution would serve no public purpose, would defeat the underlying purpose of the law in question, or would result in decreased respect for the law. The decision not to prosecute or divert shall not be influenced by the race, gender, religion, or creed of the suspect.

GUIDELINES/COMMENTARY:

Examples

The following are examples of reasons not to prosecute which could satisfy the standard.

(a) Contrary to Legislative Intent - It may be proper to decline to charge where the application of criminal sanctions would be clearly contrary to the intent of the legislature in enacting the particular statute.

(b) Antiquated Statute - It may be proper to decline to charge where the statute in question is antiquated in that:

(i) It has not been enforced for many years;

(ii) Most members of society act as if it were no longer in existence;

(iii) It serves no deterrent or protective purpose in today's society; and

(iv) The statute has not been recently reconsidered by the legislature.

This reason is not to be construed as the basis for declining cases because the law in question is unpopular or because it is difficult to enforce.

(c) De Minimis Violation - It may be proper to decline to charge where the violation of law is only technical or insubstantial and where no public interest or deterrent purpose would be served by prosecution.

(d) Confinement on Other Charges - It may be proper to decline to charge because the accused has been sentenced on another charge to a lengthy period of confinement; and

(i) Conviction of the new offense would not merit any additional direct or collateral punishment;

(ii) The new offense is either a misdemeanor or a felony which is not particularly aggravated; and

(iii) Conviction of the new offense would not serve any significant deterrent purpose.

(e) Pending Conviction on Another Charge - It may be proper to decline to charge because the accused is facing a pending prosecution in the same or another county; and

(i) Conviction of the new offense would not merit any additional direct or collateral punishment;

(ii) Conviction in the pending prosecution is imminent;

(iii) The new offense is either a misdemeanor or a felony which is not particularly aggravated; and

(iv) Conviction of the new offense would not serve any significant deterrent purpose.

(f) High Disproportionate Cost of Prosecution - It may be proper to decline to charge where the cost of locating or transporting, or the burden on, prosecution witnesses is highly disproportionate to the importance of prosecuting the offense in question. The reason should be limited to minor cases and should not be relied upon in serious cases.

(g) Improper Motives of Complainant - It may be proper to decline charges because the motives of the complainant are improper and prosecution would serve no public purpose, would defeat the underlying purpose of the law in question, or would result in decreased respect for the law.

(h) Immunity - It may be proper to decline to charge where immunity is to be given to an accused in order to prosecute another where the accused information or testimony will reasonably lead to the conviction of others who are responsible for more serious criminal conduct or who represent a greater danger to the public interest.

(i) Victim Request - It may be proper to decline to charge because the victim requests that no criminal charges be filed and the case involves the following crimes or situations:

(i) Assault cases where the victim has suffered little or no injury;

(ii) Crimes against property, not involving violence, where no major loss was suffered;

(iii) Where doing so would not jeopardize the safety of society.

Care should be taken to insure that the victim's request is freely made and is not the product of threats or pressure by the accused.

The presence of these factors may also justify the decision to dismiss a prosecution which has been commenced.

Notification

The prosecutor is encouraged to notify the victim, when practical, and the law enforcement personnel, of the decision not to prosecute.

(2) Decision to prosecute.

STANDARD:

Crimes against persons will be filed if sufficient admissible evidence exists, which, when considered with the most plausible, reasonably foreseeable defense that could be raised under the evidence, would justify conviction by a reasonable and objective fact finder. With regard to offenses prohibited by RCW 9A.44.040, 9A.44.050, 9A.44.073, 9A.44.076, 9A.44.079, 9A.44.083, 9A.44.086, 9A.44.089, and 9A.64.020 the prosecutor should avoid prefiling agreements or diversions intended to place the accused in a program of treatment or counseling, so that treatment, if determined to be beneficial, can be proved under *RCW 13.40.160(4).

Crimes against property/other crimes will be filed if the admissible evidence is of such convincing force as to make it probable that a reasonable and objective fact finder would convict after hearing all the admissible evidence and the most plausible defense that could be raised.

The categorization of crimes for these charging standards shall be the same as found in RCW 9.94A.411(2).

The decision to prosecute or use diversion shall not be influenced by the race, gender, religion, or creed of the respondent.

(3) Selection of Charges/Degree of Charge

(a) The prosecutor should file charges which adequately describe the nature of the respondent's conduct. Other offenses may be charged only if they are necessary to ensure that the charges:

(i) Will significantly enhance the strength of the state's case at trial; or

(ii) Will result in restitution to all victims.

(b) The prosecutor should not overcharge to obtain a guilty plea. Overcharging includes:

(i) Charging a higher degree;

(ii) Charging additional counts.

This standard is intended to direct prosecutors to charge those crimes which demonstrate the nature and seriousness of a respondent's criminal conduct, but to decline to charge crimes which are not necessary to such an indication. Crimes which do not merge as a matter of law, but which arise from the same course of conduct, do not all have to be charged.

(4) Police Investigation

A prosecuting attorney is dependent upon law enforcement agencies to conduct the necessary factual investigation which must precede the decision to prosecute. The prosecuting attorney shall ensure that a thorough factual investigation has been conducted before a decision to prosecute is made. In ordinary circumstances the investigation should include the following:

(a) The interviewing of all material witnesses, together with the obtaining of written statements whenever possible;

(b) The completion of necessary laboratory tests; and

(c) The obtaining, in accordance with constitutional requirements, of the suspect's version of the events.

If the initial investigation is incomplete, a prosecuting attorney should insist upon further investigation before a decision to prosecute is made, and specify what the investigation needs to include.

(5) Exceptions

In certain situations, a prosecuting attorney may authorize filing of a criminal complaint before the investigation is complete if:

(a) Probable cause exists to believe the suspect is guilty; and

(b) The suspect presents a danger to the community or is likely to flee if not apprehended; or

(c) The arrest of the suspect is necessary to complete the investigation of the crime.

In the event that the exception to the standard is applied, the prosecuting attorney shall obtain a commitment from the law enforcement agency involved to complete the investigation in a timely manner. If the subsequent investigation does not produce sufficient evidence to meet the normal charging standard, the complaint should be dismissed.

(6) Investigation Techniques

The prosecutor should be fully advised of the investigatory techniques that were used in the case investigation including:

(a) Polygraph testing;

(b) Hypnosis;

(c) Electronic surveillance;

(d) Use of informants.

(7) Prefiling Discussions with Defendant

Discussions with the defendant or his or her representative regarding the selection or disposition of charges may occur prior to the filing of charges, and potential agreements can be reached.

(8) Plea dispositions:

STANDARD

(a) Except as provided in subsection (2) of this section, a respondent will normally be expected to plead guilty to the charge or charges which adequately describe the nature of his or her criminal conduct or go to trial.

(b) In certain circumstances, a plea agreement with a respondent in exchange for a plea of guilty to a charge or charges that may not fully describe the nature of his or her criminal conduct may be necessary and in the public interest. Such situations may include the following:

(i) Evidentiary problems which make conviction of the original charges doubtful;

(ii) The respondent's willingness to cooperate in the investigation or prosecution of others whose criminal conduct is more serious or represents a greater public threat;

(iii) A request by the victim when it is not the result of pressure from the respondent;

(iv) The discovery of facts which mitigate the seriousness of the respondent's conduct;

(v) The correction of errors in the initial charging decision;

(vi) The respondent's history with respect to criminal activity;

(vii) The nature and seriousness of the offense or offenses charged;

(viii) The probable effect of witnesses.

(c) No plea agreement shall be influenced by the race, gender, religion, or creed of the respondent. This includes but is not limited to the prosecutor's decision to utilize such disposition alternatives as the Special Sex Offender Disposition Alternative, the Chemical Dependency Disposition Alternative, and manifest injustice.

(9) Disposition recommendations:

STANDARD

The prosecutor may reach an agreement regarding disposition recommendations.

The prosecutor shall not agree to withhold relevant information from the court concerning the plea agreement.

[1997 c 338 § 18; 1996 c 9 § 1.]

NOTES:

      *Reviser's note: RCW 13.40.160 was amended by 1999 c 91 § 2, changing subsection (4) to subsection (3). RCW 13.40.160 was subsequently amended by 2011 c 338 § 2, deleting subsection (3).

      Finding—Evaluation—Report—1997 c 338: See note following RCW 13.40.0357.

      Severability—Effective dates—1997 c 338: See notes following RCW 5.60.060.

13.40.080
Diversion agreement—Scope—Limitations—Restitution orders—Divertee's rights—Diversion unit's powers and duties—Interpreters—Modification.

(1) A diversion agreement shall be a contract between a juvenile accused of an offense and a diversion unit whereby the juvenile agrees to fulfill certain conditions in lieu of prosecution. Such agreements may be entered into only after the prosecutor, or probation counselor pursuant to this chapter, has determined that probable cause exists to believe that a crime has been committed and that the juvenile committed it. Such agreements shall be entered into as expeditiously as possible.

(2) A diversion agreement shall be limited to one or more of the following:

(a) Community restitution not to exceed one hundred fifty hours, not to be performed during school hours if the juvenile is attending school;

(b) Restitution limited to the amount of actual loss incurred by any victim;

(c) Attendance at up to ten hours of counseling and/or up to twenty hours of educational or informational sessions at a community agency. The educational or informational sessions may include sessions relating to respect for self, others, and authority; victim awareness; accountability; self-worth; responsibility; work ethics; good citizenship; literacy; and life skills. If an assessment identifies mental health or chemical dependency needs, a youth may access up to thirty hours of counseling. The counseling sessions may include services demonstrated to improve behavioral health and reduce recidivism. For purposes of this section, "community agency" may also mean a community-based nonprofit organization, a physician, a counselor, a school, or a treatment provider, if approved by the diversion unit. The state shall not be liable for costs resulting from the diversion unit exercising the option to permit diversion agreements to mandate attendance at up to thirty hours of counseling and/or up to twenty hours of educational or informational sessions;

(d) Requirements to remain during specified hours at home, school, or work, and restrictions on leaving or entering specified geographical areas; and

(e) Upon request of any victim or witness, requirements to refrain from any contact with victims or witnesses of offenses committed by the juvenile.

(3) Notwithstanding the provisions of subsection (2) of this section, youth courts are not limited to the conditions imposed by subsection (2) of this section in imposing sanctions on juveniles pursuant to RCW 13.40.630.

(4) In assessing periods of community restitution to be performed and restitution to be paid by a juvenile who has entered into a diversion agreement, the court officer to whom this task is assigned shall consult with the juvenile's custodial parent or parents or guardian. To the extent possible, the court officer shall advise the victims of the juvenile offender of the diversion process, offer victim impact letter forms and restitution claim forms, and involve members of the community. Such members of the community shall meet with the juvenile and advise the court officer as to the terms of the diversion agreement and shall supervise the juvenile in carrying out its terms.

(5)(a) A diversion agreement may not exceed a period of six months and may include a period extending beyond the eighteenth birthday of the divertee.

(b) If additional time is necessary for the juvenile to complete restitution to a victim, the time period limitations of this subsection may be extended by an additional six months.

(c) If the juvenile has not paid the full amount of restitution by the end of the additional six-month period, then the juvenile shall be referred to the juvenile court for entry of a civil order establishing the amount of restitution still owed to the victim. In this order, the court shall also determine the terms and conditions of the restitution, including a payment plan extending up to ten years if the court determines that the juvenile does not have the means to make full restitution over a shorter period. For the purposes of this subsection (5)(c), the juvenile shall remain under the court's jurisdiction for a maximum term of ten years after the juvenile's eighteenth birthday. Prior to the expiration of the initial ten-year period, the juvenile court may extend the judgment for restitution an additional ten years. The court may relieve the juvenile of the requirement to pay full or partial restitution if the juvenile reasonably satisfies the court that he or she does not have the means to make full or partial restitution and could not reasonably acquire the means to pay the restitution over a ten-year period. If the court relieves the juvenile of the requirement to pay full or partial restitution, the court may order an amount of community restitution that the court deems appropriate. The county clerk shall make disbursements to victims named in the order. The restitution to victims named in the order shall be paid prior to any payment for other penalties or monetary assessments. A juvenile under obligation to pay restitution may petition the court for modification of the restitution order.

(6) The juvenile shall retain the right to be referred to the court at any time prior to the signing of the diversion agreement.

(7) Divertees and potential divertees shall be afforded due process in all contacts with a diversion unit regardless of whether the juveniles are accepted for diversion or whether the diversion program is successfully completed. Such due process shall include, but not be limited to, the following:

(a) A written diversion agreement shall be executed stating all conditions in clearly understandable language;

(b) Violation of the terms of the agreement shall be the only grounds for termination;

(c) No divertee may be terminated from a diversion program without being given a court hearing, which hearing shall be preceded by:

(i) Written notice of alleged violations of the conditions of the diversion program; and

(ii) Disclosure of all evidence to be offered against the divertee;

(d) The hearing shall be conducted by the juvenile court and shall include:

(i) Opportunity to be heard in person and to present evidence;

(ii) The right to confront and cross-examine all adverse witnesses;

(iii) A written statement by the court as to the evidence relied on and the reasons for termination, should that be the decision; and

(iv) Demonstration by evidence that the divertee has substantially violated the terms of his or her diversion agreement;

(e) The prosecutor may file an information on the offense for which the divertee was diverted:

(i) In juvenile court if the divertee is under eighteen years of age; or

(ii) In superior court or the appropriate court of limited jurisdiction if the divertee is eighteen years of age or older.

(8) The diversion unit shall, subject to available funds, be responsible for providing interpreters when juveniles need interpreters to effectively communicate during diversion unit hearings or negotiations.

(9) The diversion unit shall be responsible for advising a divertee of his or her rights as provided in this chapter.

(10) The diversion unit may refer a juvenile to a restorative justice program, community-based counseling, or treatment programs.

(11) The right to counsel shall inure prior to the initial interview for purposes of advising the juvenile as to whether he or she desires to participate in the diversion process or to appear in the juvenile court. The juvenile may be represented by counsel at any critical stage of the diversion process, including intake interviews and termination hearings. The juvenile shall be fully advised at the intake of his or her right to an attorney and of the relevant services an attorney can provide. For the purpose of this section, intake interviews mean all interviews regarding the diversion agreement process.

The juvenile shall be advised that a diversion agreement shall constitute a part of the juvenile's criminal history as defined by RCW 13.40.020(8). A signed acknowledgment of such advisement shall be obtained from the juvenile, and the document shall be maintained by the diversion unit together with the diversion agreement, and a copy of both documents shall be delivered to the prosecutor if requested by the prosecutor. The supreme court shall promulgate rules setting forth the content of such advisement in simple language.

(12) When a juvenile enters into a diversion agreement, the juvenile court may receive only the following information for dispositional purposes:

(a) The fact that a charge or charges were made;

(b) The fact that a diversion agreement was entered into;

(c) The juvenile's obligations under such agreement;

(d) Whether the alleged offender performed his or her obligations under such agreement; and

(e) The facts of the alleged offense.

(13) A diversion unit may refuse to enter into a diversion agreement with a juvenile. When a diversion unit refuses to enter a diversion agreement with a juvenile, it shall immediately refer such juvenile to the court for action and shall forward to the court the criminal complaint and a detailed statement of its reasons for refusing to enter into a diversion agreement. The diversion unit shall also immediately refer the case to the prosecuting attorney for action if such juvenile violates the terms of the diversion agreement.

(14) A diversion unit may, in instances where it determines that the act or omission of an act for which a juvenile has been referred to it involved no victim, or where it determines that the juvenile referred to it has no prior criminal history and is alleged to have committed an illegal act involving no threat of or instance of actual physical harm and involving not more than fifty dollars in property loss or damage and that there is no loss outstanding to the person or firm suffering such damage or loss, counsel and release or release such a juvenile without entering into a diversion agreement. A diversion unit's authority to counsel and release a juvenile under this subsection includes the authority to refer the juvenile to community-based counseling or treatment programs or a restorative justice program. Any juvenile released under this subsection shall be advised that the act or omission of any act for which he or she had been referred shall constitute a part of the juvenile's criminal history as defined by RCW 13.40.020(8). A signed

acknowledgment of such advisement shall be obtained from the juvenile, and the document shall be maintained by the unit, and a copy of the document shall be delivered to the prosecutor if requested by the prosecutor. The supreme court shall promulgate rules setting forth the content of such advisement in simple language. A juvenile determined to be eligible by a diversion unit for release as provided in this subsection shall retain the same right to counsel and right to have his or her case referred to the court for formal action as any other juvenile referred to the unit.

(15) A diversion unit may supervise the fulfillment of a diversion agreement entered into before the juvenile's eighteenth birthday and which includes a period extending beyond the divertee's eighteenth birthday.

(16) If restitution required by a diversion agreement cannot reasonably be paid due to a change of circumstance, the diversion agreement may be modified at the request of the divertee and with the concurrence of the diversion unit to convert unpaid restitution into community restitution. The modification of the diversion agreement shall be in writing and signed by the divertee and the diversion unit. The number of hours of community restitution in lieu of a monetary penalty shall be converted at the rate of the prevailing state minimum wage per hour. [2015 c 265 § 25; 2014 c 128 § 5; 2013 c 179 § 4; 2012 c 201 § 2; 2004 c 120 § 3. Prior: 2002 c 237 § 8; 2002 c 175 § 21; 1999 c 91 § 1; 1997 c 338 § 70; 1997 c 121 § 8; 1996 c 124 § 1; 1994 sp.s. c 7 § 544; 1992 c 205 § 108; 1985 c 73 § 2; 1983 c 191 § 16; 1981 c 299 § 8; 1979 c 155 § 61; 1977 ex.s. c 291 § 62.]

NOTES:

      Finding—Intent—2015 c 265: See note following RCW 13.50.010.

      Finding—2014 c 128: See note following RCW 10.31.120.

      Finding—2013 c 179: See note following RCW 13.40.042.

      Effective date—2004 c 120: See note following RCW 13.40.010.

      Effective date—2002 c 175: See note following RCW 7.80.130.

      Finding—Evaluation—Report—1997 c 338: See note following RCW 13.40.0357.

      Severability—Effective dates—1997 c 338: See notes following RCW 5.60.060.

      Finding—Intent—Severability—1994 sp.s. c 7: See notes following RCW 43.70.540.

      Application—1994 sp.s. c 7 §§ 540-545: See note following RCW 13.50.010.

      Part headings not law—Severability—1992 c 205: See notes following RCW 13.40.010.

      Effective date—1985 c 73: See note following RCW 13.40.030.

      Effective date—Severability—1979 c 155: See notes following RCW 13.04.011.

      Effective dates—Severability—1977 ex.s. c 291: See notes following RCW 13.04.005.

13.40.085
Diversion services costs—Fees—Payment by parent or legal guardian.

The county legislative authority may authorize juvenile court administrators to establish fees to cover the costs of the administration and operation of diversion services provided under this chapter. The parent or legal guardian of a juvenile who receives diversion services must pay for the services based on the parent's or guardian's ability to pay. The juvenile court administrators shall develop a fair and equitable payment schedule. No juvenile who is eligible for diversion as provided in this chapter may be denied diversion services based on an inability to pay for the services.

[1993 c 171 § 1.]

13.40.087
Youth who have been diverted—Alleged prostitution or prostitution loitering offenses—Services and treatment.

Within available funding, when a youth who has been diverted under RCW 13.40.070 for an alleged offense of prostitution or prostitution loitering is referred to the department, the department shall connect that youth with the services and treatment specified in RCW * 74.14B.060 and 74.14B.070.

[2010 c 289 § 5.]

NOTES:

      *Reviser's note: RCW 74.14B.060 was repealed by 2012 c 29 § 14.

13.40.090
Prosecuting attorney as party to juvenile court proceedings—Exception, procedure.

The county prosecuting attorney shall be a party to all juvenile court proceedings involving juvenile offenders or alleged juvenile offenders.

The prosecuting attorney may, after giving appropriate notice to the juvenile court, decline to represent the state of Washington in juvenile court matters except felonies unless requested by the court on an individual basis to represent the state at an adjudicatory hearing in which case he or she shall participate. When the prosecutor declines to represent the state, then such function may be performed by the juvenile court probation counselor authorized by the court or local court rule to serve as the prosecuting authority.

If the prosecuting attorney elects not to participate, the prosecuting attorney shall file with the county clerk each year by the first Monday in July notice of intent not to participate. In a county wherein the prosecuting attorney has elected not to participate in juvenile court, he or she shall not thereafter until the next filing date participate in juvenile court proceedings unless so requested by the court on an individual basis, in which case the prosecuting attorney shall participate.

[1977 ex.s. c 291 § 63.]

NOTES:

   Effective dates—Severability—1977 ex.s. c 291: See notes following RCW 13.04.005.

13.40.100
Summons or other notification issued upon filing of information—Procedure—Order to take juvenile into custody—Contempt of court, when.

   (1) Upon the filing of an information the alleged offender shall be notified by summons, warrant, or other method approved by the court of the next required court appearance.

   (2) If notice is by summons, the clerk of the court shall issue a summons directed to the juvenile, if the juvenile is twelve or more years of age, and another to the parents, guardian, or custodian, and such other persons as appear to the court to be proper or necessary parties to the proceedings, requiring them to appear personally before the court at the time fixed to hear the petition. Where the custodian is summoned, the parent or guardian or both shall also be served with a summons.

   (3) A copy of the information shall be attached to each summons.

   (4) The summons shall advise the parties of the right to counsel.

   (5) The judge may endorse upon the summons an order directing the parents, guardian, or custodian having the custody or control of the juvenile to bring the juvenile to the hearing.

   (6) If it appears from affidavit or sworn statement presented to the judge that there is probable cause for the issuance of a warrant of arrest or that the juvenile needs to be taken into custody pursuant to RCW 13.34.050, the judge may endorse upon the summons an order that an officer serving the summons shall at once take the juvenile into custody and take the juvenile to the place of detention or shelter designated by the court.

   (7) Service of summons may be made under the direction of the court by any law enforcement officer or probation counselor.

   (8) If the person summoned as herein provided fails without reasonable cause to appear and abide the order of the court, the person may be proceeded against as for contempt of court. In determining whether a parent, guardian, or custodian had reasonable cause not to appear, the court may consider all factors relevant to the person's ability to appear as summoned.
   [1997 c 338 § 19; 1979 c 155 § 62; 1977 ex.s. c 291 § 64.]

NOTES:

   Finding—Evaluation—Report—1997 c 338: See note following RCW 13.40.0357.
   Severability—Effective dates—1997 c 338: See notes following RCW 5.60.060.
   Effective date—Severability—1979 c 155: See notes following RCW 13.04.011.
   Effective dates—Severability—1977 ex.s. c 291: See notes following RCW 13.04.005.

13.40.110
Hearing on question of declining jurisdiction—Held, when—Findings.

(1) Discretionary decline hearing - The prosecutor, respondent, or the court on its own motion may, before a hearing on the information on its merits, file a motion requesting the court to transfer the respondent for adult criminal prosecution and the matter shall be set for a hearing on the question of declining jurisdiction.

(2) Mandatory decline hearing - Unless waived by the court, the parties, and their counsel, a decline hearing shall be held when:

(a) The respondent is sixteen or seventeen years of age and the information alleges a class A felony or an attempt, solicitation, or conspiracy to commit a class A felony;

(b) The respondent is seventeen years of age and the information alleges assault in the second degree, extortion in the first degree, indecent liberties, child molestation in the second degree, kidnapping in the second degree, or robbery in the second degree; or

(c) The information alleges an escape by the respondent and the respondent is serving a minimum juvenile sentence to age twenty-one.

(3) The court after a decline hearing may order the case transferred for adult criminal prosecution upon a finding that the declination would be in the best interest of the juvenile or the public. The court shall consider the relevant reports, facts, opinions, and arguments presented by the parties and their counsel.

(4) When the respondent is transferred for criminal prosecution or retained for prosecution in juvenile court, the court shall set forth in writing its finding which shall be supported by relevant facts and opinions produced at the hearing.
[2009 c 454 § 3; 1997 c 338 § 20; 1990 c 3 § 303; 1988 c 145 § 18; 1979 c 155 § 63; 1977 ex.s. c 291 § 65.]
NOTES:

Finding—Evaluation—Report—1997 c 338: See note following RCW 13.40.0357.

Severability—Effective dates—1997 c 338: See notes following RCW 5.60.060.

Index, part headings not law—Severability—Effective dates—Application—1990 c 3: See RCW 18.155.900 through 18.155.902.

Effective date—Savings—Application—1988 c 145: See notes following RCW 9A.44.010.

Effective date—Severability—1979 c 155: See notes following RCW 13.04.011.

Effective dates—Severability—1977 ex.s. c 291: See notes following RCW 13.04.005.

13.40.120
Hearings—Time and place.

All hearings may be conducted at any time or place within the limits of the judicial district, and such cases may not be heard in conjunction with other business of any other division of the superior court.

[1981 c 299 § 9; 1979 c 155 § 64; 1977 ex.s. c 291 § 66.]
NOTES:
      Effective date—Severability—1979 c 155: See notes following RCW 13.04.011.
      Effective dates—Severability—1977 ex.s. c 291: See notes following RCW 13.04.005.

13.40.127
Deferred disposition.

(1) A juvenile is eligible for deferred disposition unless he or she:

(a) Is charged with a sex or violent offense;

(b) Has a criminal history which includes any felony;

(c) Has a prior deferred disposition or deferred adjudication; or

(d) Has two or more adjudications.

(2) The juvenile court may, upon motion at least fourteen days before commencement of trial and, after consulting the juvenile's custodial parent or parents or guardian and with the consent of the juvenile, continue the case for disposition for a period not to exceed one year from the date the juvenile is found guilty. In all cases where the juvenile is eligible for a deferred disposition, there shall be a strong presumption that the deferred disposition will be granted. The court may waive the fourteen-day period anytime before the commencement of trial for good cause.

(3) Any juvenile who agrees to a deferral of disposition shall:

(a) Stipulate to the admissibility of the facts contained in the written police report;

(b) Acknowledge that the report will be entered and used to support a finding of guilt and to impose a disposition if the juvenile fails to comply with terms of supervision;

(c) Waive the following rights to: (i) A speedy disposition; and (ii) call and confront witnesses; and

(d) Acknowledge the direct consequences of being found guilty and the direct consequences that will happen if an order of disposition is entered.

The adjudicatory hearing shall be limited to a reading of the court's record.

(4) Following the stipulation, acknowledgment, waiver, and entry of a finding or plea of guilt, the court shall defer entry of an order of disposition of the juvenile.

(5) Any juvenile granted a deferral of disposition under this section shall be placed under community supervision. The court may impose any conditions of supervision that it deems appropriate including posting a probation bond. Payment of restitution under RCW 13.40.190 shall be a condition of community supervision under this section.

The court may require a juvenile offender convicted of animal cruelty in the first degree to submit to a mental health evaluation to determine if the offender would benefit from treatment and such intervention would promote the safety of the community. After consideration of the results of the evaluation, as a condition of community supervision, the court may order the offender to attend treatment to address issues pertinent to the offense.

The court may require the juvenile to undergo a mental health or substance abuse assessment, or both. If the assessment identifies a need for treatment, conditions of supervision may include treatment for the assessed need that has been demonstrated to improve behavioral health and reduce recidivism.

The court shall require a juvenile granted a deferral of disposition for unlawful possession of a firearm in violation of RCW 9.41.040 to participate in a qualifying program as described in RCW 13.40.193(2)(b), when available, unless the court makes a written finding based on the outcome of the juvenile court risk assessment that participation in a qualifying program would not be appropriate.

(6) A parent who signed for a probation bond has the right to notify the counselor if the juvenile fails to comply with the bond or conditions of supervision. The counselor shall notify the court and surety of any failure to comply. A surety shall notify the court of the juvenile's failure to comply with the probation bond. The state shall bear the burden to prove, by a preponderance of the evidence, that the juvenile has failed to comply with the terms of community supervision.

(7)(a) Anytime prior to the conclusion of the period of supervision, the prosecutor or the juvenile's juvenile court community supervision counselor may file a motion with the court requesting the court revoke the deferred disposition based on the juvenile's lack of compliance or treat the juvenile's lack of compliance as a violation pursuant to RCW 13.40.200.

(b) If the court finds the juvenile failed to comply with the terms of the deferred disposition, the court may:

(i) Revoke the deferred disposition and enter an order of disposition; or

(ii) Impose sanctions for the violation pursuant to RCW 13.40.200.

(8) At any time following deferral of disposition the court may, following a hearing, continue supervision for an additional one-year period for good cause.

(9)(a) At the conclusion of the period of supervision, the court shall determine whether the juvenile is entitled to dismissal of the deferred disposition only when the court finds:

(i) The deferred disposition has not been previously revoked;

(ii) The juvenile has completed the terms of supervision;

(iii) There are no pending motions concerning lack of compliance pursuant to subsection (7) of this section; and

(iv) The juvenile has either paid the full amount of restitution, or, made a good faith effort to pay the full amount of restitution during the period of supervision.

(b) If the court finds the juvenile is entitled to dismissal of the deferred disposition pursuant to (a) of this subsection, the juvenile's conviction shall be vacated and the court shall dismiss the case with prejudice, except that a conviction under RCW 16.52.205 shall not be vacated. Whenever a case is dismissed with restitution still owing, the court shall enter a restitution order pursuant to RCW 7.80.130 for any unpaid restitution. Jurisdiction to enforce payment and modify terms of the restitution order shall be the same as those set forth in RCW 7.80.130.

(c) If the court finds the juvenile is not entitled to dismissal of the deferred disposition pursuant to (a) of this subsection, the court shall revoke the deferred disposition and enter an order of disposition. A deferred disposition shall remain a conviction unless the case is dismissed and the conviction is vacated pursuant to (b) of this subsection or sealed pursuant to RCW 13.50.260.

(10)(a)(i) Any time the court vacates a conviction pursuant to subsection (9) of this section, if the juvenile is eighteen years of age or older and the full amount of restitution owing to the

---

individual victim named in the restitution order, excluding restitution owed to any insurance provider authorized under Title 48 RCW has been paid, the court shall enter a written order sealing the case.

(ii) Any time the court vacates a conviction pursuant to subsection (9) of this section, if the juvenile is not eighteen years of age or older and full restitution ordered has been paid, the court shall schedule an administrative sealing hearing to take place no later than thirty days after the respondent's eighteenth birthday, at which time the court shall enter a written order sealing the case. The respondent's presence at the administrative sealing hearing is not required.

(iii) Any deferred disposition vacated prior to June 7, 2012, is not subject to sealing under this subsection.

(b) Nothing in this subsection shall preclude a juvenile from petitioning the court to have the records of his or her deferred dispositions sealed under RCW 13.50.260.

(c) Records sealed under this provision shall have the same legal status as records sealed under RCW 13.50.260.

[2016 c 136 § 3; 2015 c 265 § 26. Prior: 2014 c 175 § 6; 2014 c 117 § 2; 2013 c 179 § 5; 2012 c 177 § 1; 2009 c 236 § 1; 2004 c 117 § 2; 2001 c 175 § 3; 1997 c 338 § 21.]

NOTES:

    Finding—Intent—2015 c 265: See note following RCW 13.50.010.
    Findings—Intent—2014 c 175: See note following RCW 13.50.010.
    Finding—2013 c 179: See note following RCW 13.40.042.
    Effective date—2004 c 117: See note following RCW 13.40.0357.
    Finding—Evaluation—Report—1997 c 338: See note following RCW 13.40.0357.
    Severability—Effective dates—1997 c 338: See notes following RCW 5.60.060.

13.40.130
Procedure upon plea of guilty or not guilty to information allegations—Notice—Adjudicatory and disposition hearing—Disposition standards used in sentencing.

(1) The respondent shall be advised of the allegations in the information and shall be required to plead guilty or not guilty to the allegation(s). The state or the respondent may make preliminary motions up to the time of the plea.

(2) If the respondent pleads guilty, the court may proceed with disposition or may continue the case for a dispositional hearing. If the respondent denies guilt, an adjudicatory hearing date shall be set. The court shall notify the parent, guardian, or custodian who has custody of a juvenile described in the charging document of the dispositional or adjudicatory hearing and shall require attendance.

(3) At the adjudicatory hearing it shall be the burden of the prosecution to prove the allegations of the information beyond a reasonable doubt.

(4) The court shall record its findings of fact and shall enter its decision upon the record. Such findings shall set forth the evidence relied upon by the court in reaching its decision.

(5) If the respondent is found not guilty he or she shall be released from detention.

(6) If the respondent is found guilty the court may immediately proceed to disposition or may continue the case for a dispositional hearing. Notice of the time and place of the continued hearing may be given in open court. If notice is not given in open court to a party, the party and the parent, guardian, or custodian who has custody of the juvenile shall be notified by mail of the time and place of the continued hearing.

(7) The court following an adjudicatory hearing may request that a predisposition study be prepared to aid the court in its evaluation of the matters relevant to disposition of the case.

(8) The disposition hearing shall be held within fourteen days after the adjudicatory hearing or plea of guilty unless good cause is shown for further delay, or within twenty-one days if the juvenile is not held in a detention facility, unless good cause is shown for further delay.

(9) In sentencing an offender, the court shall use the disposition standards in effect on the date of the offense.

(10) A person notified under this section who fails without reasonable cause to appear and abide by the order of the court may be proceeded against as for contempt of court. In determining whether a parent, guardian, or custodian had reasonable cause not to appear, the court may consider all factors relevant to the person's ability to appear as summoned.

[1997 c 338 § 22; 1981 c 299 § 10; 1979 c 155 § 65; 1977 ex.s. c 291 § 67.]

NOTES:

> **Finding—Evaluation—Report—1997 c 338:** See note following RCW 13.40.0357.
> **Severability—Effective dates—1997 c 338:** See notes following RCW 5.60.060.
> **Effective date—Severability—1979 c 155:** See notes following RCW 13.04.011.
> **Effective dates—Severability—1977 ex.s. c 291:** See notes following RCW 13.04.005.

13.40.135
Sexual motivation special allegation—Procedures.

(1) The prosecuting attorney shall file a special allegation of sexual motivation in every juvenile offense other than sex offenses as defined in RCW 9.94A.030 when sufficient admissible evidence exists, which, when considered with the most plausible, reasonably consistent defense that could be raised under the evidence, would justify a finding of sexual motivation by a reasonable and objective fact finder.

(2) In a juvenile case wherein there has been a special allegation the state shall prove beyond a reasonable doubt that the juvenile committed the offense with a sexual motivation. The court shall make a finding of fact of whether or not the sexual motivation was present at the time of the commission of the offense. This finding shall not be applied to sex offenses as defined in RCW 9.94A.030.

(3) The prosecuting attorney shall not withdraw the special allegation of "sexual motivation" without approval of the court through an order of dismissal. The court shall not dismiss the special allegation unless it finds that such an order is necessary to correct an error in the initial charging decision or unless there are evidentiary problems which make proving the special allegation doubtful.

[2009 c 28 § 33; 1997 c 338 § 23; 1990 c 3 § 604.]
NOTES:

      Effective date—2009 c 28: See note following RCW 2.24.040.

      Finding—Evaluation—Report—1997 c 338: See note following RCW 13.40.0357.

      Severability—Effective dates—1997 c 338: See notes following RCW 5.60.060.

      Effective date—Application—1990 c 3 §§ 601-605: See note following RCW 9.94A.835.

      Index, part headings not law—Severability—Effective dates—Application—1990 c 3: See RCW 18.155.900 through 18.155.902.

13.40.140
Juveniles entitled to usual judicial rights—Notice of—Open court—Privilege against self-incrimination—Waiver of rights, when.

(1) A juvenile shall be advised of his or her rights when appearing before the court.

(2) A juvenile and his or her parent, guardian, or custodian shall be advised by the court or its representative that the juvenile has a right to be represented by counsel at all critical stages of the proceedings. Unless waived, counsel shall be provided to a juvenile who is financially unable to obtain counsel without causing substantial hardship to himself or herself or the juvenile's family, in any proceeding where the juvenile may be subject to transfer for criminal prosecution, or in any proceeding where the juvenile may be in danger of confinement. The ability to pay part of the cost of counsel does not preclude assignment. In no case may a juvenile be deprived of counsel because of a parent, guardian, or custodian refusing to pay therefor. The juvenile shall be fully advised of his or her right to an attorney and of the relevant services an attorney can provide.

(3) The right to counsel includes the right to the appointment of experts necessary, and the experts shall be required pursuant to the procedures and requirements established by the supreme court.

(4) Upon application of a party, the clerk of the court shall issue, and the court on its own motion may issue, subpoenas requiring attendance and testimony of witnesses and production of records, documents, or other tangible objects at any hearing, or such subpoenas may be issued by an attorney of record.

(5) All proceedings shall be transcribed verbatim by means which will provide an accurate record.

(6) The general public and press shall be permitted to attend any hearing unless the court, for good cause, orders a particular hearing to be closed. The presumption shall be that all such hearings will be open.

(7) In all adjudicatory proceedings before the court, all parties shall have the right to adequate notice, discovery as provided in criminal cases, opportunity to be heard, confrontation of witnesses except in such cases as this chapter expressly permits the use of hearsay testimony, findings based solely upon the evidence adduced at the hearing, and an unbiased fact finder.

(8) A juvenile shall be accorded the same privilege against self-incrimination as an adult. An extrajudicial statement which would be constitutionally inadmissible in a criminal proceeding may not be received in evidence at an adjudicatory hearing over objection. Evidence illegally seized or obtained may not be received in evidence over objection at an adjudicatory hearing to prove the allegations against the juvenile if the evidence would be inadmissible in an adult criminal proceeding. An extrajudicial admission or confession made by the juvenile out of court is insufficient to support a finding that the juvenile committed the acts alleged in the information unless evidence of a corpus delicti is first independently established in the same manner as required in an adult criminal proceeding.

(9) Statements, admissions, or confessions made by a juvenile in the course of a mental health or chemical dependency screening or assessment, whether or not the screening or assessment was ordered by the court, shall not be admissible into evidence against the juvenile on the issue of guilt in any juvenile offense matter or adult criminal proceeding, unless the juvenile has placed his or her mental health at issue. The statement is admissible for any other purpose or proceeding allowed by law. This prohibition does not apply to statements, admissions, or confessions made to law enforcement, and may not be used to argue for derivative suppression of other evidence lawfully obtained as a result of an otherwise inadmissible statement, admission, or confession.

(10) Waiver of any right which a juvenile has under this chapter must be an express waiver intelligently made by the juvenile after the juvenile has been fully informed of the right being waived.

(11) Whenever this chapter refers to waiver or objection by a juvenile, the word juvenile shall be construed to refer to a juvenile who is at least twelve years of age. If a juvenile is under twelve years of age, the juvenile's parent, guardian, or custodian shall give any waiver or offer any objection contemplated by this chapter.

[2014 c 110 § 2; 1981 c 299 § 11; 1979 c 155 § 66; 1977 ex.s. c 291 § 68.]

NOTES:

> **Effective date—Severability—1979 c 155:** See notes following RCW 13.04.011.
> **Effective dates—Severability—1977 ex.s. c 291:** See notes following RCW 13.04.005.

13.40.150

Disposition hearing—Scope—Factors to be considered prior to entry of dispositional order.

(1) In disposition hearings all relevant and material evidence, including oral and written reports, may be received by the court and may be relied upon to the extent of its probative value, even though such evidence may not be admissible in a hearing on the information. The youth or the youth's counsel and the prosecuting attorney shall be afforded an opportunity to examine and controvert written reports so received and to cross-examine individuals making reports when such individuals are reasonably available, but sources of confidential information need not be

disclosed. The prosecutor and counsel for the juvenile may submit recommendations for disposition.

(2) For purposes of disposition:

(a) Violations which are current offenses count as misdemeanors;

(b) Violations may not count as part of the offender's criminal history;

(c) In no event may a disposition for a violation include confinement.

(3) Before entering a dispositional order as to a respondent found to have committed an offense, the court shall hold a disposition hearing, at which the court shall:

(a) Consider the facts supporting the allegations of criminal conduct by the respondent;

(b) Consider information and arguments offered by parties and their counsel;

(c) Consider any predisposition reports;

(d) Consult with the respondent's parent, guardian, or custodian on the appropriateness of dispositional options under consideration and afford the respondent and the respondent's parent, guardian, or custodian an opportunity to speak in the respondent's behalf;

(e) Allow the victim or a representative of the victim and an investigative law enforcement officer to speak;

(f) Determine the amount of restitution owing to the victim, if any, or set a hearing for a later date not to exceed one hundred eighty days from the date of the disposition hearing to determine the amount, except that the court may continue the hearing beyond the one hundred eighty days for good cause;

(g) Determine the respondent's offender score;

(h) Consider whether or not any of the following mitigating factors exist:

(i) The respondent's conduct neither caused nor threatened serious bodily injury or the respondent did not contemplate that his or her conduct would cause or threaten serious bodily injury;

(ii) The respondent acted under strong and immediate provocation;

(iii) The respondent was suffering from a mental or physical condition that significantly reduced his or her culpability for the offense though failing to establish a defense;

(iv) Prior to his or her detection, the respondent compensated or made a good faith attempt to compensate the victim for the injury or loss sustained; and

(v) There has been at least one year between the respondent's current offense and any prior criminal offense;

(i) Consider whether or not any of the following aggravating factors exist:

(i) In the commission of the offense, or in flight therefrom, the respondent inflicted or attempted to inflict serious bodily injury to another;

(ii) The offense was committed in an especially heinous, cruel, or depraved manner;

(iii) The victim or victims were particularly vulnerable;

(iv) The respondent has a recent criminal history or has failed to comply with conditions of a recent dispositional order or diversion agreement;

(v) The current offense included a finding of sexual motivation pursuant to RCW 13.40.135;

(vi) The respondent was the leader of a criminal enterprise involving several persons;

(vii) There are other complaints which have resulted in diversion or a finding or plea of guilty but which are not included as criminal history; and

(viii) The standard range disposition is clearly too lenient considering the seriousness of the juvenile's prior adjudications.

(4) The following factors may not be considered in determining the punishment to be imposed:

(a) The sex of the respondent;

(b) The race or color of the respondent or the respondent's family;

(c) The creed or religion of the respondent or the respondent's family;

(d) The economic or social class of the respondent or the respondent's family; and

(e) Factors indicating that the respondent may be or is a dependent child within the meaning of this chapter.

(5) A court may not commit a juvenile to a state institution solely because of the lack of facilities, including treatment facilities, existing in the community.

[1998 c 86 § 1; 1997 c 338 § 24; 1995 c 268 § 5; 1992 c 205 § 109; 1990 c 3 § 605; 1981 c 299 § 12; 1979 c 155 § 67; 1977 ex.s. c 291 § 69.]

NOTES:

> **Effective date—1998 c 86:** "This act takes effect July 1, 1998." [1998 c 86 § 2.]
> **Finding—Evaluation—Report—1997 c 338:** See note following RCW 13.40.0357.
> **Severability—Effective dates—1997 c 338:** See notes following RCW 5.60.060.
> **Purpose—1995 c 268:** See note following RCW 9.94A.030.
> **Part headings not law—Severability—1992 c 205:** See notes following RCW 13.40.010.
> **Effective date—Application—1990 c 3 §§ 601-605:** See note following RCW 9.94A.835.
> **Index, part headings not law—Severability—Effective dates—Application—1990 c 3:** See RCW 18.155.900 through 18.155.902.
> **Effective date—Severability—1979 c 155:** See notes following RCW 13.04.011.
> **Effective dates—Severability—1977 ex.s. c 291:** See notes following RCW 13.04.005.

13.40.160

Disposition order—Court's action prescribed—Disposition outside standard range—Right of appeal—Special sex offender disposition alternative.

(1) The standard range disposition for a juvenile adjudicated of an offense is determined according to RCW 13.40.0357.

(a) When the court sentences an offender to a local sanction as provided in RCW 13.40.0357 option A, the court shall impose a determinate disposition within the standard ranges, except as provided in subsection (2), (3), (4), (5), or (6) of this section. The disposition may be comprised of one or more local sanctions.

(b) When the court sentences an offender to a standard range as provided in RCW 13.40.0357 option A that includes a term of confinement exceeding thirty days, commitment

---

shall be to the department for the standard range of confinement, except as provided in subsection (2), (3), (4), (5), or (6) of this section.

(2) If the court concludes, and enters reasons for its conclusion, that disposition within the standard range would effectuate a manifest injustice the court shall impose a disposition outside the standard range, as indicated in option D of RCW 13.40.0357. The court's finding of manifest injustice shall be supported by clear and convincing evidence.

A disposition outside the standard range shall be determinate and shall be comprised of confinement or community supervision, or a combination thereof. When a judge finds a manifest injustice and imposes a sentence of confinement exceeding thirty days, the court shall sentence the juvenile to a maximum term, and the provisions of RCW 13.40.030(2) shall be used to determine the range. A disposition outside the standard range is appealable under RCW 13.40.230 by the state or the respondent. A disposition within the standard range is not appealable under RCW 13.40.230.

(3) If a juvenile offender is found to have committed a sex offense, other than a sex offense that is also a serious violent offense as defined by RCW 9.94A.030, and has no history of a prior sex offense, the court may impose the special sex offender disposition alternative under RCW 13.40.162.

(4) If the juvenile offender is subject to a standard range disposition of local sanctions or 15 to 36 weeks of confinement and has not committed an A- or B+ offense, the court may impose the disposition alternative under RCW 13.40.165.

(5) If a juvenile is subject to a commitment of 15 to 65 weeks of confinement, the court may impose the disposition alternative under *RCW 13.40.167.

(6) When the offender is subject to a standard range commitment of 15 to 36 weeks and is ineligible for a suspended disposition alternative, a manifest injustice disposition below the standard range, special sex offender disposition alternative, chemical dependency disposition alternative, or mental health disposition alternative, the court in a county with a pilot program under **RCW 13.40.169 may impose the disposition alternative under **RCW 13.40.169.

(7) RCW 13.40.193 shall govern the disposition of any juvenile adjudicated of possessing a firearm in violation of ***RCW 9.41.040(2)(a)(iii) or any crime in which a special finding is entered that the juvenile was armed with a firearm.

(8) RCW 13.40.308 shall govern the disposition of any juvenile adjudicated of theft of a motor vehicle as defined under RCW 9A.56.065, possession of a stolen motor vehicle as defined under RCW 9A.56.068, taking a motor vehicle without permission in the first degree under RCW 9A.56.070, and taking a motor vehicle without permission in the second degree under RCW 9A.56.075.

(9) Whenever a juvenile offender is entitled to credit for time spent in detention prior to a dispositional order, the dispositional order shall specifically state the number of days of credit for time served.

(10) Except as provided under subsection (3), (4), (5), or (6) of this section, or option B of RCW 13.40.0357, or RCW 13.40.127, the court shall not suspend or defer the imposition or the execution of the disposition.

(11) In no case shall the term of confinement imposed by the court at disposition exceed that to which an adult could be subjected for the same offense.

[2011 c 338 § 2; 2007 c 199 § 14. Prior: 2004 c 120 § 4; 2004 c 38 § 11; prior: 2003 c 378 § 3; 2003 c 53 § 99; 2002 c 175 § 22; 1999 c 91 § 2; prior: 1997 c 338 § 25; 1997 c 265 § 1; 1995 c 395 § 7; 1994 sp.s. c 7 § 523; 1992 c 45 § 6; 1990 c 3 § 302; 1989 c 407 § 4; 1983 c 191 § 8; 1981 c 299 § 13; 1979 c 155 § 68; 1977 ex.s. c 291 § 70.]

NOTES:

      Reviser's note: *(1) RCW 13.40.167 was repealed by 2016 c 106 § 4.

      **(2) RCW 13.40.169 expired July 1, 2005.

      ***(3) RCW 9.41.040 was amended by 2014 c 111 § 1, changing subsection (2)(a)(iii) to subsection (2)(a)(iv).

      Findings—Intent—Short title—2007 c 199: See notes following RCW 9A.56.065.

      Effective date—2004 c 120: See note following RCW 13.40.010.

      Effective date—2004 c 38: See note following RCW 18.155.075.

      Intent—Effective date—2003 c 53: See notes following RCW 2.48.180.

      Effective date—2002 c 175: See note following RCW 7.80.130.

      Finding—Evaluation—Report—1997 c 338: See note following RCW 13.40.0357.

      Severability—Effective dates—1997 c 338: See notes following RCW 5.60.060.

      Severability—1997 c 265: "If any provision of this act or its application to any person or circumstance is held invalid, the remainder of the act or the application of the provision to other persons or circumstances is not affected." [1997 c 265 § 9.]

      Finding—Intent—Severability—1994 sp.s. c 7: See notes following RCW 43.70.540.

      Severability—Application—1992 c 45: See notes following RCW 9.94A.840.

      Index, part headings not law—Severability—Effective dates—Application—1990 c 3: See RCW 18.155.900 through 18.155.902.

      Effective date—Severability—1979 c 155: See notes following RCW 13.04.011.

      Effective dates—Severability—1977 ex.s. c 291: See notes following RCW 13.04.005.

13.40.162
Special sex offender disposition alternative.

(1) A juvenile offender is eligible for the special sex offender disposition alternative when:

(a) The offender is found to have committed a sex offense, other than a sex offense that is also a serious violent offense as defined by RCW 9.94A.030; and

(b) The offender has no history of a prior sex offense.

(2) If the court finds the offender is eligible for this alternative, the court, on its own motion or the motion of the state or the respondent, may order an examination to determine whether the respondent is amenable to treatment.

(a) The report of the examination shall include at a minimum the following:

(i) The respondent's version of the facts and the official version of the facts;

(ii) The respondent's offense history;

(iii) An assessment of problems in addition to alleged deviant behaviors;

(iv) The respondent's social, educational, and employment situation;

(v) Other evaluation measures used.

The report shall set forth the sources of the evaluator's information.

(b) The examiner shall assess and report regarding the respondent's amenability to treatment and relative risk to the community. A proposed treatment plan shall be provided and shall include, at a minimum:

(i) The frequency and type of contact between the offender and therapist;

(ii) Specific issues to be addressed in the treatment and description of planned treatment modalities;

(iii) Monitoring plans, including any requirements regarding living conditions, lifestyle requirements, and monitoring by family members, legal guardians, or others;

(iv) Anticipated length of treatment; and

(v) Recommended crime-related prohibitions.

(c) The court on its own motion may order, or on a motion by the state shall order, a second examination regarding the offender's amenability to treatment. The evaluator shall be selected by the party making the motion. The defendant shall pay the cost of any second examination ordered unless the court finds the defendant to be indigent in which case the state shall pay the cost.

(3) After receipt of reports of the examination, the court shall then consider whether the offender and the community will benefit from use of this special sex offender disposition alternative and consider the victim's opinion whether the offender should receive a treatment disposition under this section. If the court determines that this special sex offender disposition alternative is appropriate, then the court shall impose a determinate disposition within the standard range for the offense, or if the court concludes, and enters reasons for its conclusions, that such disposition would cause a manifest injustice, the court shall impose a disposition under option D, and the court may suspend the execution of the disposition and place the offender on community supervision for at least two years.

(4) As a condition of the suspended disposition, the court may impose the conditions of community supervision and other conditions, including up to thirty days of confinement and requirements that the offender do any one or more of the following:

(a) Devote time to a specific education, employment, or occupation;

(b) Undergo available outpatient sex offender treatment for up to two years, or inpatient sex offender treatment not to exceed the standard range of confinement for that offense. A community mental health center may not be used for such treatment unless it has an appropriate program designed for sex offender treatment. The respondent shall not change sex offender treatment providers or treatment conditions without first notifying the prosecutor, the probation counselor, and the court, and shall not change providers without court approval after a hearing if the prosecutor or probation counselor object to the change;

(c) Remain within prescribed geographical boundaries and notify the court or the probation counselor prior to any change in the offender's address, educational program, or employment;

(d) Report to the prosecutor and the probation counselor prior to any change in a sex offender treatment provider. This change shall have prior approval by the court;

(e) Report as directed to the court and a probation counselor;

(f) Pay all court-ordered legal financial obligations, perform community restitution, or any combination thereof;

(g) Make restitution to the victim for the cost of any counseling reasonably related to the offense; or

(h) Comply with the conditions of any court-ordered probation bond.

(5) If the court orders twenty-four hour, continuous monitoring of the offender while on probation, the court shall include the basis for this condition in its findings.

(6)(a) The court must order the offender not to attend the public or approved private elementary, middle, or high school attended by the victim or the victim's siblings.

(b) The parents or legal guardians of the offender are responsible for transportation or other costs associated with the offender's change of school that would otherwise be paid by the school district.

(c) The court shall send notice of the disposition and restriction on attending the same school as the victim or victim's siblings to the public or approved private school the juvenile will attend, if known, or if unknown, to the approved private schools and the public school district board of directors of the district in which the juvenile resides or intends to reside. This notice must be sent at the earliest possible date but not later than ten calendar days after entry of the disposition.

(7)(a) The sex offender treatment provider shall submit quarterly reports on the respondent's progress in treatment to the court and the parties. The reports shall reference the treatment plan and include at a minimum the following: Dates of attendance, respondent's compliance with requirements, treatment activities, the respondent's relative progress in treatment, and any other material specified by the court at the time of the disposition.

(b) At the time of the disposition, the court may set treatment review hearings as the court considers appropriate.

(c) Except as provided in this subsection, examinations and treatment ordered pursuant to this subsection shall only be conducted by certified sex offender treatment providers or certified affiliate sex offender treatment providers under chapter 18.155 RCW.

(d) A sex offender therapist who examines or treats a juvenile sex offender pursuant to this subsection does not have to be certified by the department of health pursuant to chapter 18.155 RCW if the court finds that: (i) The offender has already moved to another state or plans to move to another state for reasons other than circumventing the certification requirements; (ii) no certified sex offender treatment providers or certified affiliate sex offender treatment providers are available for treatment within a reasonable geographical distance of the offender's home; and (iii) the evaluation and treatment plan comply with this subsection and the rules adopted by the department of health.

(8)(a) If the offender violates any condition of the disposition or the court finds that the respondent is failing to make satisfactory progress in treatment, the court may revoke the suspension and order execution of the disposition or the court may impose a penalty of up to thirty days confinement for violating conditions of the disposition.

(b) The court may order both execution of the disposition and up to thirty days confinement for the violation of the conditions of the disposition.

(c) The court shall give credit for any confinement time previously served if that confinement was for the offense for which the suspension is being revoked.

(9) For purposes of this section, "victim" means any person who has sustained emotional, psychological, physical, or financial injury to person or property as a direct result of the crime

charged. "Victim" may also include a known parent or guardian of a victim who is a minor child unless the parent or guardian is the perpetrator of the offense.

(10) A disposition entered under this section is not appealable under RCW 13.40.230. [2011 c 338 § 3.]

13.40.165
Chemical dependency disposition alternative.

(1) The purpose of this disposition alternative is to ensure that successful treatment options to reduce recidivism are available to eligible youth, pursuant to *RCW 70.96A.520. It is also the purpose of the disposition alternative to assure that minors in need of chemical dependency, mental health, and/or co-occurring disorder treatment receive an appropriate continuum of culturally relevant care and treatment, including prevention and early intervention, self-directed care, parent-directed care, and residential treatment. To facilitate the continuum of care and treatment to minors in out-of-home placements, all divisions of the department that provide these services to minors shall jointly plan and deliver these services. It is also the purpose of the disposition alternative to protect the rights of minors against needless hospitalization and deprivations of liberty and to enable treatment decisions to be made in response to clinical needs and in accordance with sound professional judgment. The mental health, substance abuse, and co-occurring disorder treatment providers shall, to the extent possible, offer services that involve minors' parents, guardians, and family.

(2) The court must consider eligibility for the chemical dependency or mental health disposition alternative when a juvenile offender is subject to a standard range disposition of local sanctions or 15 to 36 weeks of confinement and has not committed an A- or B+ offense, other than a first time B+ offense under chapter 69.50 RCW. The court, on its own motion or the motion of the state or the respondent if the evidence shows that the offender may be chemically dependent, substance abusing, or has significant mental health or co-occurring disorders may order an examination by a chemical dependency counselor from a chemical dependency treatment facility approved under **chapter 70.96A RCW or a mental health professional as defined in chapter 71.34 RCW to determine if the youth is chemically dependent, substance abusing, or suffers from significant mental health or co-occurring disorders. The offender shall pay the cost of any examination ordered under this subsection unless the court finds that the offender is indigent and no third party insurance coverage is available, in which case the state shall pay the cost.

(3) The report of the examination shall include at a minimum the following: The respondent's version of the facts and the official version of the facts, the respondent's offense history, an assessment of drug-alcohol problems, mental health diagnoses, previous treatment attempts, the respondent's social, educational, and employment situation, and other evaluation measures used. The report shall set forth the sources of the examiner's information.

(4) The examiner shall assess and report regarding the respondent's relative risk to the community. A proposed treatment plan shall be provided and shall include, at a minimum:

(a) Whether inpatient and/or outpatient treatment is recommended;

(b) Availability of appropriate treatment;

(c) Monitoring plans, including any requirements regarding living conditions, lifestyle requirements, and monitoring by family members, legal guardians, or others;

(d) Anticipated length of treatment; and

(e) Recommended crime-related prohibitions.

(5) The court on its own motion may order, or on a motion by the state or the respondent shall order, a second examination. The evaluator shall be selected by the party making the motion. The requesting party shall pay the cost of any examination ordered under this subsection unless the requesting party is the offender and the court finds that the offender is indigent and no third party insurance coverage is available, in which case the state shall pay the cost.

(6)(a) After receipt of reports of the examination, the court shall then consider whether the offender and the community will benefit from use of this disposition alternative and consider the victim's opinion whether the offender should receive a treatment disposition under this section.

(b) If the court determines that this disposition alternative is appropriate, then the court shall impose the standard range for the offense, or if the court concludes, and enters reasons for its conclusion, that such disposition would effectuate a manifest injustice, the court shall impose a disposition above the standard range as indicated in option D of RCW 13.40.0357 if the disposition is an increase from the standard range and the confinement of the offender does not exceed a maximum of fifty-two weeks, suspend execution of the disposition, and place the offender on community supervision for up to one year. As a condition of the suspended disposition, the court shall require the offender to undergo available outpatient drug/alcohol, mental health, or co-occurring disorder treatment and/or inpatient mental health or drug/alcohol treatment. The court shall only order inpatient treatment under this section if a funded bed is available. If the inpatient treatment is longer than ninety days, the court shall hold a review hearing every thirty days beyond the initial ninety days. The respondent may appear telephonically at these review hearings if in compliance with treatment. As a condition of the suspended disposition, the court may impose conditions of community supervision and other sanctions, including up to thirty days of confinement, one hundred fifty hours of community restitution, and payment of legal financial obligations and restitution.

(7) The mental health/co-occurring disorder/drug/alcohol treatment provider shall submit monthly reports on the respondent's progress in treatment to the court and the parties. The reports shall reference the treatment plan and include at a minimum the following: Dates of attendance, respondent's compliance with requirements, treatment activities, the respondent's relative progress in treatment, and any other material specified by the court at the time of the disposition.

At the time of the disposition, the court may set treatment review hearings as the court considers appropriate.

If the offender violates any condition of the disposition or the court finds that the respondent is failing to make satisfactory progress in treatment, the court may impose sanctions pursuant to RCW 13.40.200 or revoke the suspension and order execution of the disposition. The court shall give credit for any confinement time previously served if that confinement was for the offense for which the suspension is being revoked.

(8) For purposes of this section, "victim" means any person who has sustained emotional, psychological, physical, or financial injury to person or property as a direct result of the offense

---

charged. "Victim" may also include a known parent or guardian of a victim who is a minor child or is not a minor child but is incapacitated, incompetent, disabled, or deceased.

(9) Whenever a juvenile offender is entitled to credit for time spent in detention prior to a dispositional order, the dispositional order shall specifically state the number of days of credit for time served.

(10) In no case shall the term of confinement imposed by the court at disposition exceed that to which an adult could be subjected for the same offense.

(11) A disposition under this section is not appealable under RCW 13.40.230.

(12) Subject to funds appropriated for this specific purpose, the costs incurred by the juvenile courts for the mental health, chemical dependency, and/or co-occurring disorder evaluations, treatment, and costs of supervision required under this section shall be paid by the department. [2016 c 106 § 3; 2004 c 120 § 5; 2003 c 378 § 6. Prior: 2002 c 175 § 23; 2002 c 42 § 1; 2001 c 164 § 1; 1997 c 338 § 26.]

NOTES:

Reviser's note: *(1) RCW 70.96A.520 was recodified as RCW 71.24.615 pursuant to 2016 sp.s. c 29 § 701.

**(2) Many sections in chapter 70.96A RCW were recodified in chapter 71.24 RCW pursuant to 2016 sp.s. c 29 § 701.

Effective date—2004 c 120: See note following RCW 13.40.010.

Effective date—2002 c 175: See note following RCW 7.80.130.

Effectiveness standards—1997 c 338 § 26: "The University of Washington shall develop standards for measuring effectiveness of treatment programs established under section 26 of this act. The standards shall be developed and presented to the governor and legislature not later than January 1, 1998. The standards shall include methods for measuring success factors following treatment. Success factors shall include, but need not be limited to, continued use of alcohol or controlled substances, arrests, violations of terms of community supervision, and convictions for subsequent offenses." [1997 c 338 § 27.]

Finding—Evaluation—Report—1997 c 338: See note following RCW 13.40.0357.

Severability—Effective dates—1997 c 338: See notes following RCW 5.60.060.

13.40.180
Single disposition order—Consecutive terms when two or more offenses—Limitations—Separate disposition order—Concurrent period of community supervision.

(1) Where a disposition in a single disposition order is imposed on a youth for two or more offenses, the terms shall run consecutively, subject to the following limitations:

(a) Where the offenses were committed through a single act or omission, omission, or through an act or omission which in itself constituted one of the offenses and also was an element of the other, the aggregate of all the terms shall not exceed one hundred fifty percent of the term imposed for the most serious offense;

(b) The aggregate of all consecutive terms shall not exceed three hundred percent of the term imposed for the most serious offense; and

(c) The aggregate of all consecutive terms of community supervision shall not exceed two years in length, or require payment of more than two hundred dollars in fines or the performance of more than two hundred hours of community restitution.

(2) Where disposition in separate disposition orders is imposed on a youth, the periods of community supervision contained in separate orders, if any, shall run concurrently. All other terms contained in separate disposition orders shall run consecutively.

[2012 c 177 § 3; 2002 c 175 § 24; 1981 c 299 § 14; 1977 ex.s. c 291 § 72.]

NOTES:

> **Effective date—2002 c 175:** See note following RCW 7.80.130.
>
> **Effective dates—Severability—1977 ex.s. c 291:** See notes following RCW 13.04.005.

13.40.185

Disposition order—Confinement under departmental supervision or in juvenile facility, when.

(1) Any term of confinement imposed for an offense which exceeds thirty days shall be served under the supervision of the department. If the period of confinement imposed for more than one offense exceeds thirty days but the term imposed for each offense is less than thirty days, the confinement may, in the discretion of the court, be served in a juvenile facility operated by or pursuant to a contract with the state or a county.

(2) Whenever a juvenile is confined in a detention facility or is committed to the department, the court may not directly order a juvenile into a particular county or state facility. The juvenile court administrator and the secretary, assistant secretary, or the secretary's designee, as appropriate, has the sole discretion to determine in which facility a juvenile should be confined or committed. The counties may operate a variety of detention facilities as determined by the county legislative authority subject to available funds.

[1994 sp.s. c 7 § 524; 1981 c 299 § 15.]

NOTES:

> **Finding—Intent—Severability—1994 sp.s. c 7:** See notes following RCW 43.70.540.

13.40.190

Disposition order—Restitution for loss or damage—Modification of restitution order.

(1)(a) In its dispositional order, the court shall require the respondent to make restitution to any persons who have suffered loss or damage as a result of the offense committed by the respondent. In addition, restitution may be ordered for loss or damage if the offender pleads guilty to a lesser offense or fewer offenses and agrees with the prosecutor's recommendation that the offender be required to pay restitution to a victim of an offense or offenses which, pursuant to a plea agreement, are not prosecuted.

(b) Restitution may include the costs of counseling reasonably related to the offense.

(c) The payment of restitution shall be in addition to any punishment which is imposed pursuant to the other provisions of this chapter.

(d) The court may determine the amount, terms, and conditions of the restitution including a payment plan extending up to ten years if the court determines that the respondent does not have the means to make full restitution over a shorter period. If the court determines that a juvenile has insufficient funds to pay and upon agreement of the victim, the court may order performance of a number of hours of community restitution in lieu of monetary penalty, at the rate of the then state minimum wage per hour. The court shall allow the victim to determine the nature of the community restitution to be completed when it is practicable and appropriate to do so. For the purposes of this section, the respondent shall remain under the court's jurisdiction for a maximum term of ten years after the respondent's eighteenth birthday and, during this period, the restitution portion of the dispositional order may be modified as to amount, terms, and conditions at any time. Prior to the expiration of the ten-year period, the juvenile court may extend the judgment for the payment of restitution for an additional ten years. If the court grants a respondent's petition pursuant to RCW 13.50.260, the court's jurisdiction under this subsection shall terminate.

(e) Nothing in this section shall prevent a respondent from petitioning the court pursuant to RCW 13.50.260 if the respondent has paid the full restitution amount stated in the court's order and has met the statutory criteria.

(f) If the respondent participated in the crime with another person or other persons, the court may either order joint and several restitution or may divide restitution equally among the respondents. In determining whether restitution should be joint and several or equally divided, the court shall consider the interest and circumstances of the victim or victims, the circumstances of the respondents, and the interest of justice.

(g) At any time, the court may determine that the respondent is not required to pay, or may relieve the respondent of the requirement to pay, full or partial restitution to any insurance provider authorized under Title 48 RCW if the respondent reasonably satisfies the court that he or she does not have the means to make full or partial restitution to the insurance provider.

(2) Regardless of the provisions of subsection (1) of this section, the court shall order restitution in all cases where the victim is entitled to benefits under the crime victims' compensation act, chapter 7.68 RCW. If the court does not order restitution and the victim of the crime has been determined to be entitled to benefits under the crime victims' compensation act, the department of labor and industries, as administrator of the crime victims' compensation program, may petition the court within one year of entry of the disposition order for entry of a restitution order. Upon receipt of a petition from the department of labor and industries, the court shall hold a restitution hearing and shall enter a restitution order.

(3) If an order includes restitution as one of the monetary assessments, the county clerk shall make disbursements to victims named in the order. The restitution to victims named in the order shall be paid prior to any payment for other penalties or monetary assessments. The county clerk

shall make restitution disbursements to victims prior to payments to any insurance provider under Title 48 RCW.

(4) For purposes of this section, "victim" means any person who has sustained emotional, psychological, physical, or financial injury to person or property as a direct result of the offense charged. "Victim" may also include a known parent or guardian of a victim who is a minor child or is not a minor child but is incapacitated, incompetent, disabled, or deceased.

(5) A respondent under obligation to pay restitution may petition the court for modification of the restitution order for good cause shown, including inability to pay.

[2015 c 265 § 6; 2014 c 175 § 7; 2010 c 134 § 1; 2004 c 120 § 6. Prior: 1997 c 338 § 29; 1997 c 121 § 9; 1996 c 124 § 2; 1995 c 33 § 5; 1994 sp.s. c 7 § 528; 1987 c 281 § 5; 1985 c 257 § 2; 1983 c 191 § 9; 1979 c 155 § 69; 1977 ex.s. c 291 § 73.]

NOTES:

> **Finding—Intent—2015 c 265:** See note following RCW 13.50.010.
> **Findings—Intent—2014 c 175:** See note following RCW 13.50.010.
> **Effective date—2004 c 120:** See note following RCW 13.40.010.
> **Finding—Evaluation—Report—1997 c 338:** See note following RCW 13.40.0357.
> **Severability—Effective dates—1997 c 338:** See notes following RCW 5.60.060.
> **Finding—Intent—Severability—1994 sp.s. c 7:** See notes following RCW 43.70.540.
> **Effective date—1987 c 281:** See note following RCW 7.68.020.
> **Severability—1985 c 257:** See note following RCW 13.34.165.
> **Effective date—Severability—1979 c 155:** See notes following RCW 13.04.011.
> **Effective dates—Severability—1977 ex.s. c 291:** See notes following RCW 13.04.005.

13.40.192
Legal financial obligations—Enforceability—Treatment of obligations upon age of eighteen or conclusion of juvenile court jurisdiction—Extension of judgment—Petition for modification or relief.

(1) If a juvenile is ordered to pay legal financial obligations, including fines, penalty assessments, attorneys' fees, court costs, and restitution, the money judgment remains enforceable for a period of ten years. When the juvenile reaches the age of eighteen years or at the conclusion of juvenile court jurisdiction, whichever occurs later, the superior court clerk must docket the remaining balance of the juvenile's legal financial obligations in the same manner as other judgments for the payment of money. The judgment remains valid and enforceable until ten years from the date of its imposition. The clerk of the superior court may seek extension of the judgment for legal financial obligations, including crime victims' assessments, in the same manner as RCW 6.17.020 for purposes of collection as allowed under RCW 36.18.190.

(2) A respondent under obligation to pay legal financial obligations other than restitution, the victim penalty assessment set forth in RCW 7.68.035, or the crime laboratory analysis fee set forth in RCW 43.43.690 may petition the court for modification or relief from those legal

financial obligations and interest accrued on those obligations for good cause shown, including inability to pay. The court shall consider factors such as, but not limited to incarceration and a respondent's other debts, including restitution, when determining a respondent's ability to pay. [2015 c 265 § 7; 1997 c 121 § 7.]

NOTES:

      Finding—Intent—2015 c 265: See note following RCW 13.50.010.

13.40.193
Firearms—Length of confinement.

(1) If a respondent is found to have been in possession of a firearm in violation of *RCW 9.41.040(2)(a)(iii), the court shall impose a minimum disposition of ten days of confinement. If the offender's standard range of disposition for the offense as indicated in RCW 13.40.0357 is more than thirty days of confinement, the court shall commit the offender to the department for the standard range disposition. The offender shall not be released until the offender has served a minimum of ten days in confinement.

(2)(a) If a respondent is found to have been in possession of a firearm in violation of RCW 9.41.040, the disposition must include a requirement that the respondent participate in a qualifying program as described in (b) of this subsection, when available, unless the court makes a written finding based on the outcome of the juvenile court risk assessment that participation in a qualifying program would not be appropriate.

(b) For purposes of this section, "qualifying program" means an aggression replacement training program, a functional family therapy program, or another program applicable to the juvenile firearm offender population that has been identified as evidence-based or research-based and cost-beneficial in the current list prepared at the direction of the legislature by the Washington state institute for public policy.

(3) If the court finds that the respondent or an accomplice was armed with a firearm, the court shall determine the standard range disposition for the offense pursuant to RCW 13.40.160. If the offender or an accomplice was armed with a firearm when the offender committed any felony other than possession of a machine gun, possession of a stolen firearm, drive-by shooting, theft of a firearm, unlawful possession of a firearm in the first and second degree, or use of a machine gun in a felony, the following periods of total confinement must be added to the sentence: For a class A felony, six months; for a class B felony, four months; and for a class C felony, two months. The additional time shall be imposed regardless of the offense's juvenile disposition offense category as designated in RCW 13.40.0357.

(4) When a disposition under this section would effectuate a manifest injustice, the court may impose another disposition. When a judge finds a manifest injustice and imposes a disposition of confinement exceeding thirty days, the court shall commit the juvenile to a maximum term, and the provisions of RCW 13.40.030(2) shall be used to determine the range. When a judge finds a manifest injustice and imposes a disposition of confinement less than thirty days, the disposition shall be comprised of confinement or community supervision or both.

(5) Any term of confinement ordered pursuant to this section shall run consecutively to any term of confinement imposed in the same disposition for other offenses.
[2014 c 117 § 1; 2003 c 53 § 100; 1997 c 338 § 30; 1994 sp.s. c 7 § 525.]
NOTES:

*Reviser's note: RCW 9.41.040 was amended by 2014 c 111 § 1, changing subsection (2)(a)(iii) to subsection (2)(a)(iv).

Intent—Effective date—2003 c 53: See notes following RCW 2.48.180.

Finding—Evaluation—Report—1997 c 338: See note following RCW 13.40.0357.

Severability—Effective dates—1997 c 338: See notes following RCW 5.60.060.

Finding—Intent—Severability—Effective dates—Contingent expiration date—1994 sp.s. c 7: See notes following RCW 43.70.540.

13.40.196
Firearms—Special allegation.

A prosecutor may file a special allegation that the offender or an accomplice was armed with a firearm when the offender committed the alleged offense. If a special allegation has been filed and the court finds that the offender committed the alleged offense, the court shall also make a finding whether the offender or an accomplice was armed with a firearm when the offender committed the offense.
[1994 sp.s. c 7 § 526.]
NOTES:

Finding—Intent—Severability—1994 sp.s. c 7: See notes following RCW 43.70.540.

13.40.198
Penalty assessments—Jurisdiction of court.

If a respondent is ordered to pay a penalty assessment pursuant to a dispositional order entered under this chapter, he or she shall remain under the court's jurisdiction for a maximum term of ten years after the respondent's eighteenth birthday. Prior to the expiration of the ten-year period, the juvenile court may extend the judgment for the payment of a penalty assessment for an additional ten years.
[2000 c 71 § 1.]
NOTES:

Effective date—2000 c 71: "This act is necessary for the immediate preservation of the public peace, health, or safety, or support of the state government and its existing public institutions, and takes effect immediately [March 22, 2000]." [2000 c 71 § 4.]

13.40.200

Violation of order of restitution, community supervision, fines, penalty assessments, or confinement—Modification of order after hearing—Scope—Rights—Use of fines.

(1) When a respondent fails to comply with an order of restitution, community supervision, penalty assessments, or confinement of less than thirty days, the court upon motion of the prosecutor or its own motion, may modify the order after a hearing on the violation.

(2) The hearing shall afford the respondent the same due process of law as would be afforded an adult probationer. The court may issue a summons or a warrant to compel the respondent's appearance. The state shall have the burden of proving by a preponderance of the evidence the fact of the violation. The respondent shall have the burden of showing that the violation was not a willful refusal to comply with the terms of the order. If a respondent has failed to pay a fine, penalty assessments, or restitution or to perform community restitution hours, as required by the court, it shall be the respondent's burden to show that he or she did not have the means and could not reasonably have acquired the means to pay the fine, penalty assessments, or restitution or perform community restitution.

(3) If the court finds that a respondent has willfully violated the terms of an order pursuant to subsections (1) and (2) of this section, it may impose a penalty of up to thirty days' confinement. Penalties for multiple violations occurring prior to the hearing shall not be aggregated to exceed thirty days' confinement. Regardless of the number of times a respondent is brought to court for violations of the terms of a single disposition order, the combined total number of days spent by the respondent in detention shall never exceed the maximum term to which an adult could be sentenced for the underlying offense.

(4) If a respondent has been ordered to pay a fine or monetary penalty and due to a change of circumstance cannot reasonably comply with the order, the court, upon motion of the respondent, may order that the unpaid fine or monetary penalty be converted to community restitution unless the monetary penalty is the crime victim penalty assessment, which cannot be converted, waived, or otherwise modified, except for schedule of payment. The number of hours of community restitution in lieu of a monetary penalty or fine shall be converted at the rate of the prevailing state minimum wage per hour. The monetary penalties or fines collected shall be deposited in the county general fund. A failure to comply with an order under this subsection shall be deemed a failure to comply with an order of community supervision and may be proceeded against as provided in this section.

(5) When a respondent has willfully violated the terms of a probation bond, the court may modify, revoke, or retain the probation bond as provided in RCW 13.40.054.
[2004 c 120 § 7; 2002 c 175 § 25; 1997 c 338 § 31; 1995 c 395 § 8; 1986 c 288 § 5; 1983 c 191 § 15; 1979 c 155 § 70; 1977 ex.s. c 291 § 74.]
NOTES:
    Effective date—2004 c 120: See note following RCW 13.40.010.
    Effective date—2002 c 175: See note following RCW 7.80.130.
    Finding—Evaluation—Report—1997 c 338: See note following RCW 13.40.0357.

Severability—Effective dates—1997 c 338: See notes following RCW 5.60.060.
Severability—1986 c 288: See note following RCW 43.185C.260.
Effective date—Severability—1979 c 155: See notes following RCW 13.04.011.
Effective dates—Severability—1977 ex.s. c 291: See notes following RCW 13.04.005.

13.40.205
Release from physical custody, when—Authorized leaves—Leave plan and order—Notice.

(1) A juvenile sentenced to a term of confinement to be served under the supervision of the department shall not be released from the physical custody of the department prior to the release date established under RCW 13.40.210 except as otherwise provided in this section.

(2) A juvenile serving a term of confinement under the supervision of the department may be released on authorized leave from the physical custody of the department only if consistent with public safety and if:

(a) Sixty percent of the minimum term of confinement has been served; and

(b) The purpose of the leave is to enable the juvenile:

(i) To visit the juvenile's family for the purpose of strengthening or preserving family relationships;

(ii) To make plans for parole or release which require the juvenile's personal appearance in the community and which will facilitate the juvenile's reintegration into the community; or

(iii) To make plans for a residential placement out of the juvenile's home which requires the juvenile's personal appearance in the community.

(3) No authorized leave may exceed seven consecutive days. The total of all pre-minimum term authorized leaves granted to a juvenile prior to final discharge from confinement shall not exceed thirty days.

(4) Prior to authorizing a leave, the secretary shall require a written leave plan, which shall detail the purpose of the leave and how it is to be achieved, the address at which the juvenile shall reside, the identity of the person responsible for supervising the juvenile during the leave, and a statement by such person acknowledging familiarity with the leave plan and agreeing to supervise the juvenile and to notify the secretary immediately if the juvenile violates any terms or conditions of the leave. The leave plan shall include such terms and conditions as the secretary deems appropriate and shall be signed by the juvenile.

(5) Upon authorizing a leave, the secretary shall issue to the juvenile an authorized leave order which shall contain the name of the juvenile, the fact that the juvenile is on leave from a designated facility, the time period of the leave, and the identity of an appropriate official of the department to contact when necessary. The authorized leave order shall be carried by the juvenile at all times while on leave.

(6) Prior to the commencement of any authorized leave, the secretary shall give notice of the leave to the appropriate law enforcement agency in the jurisdiction in which the juvenile will reside during the leave period. The notice shall include the identity of the juvenile, the time

period of the leave, the residence of the juvenile during the leave, and the identity of the person responsible for supervising the juvenile during the leave.

(7) The secretary may authorize a leave, which shall not exceed forty-eight hours plus travel time, to meet an emergency situation such as a death or critical illness of a member of the juvenile's family. The secretary may authorize a leave, which shall not exceed the period of time medically necessary, to obtain medical care not available in a juvenile facility maintained by the department. In cases of emergency or medical leave the secretary may waive all or any portions of subsections (2)(a), (3), (4), (5), and (6) of this section.

(8) If requested by the juvenile's victim or the victim's immediate family, the secretary shall give notice of any leave to the victim or the victim's immediate family.

(9) A juvenile who violates any condition of an authorized leave plan may be taken into custody and returned to the department in the same manner as an adult in identical circumstances.

(10) Notwithstanding the provisions of this section, a juvenile placed in minimum security status may participate in work, educational, community restitution, or treatment programs in the community up to twelve hours a day if approved by the secretary. Such a release shall not be deemed a leave of absence.

(11) Subsections (6), (7), and (8) of this section do not apply to juveniles covered by RCW 13.40.215.
[2002 c 175 § 26; 1990 c 3 § 103; 1983 c 191 § 10.]
NOTES:
>   **Effective date—2002 c 175:** See note following RCW 7.80.130.
>
>   **Index, part headings not law—Severability—Effective dates—Application—1990 c 3:** See RCW 18.155.900 through 18.155.902.

13.40.210

Setting of release date—Administrative release authorized, when—Parole program, revocation or modification of, scope—Intensive supervision program—Parole officer's right of arrest.

(1) The secretary shall set a release date for each juvenile committed to its custody. The release date shall be within the prescribed range to which a juvenile has been committed under RCW 13.40.0357 or 13.40.030 except as provided in RCW 13.40.320 concerning offenders the department determines are eligible for the juvenile offender basic training camp program. Such dates shall be determined prior to the expiration of sixty percent of a juvenile's minimum term of confinement included within the prescribed range to which the juvenile has been committed. The secretary shall release any juvenile committed to the custody of the department within four calendar days prior to the juvenile's release date or on the release date set under this chapter. Days spent in the custody of the department shall be tolled by any period of time during which a juvenile has absented himself or herself from the department's supervision without the prior approval of the secretary or the secretary's designee.

(2) The secretary shall monitor the average daily population of the state's juvenile residential facilities. When the secretary concludes that in-residence population of residential facilities exceeds one hundred five percent of the rated bed capacity specified in statute, or in absence of such specification, as specified by the department in rule, the secretary may recommend reductions to the governor. On certification by the governor that the recommended reductions are necessary, the secretary has authority to administratively release a sufficient number of offenders to reduce in-residence population to one hundred percent of rated bed capacity. The secretary shall release those offenders who have served the greatest proportion of their sentence. However, the secretary may deny release in a particular case at the request of an offender, or if the secretary finds that there is no responsible custodian, as determined by the department, to whom to release the offender, or if the release of the offender would pose a clear danger to society. The department shall notify the committing court of the release at the time of release if any such early releases have occurred as a result of excessive in-residence population. In no event shall an offender adjudicated of a violent offense be granted release under the provisions of this subsection.

(3)(a) Following the release of any juvenile under subsection (1) of this section, the secretary may require the juvenile to comply with a program of parole to be administered by the department in his or her community which shall last no longer than eighteen months, except that in the case of a juvenile sentenced for rape in the first or second degree, rape of a child in the first or second degree, child molestation in the first degree, or indecent liberties with forcible compulsion, the period of parole shall be twenty-four months and, in the discretion of the secretary, may be up to thirty-six months when the secretary finds that an additional period of parole is necessary and appropriate in the interests of public safety or to meet the ongoing needs of the juvenile. A parole program is mandatory for offenders released under subsection (2) of this section and for offenders who receive a juvenile residential commitment sentence for theft of a motor vehicle, possession of a stolen motor vehicle, or taking a motor vehicle without permission 1. A juvenile adjudicated for unlawful possession of a firearm, possession of a stolen firearm, theft of a firearm, or drive-by shooting may participate in aggression replacement training, functional family therapy, or functional family parole aftercare if the juvenile meets eligibility requirements for these services. The decision to place an offender in an evidence-based parole program shall be based on an assessment by the department of the offender's risk for reoffending upon release and an assessment of the ongoing treatment needs of the juvenile. The department shall prioritize available parole resources to provide supervision and services to offenders at moderate to high risk for reoffending.

(b) The secretary shall, for the period of parole, facilitate the juvenile's reintegration into his or her community and to further this goal shall require the juvenile to refrain from possessing a firearm or using a deadly weapon and refrain from committing new offenses and may require the juvenile to: (i) Undergo available medical, psychiatric, drug and alcohol, sex offender, mental health, and other offense-related treatment services; (ii) report as directed to a parole officer and/or designee; (iii) pursue a course of study, vocational training, or employment; (iv) notify the parole officer of the current address where he or she resides; (v) be present at a particular address during specified hours; (vi) remain within prescribed geographical boundaries; (vii) submit to electronic monitoring; (viii) refrain from using illegal drugs and alcohol, and submit to random urinalysis when requested by the assigned parole officer; (ix) refrain from contact with specific individuals or a specified class of individuals; (x) meet other conditions determined by the parole officer to further enhance the juvenile's reintegration into the community; (xi) pay any court-ordered fines or restitution; and (xii) perform community restitution. Community restitution for the purpose of this section means compulsory service, without compensation, performed for the benefit of the community by the offender. Community restitution may be performed through public or private organizations or through work crews.

(c) The secretary may further require up to twenty-five percent of the highest risk juvenile offenders who are placed on parole to participate in an intensive supervision program. Offenders participating in an intensive supervision program shall be required to comply with all terms and conditions listed in (b) of this subsection and shall also be required to comply with the following additional terms and conditions: (i) Obey all laws and refrain from any conduct that threatens public safety; (ii) report at least once a week to an assigned community case manager; and (iii) meet all other requirements imposed by the community case manager related to participating in the intensive supervision program. As a part of the intensive supervision program, the secretary may require day reporting.

(d) After termination of the parole period, the juvenile shall be discharged from the department's supervision.

(4)(a) The department may also modify parole for violation thereof. If, after affording a juvenile all of the due process rights to which he or she would be entitled if the juvenile were an adult, the secretary finds that a juvenile has violated a condition of his or her parole, the secretary shall order one of the following which is reasonably likely to effectuate the purpose of the parole and to protect the public: (i) Continued supervision under the same conditions previously imposed; (ii) intensified supervision with increased reporting requirements; (iii) additional conditions of supervision authorized by this chapter; (iv) except as provided in (a)(v) and (vi) of this subsection, imposition of a period of confinement not to exceed thirty days in a facility operated by or pursuant to a contract with the state of Washington or any city or county for a portion of each day or for a certain number of days each week with the balance of the days or weeks spent under supervision; (v) the secretary may order any of the conditions or may return the offender to confinement for the remainder of the sentence range if the offense for which the offender was sentenced is rape in the first or second degree, rape of a child in the first or second degree, child molestation in the first degree, indecent liberties with forcible compulsion, or a sex offense that is also a serious violent offense as defined by RCW 9.94A.030; and (vi) the secretary may order any of the conditions or may return the offender to confinement for the remainder of the sentence range if the youth has completed the basic training camp program as described in RCW 13.40.320.

(b) The secretary may modify parole and order any of the conditions or may return the offender to confinement for up to twenty-four weeks if the offender was sentenced for a sex offense as defined under *RCW 9A.44.130 and is known to have violated the terms of parole. Confinement beyond thirty days is intended to only be used for a small and limited number of sex offenders. It shall only be used when other graduated sanctions or interventions have not been effective or the behavior is so egregious it warrants the use of the higher level intervention and the violation: (i) Is a known pattern of behavior consistent with a previous sex offense that puts the youth at high risk for reoffending sexually; (ii) consists of sexual behavior that is determined to be predatory as defined in RCW 71.09.020; or (iii) requires a review under chapter

71.09 RCW, due to a recent overt act. The total number of days of confinement for violations of parole conditions during the parole period shall not exceed the number of days provided by the maximum sentence imposed by the disposition for the underlying offense pursuant to RCW 13.40.0357. The department shall not aggregate multiple parole violations that occur prior to the parole revocation hearing and impose consecutive twenty-four week periods of confinement for each parole violation. The department is authorized to engage in rule making pursuant to chapter 34.05 RCW, to implement this subsection, including narrowly defining the behaviors that could lead to this higher level intervention.

(c) If the department finds that any juvenile in a program of parole has possessed a firearm or used a deadly weapon during the program of parole, the department shall modify the parole under (a) of this subsection and confine the juvenile for at least thirty days. Confinement shall be in a facility operated by or pursuant to a contract with the state or any county.

(5) A parole officer of the department of social and health services shall have the power to arrest a juvenile under his or her supervision on the same grounds as a law enforcement officer would be authorized to arrest the person.

(6) If so requested and approved under chapter 13.06 RCW, the secretary shall permit a county or group of counties to perform functions under subsections (3) through (5) of this section.

[2014 c 117 § 3; 2009 c 187 § 1. Prior: 2007 c 203 § 1; 2007 c 199 § 13; 2002 c 175 § 27; prior: 2001 c 137 § 2; 2001 c 51 § 1; 1997 c 338 § 32; 1994 sp.s. c 7 § 527; 1990 c 3 § 304; 1987 c 505 § 4; 1985 c 287 § 1; 1985 c 257 § 4; 1983 c 191 § 11; 1979 c 155 § 71; 1977 ex.s. c 291 § 75.]

NOTES:

*Reviser's note: RCW 9A.44.130 was amended by 2010 c 267 § 2, removing the definition of "sex offense" and "kidnapping offense." Those terms are now defined in RCW 9A.44.128.

Applicability—2007 c 203: "This act applies prospectively only and not retroactively. It applies only to juvenile offenders who have been adjudicated for an offense that occurred on or after October 1, 2007." [2007 c 203 § 2.]

Effective date—2007 c 203: "This act takes effect October 1, 2007." [2007 c 203 § 3.]

Findings—Intent—Short title—2007 c 199: See notes following RCW 9A.56.065.

Effective date—2002 c 175: See note following RCW 7.80.130.

Effective date—2001 c 51: "This act is necessary for the immediate preservation of the public peace, health, or safety, or support of the state government and its existing public institutions, and takes effect immediately [April 17, 2001]." [2001 c 51 § 2.]

Findings—Intent—1997 c 338 §§ 32 and 34: See note following RCW 13.40.212.

Finding—Evaluation—Report—1997 c 338: See note following RCW 13.40.0357.

Severability—Effective dates—1997 c 338: See notes following RCW 5.60.060.

Finding—Intent—Severability—Effective dates—Contingent expiration date—1994 sp.s. c 7: See notes following RCW 43.70.540.

Index, part headings not law—Severability—Effective dates—Application—1990 c 3: See RCW 18.155.900 through 18.155.902.

Intent—1985 c 257 § 4: "To promote both public safety and the welfare of juvenile offenders, it is the intent of the legislature that services to juvenile offenders be delivered in the most effective and efficient means possible. Section 4 of this act facilitates those objectives by permitting counties to supervise parole of juvenile offenders. This is consistent with the philosophy of chapter 13.06 RCW to deliver community services to juvenile offenders comprehensively at the county level." [1985 c 257 § 3.]

      Severability—1985 c 257: See note following RCW 13.34.165.
      Effective date—Severability—1979 c 155: See notes following RCW 13.04.011.
      Effective dates—Severability—1977 ex.s. c 291: See notes following RCW 13.04.005.

13.40.212
Intensive supervision program—Elements—Report.

(1) The department shall, no later than January 1, 1999, implement an intensive supervision program as a part of its parole services that includes, at a minimum, the following program elements:

(a) A process of case management involving coordinated and comprehensive planning, information exchange, continuity and consistency, service provision and referral, and monitoring. The components of the case management system shall include assessment, classification, and selection criteria; individual case planning that incorporates a family and community perspective; a mixture of intensive surveillance and services; a balance of incentives and graduated consequences coupled with the imposition of realistic, enforceable conditions; and service brokerage with community resources and linkage with social networks;

(b) Administration of transition services that transcend traditional agency boundaries and professional interests and include courts, institutions, aftercare, education, social and mental health services, substance abuse treatment, and employment and vocational training; and

(c) A plan for information management and program evaluation that maintains close oversight over implementation and quality control, and determines the effectiveness of both the processes and outcomes of the program.

(2) The department shall report annually to the legislature, beginning December 1, 1999, on the department's progress in meeting the intensive supervision program evaluation goals required under subsection (1)(c) of this section.
[1997 c 338 § 34.]
NOTES:

      Findings—Intent—1997 c 338 §§ 32 and 34: "The legislature finds the present system of transitioning youths from residential status to parole status to discharge is insufficient to provide adequate rehabilitation and public safety in many instances, particularly in cases of offenders at highest risk of reoffending. The legislature further finds that an intensive supervision program based on the following principles holds much promise for positively impacting recidivism rates for juvenile offenders: (1) Progressive increase in responsibility and freedom in the community; (2) facilitation of youths' interaction and involvement with their communities; (3) involvement of both the youth and targeted community support systems such as family, peers, schools, and employers, on the qualities needed for constructive interaction and successful adjustment with the community; (4) development of new resources, supports, and opportunities where necessary; and (5) ongoing monitoring and testing of youth on their ability to abide by community rules and standards.

The legislature intends for the department to create an intensive supervision program based on the principles stated in this section that will be available to the highest risk juvenile offenders placed on parole." [1997 c 338 § 33.]

Finding—Evaluation—Report—1997 c 338: See note following RCW 13.40.0357.
Severability—Effective dates—1997 c 338: See notes following RCW 5.60.060.

13.40.213
Juveniles alleged to have committed offenses of prostitution or prostitution loitering—Diversion.

(1) When a juvenile is alleged to have committed the offenses of prostitution or prostitution loitering, and the allegation, if proved, would not be the juvenile's first offense, a prosecutor may divert the offense if the county in which the offense is alleged to have been committed has a comprehensive program that provides:

(a) Safe and stable housing;

(b) Comprehensive on-site case management;

(c) Integrated mental health and chemical dependency services, including specialized trauma recovery services;

(d) Education and employment training delivered on-site; and

(e) Referrals to off-site specialized services, as appropriate.

(2) A prosecutor may divert a case for prostitution or prostitution loitering into the comprehensive program described in this section, notwithstanding the filing criteria set forth in RCW 13.40.070(5).

(3) A diversion agreement under this section may extend to twelve months.

(4)(a) The administrative office of the courts shall compile data regarding:

(i) The number of juveniles whose cases are diverted into the comprehensive program described in this section;

(ii) Whether the juveniles complete their diversion agreements under this section; and

(iii) Whether juveniles whose cases have been diverted under this section have been subsequently arrested or committed subsequent offenses.

(b) An annual report of the data compiled shall be provided to the governor and the appropriate committee of the legislature. The first report is due by November 1, 2010. [2010 c 289 § 8; 2009 c 252 § 2.]

NOTES:

Findings—2009 c 252: "The legislature finds that juveniles involved in the commercial sex trade are sexually exploited and that they face extreme threats to their physical and emotional well-being. In order to help them break out of the isolation, fear, and danger of the commercial sex trade and to assist them in their recovery from the resulting mental and physical harm and in the development of skills that will allow them to become independent and achieve long-term security, these juveniles are in critical need of comprehensive services, including housing, mental health counseling, education, employment, chemical dependency treatment, and skill building. The legislature further finds that a diversion program to provide these comprehensive services, working within existing resources in the counties which prosecute juveniles for prostitution and prostitution loitering, may be an appropriate alternative to the prosecution of juveniles involved in the commercial sex trade." [2009 c 252 § 1.]

13.40.215
Juveniles found to have committed violent or sex offense or stalking— Notification of discharge, parole, leave, release, transfer, or escape—To whom given—School attendance—Definitions.

(1)(a) Except as provided in subsection (2) of this section, at the earliest possible date, and in no event later than thirty days before discharge, parole, or any other authorized leave or release, or before transfer to a community residential facility, the secretary shall send written notice of the discharge, parole, authorized leave or release, or transfer of a juvenile found to have committed a violent offense, a sex offense, or stalking, to the following:

(i) The chief of police of the city, if any, in which the juvenile will reside;

(ii) The sheriff of the county in which the juvenile will reside; and

(iii) The approved private schools and the common school district board of directors of the district in which the juvenile intends to reside or the approved private school or public school district in which the juvenile last attended school, whichever is appropriate, except when it has been determined by the department that the juvenile is twenty-one years old or will be in the community for less than seven consecutive days on approved leave and will not be attending school during that time.

(b) After July 25, 1999, the department shall send a written notice to approved private and public schools under the same conditions identified in subsection (1)(a)(iii) of this section when a juvenile adjudicated of any offense is transferred to a community residential facility, discharged, paroled, released, or granted a leave. The community residential facility shall provide written notice of the offender's criminal history to any school that the offender attends while residing at the community residential facility and to any employer that employs the offender while residing at the community residential facility.

(c) The same notice as required by (a) of this subsection shall be sent to the following, if such notice has been requested in writing about a specific juvenile:

(i) The victim of the offense for which the juvenile was found to have committed or the victim's next of kin if the crime was a homicide;

(ii) Any witnesses who testified against the juvenile in any court proceedings involving the offense; and

(iii) Any person specified in writing by the prosecuting attorney.
Information regarding victims, next of kin, or witnesses requesting the notice, information regarding any other person specified in writing by the prosecuting attorney to receive the notice,

and the notice are confidential and shall not be available to the juvenile. The notice to the chief of police or the sheriff shall include the identity of the juvenile, the residence where the juvenile will reside, the identity of the person, if any, responsible for supervising the juvenile, and the time period of any authorized leave.

(d) The thirty-day notice requirements contained in this subsection shall not apply to emergency medical furloughs.

(e) The existence of the notice requirements in this subsection will not require any extension of the release date in the event the release plan changes after notification.

(2)(a) If a juvenile found to have committed a violent offense, a sex offense, or stalking escapes from a facility of the department, the secretary shall immediately notify, by the most reasonable and expedient means available, the chief of police of the city and the sheriff of the county in which the juvenile resided immediately before the juvenile's arrest. If previously requested, the secretary shall also notify the witnesses and the victim of the offense which the juvenile was found to have committed or the victim's next of kin if the crime was a homicide. If the juvenile is recaptured, the secretary shall send notice to the persons designated in this subsection as soon as possible but in no event later than two working days after the department learns of such recapture.

(b) The secretary may authorize a leave, for a juvenile found to have committed a violent offense, a sex offense, or stalking, which shall not exceed forty-eight hours plus travel time, to meet an emergency situation such as a death or critical illness of a member of the juvenile's family. The secretary may authorize a leave, which shall not exceed the time medically necessary, to obtain medical care not available in a juvenile facility maintained by the department. Prior to the commencement of an emergency or medical leave, the secretary shall give notice of the leave to the appropriate law enforcement agency in the jurisdiction in which the juvenile will be during the leave period. The notice shall include the identity of the juvenile, the time period of the leave, the residence of the juvenile during the leave, and the identity of the person responsible for supervising the juvenile during the leave. If previously requested, the department shall also notify the witnesses and victim of the offense which the juvenile was found to have committed or the victim's next of kin if the offense was a homicide.

In case of an emergency or medical leave the secretary may waive all or any portion of the requirements for leaves pursuant to RCW 13.40.205 (2)(a), (3), (4), and (5).

(3) If the victim, the victim's next of kin, or any witness is under the age of sixteen, the notice required by this section shall be sent to the parents or legal guardian of the child.

(4) The secretary shall send the notices required by this chapter to the last address provided to the department by the requesting party. The requesting party shall furnish the department with a current address.

(5) Upon discharge, parole, transfer to a community residential facility, or other authorized leave or release, a convicted juvenile sex offender shall not attend a public or approved private elementary, middle, or high school that is attended by a victim or a sibling of a victim of the sex offender. The parents or legal guardians of the convicted juvenile sex offender shall be responsible for transportation or other costs associated with or required by the sex offender's change in school that otherwise would be paid by a school district. Upon discharge, parole, transfer to a community residential facility, or other authorized leave or release of a convicted juvenile sex offender, the secretary shall send written notice of the discharge, parole, or other

---

authorized leave or release and the requirements of this subsection to the common school district board of directors of the district in which the sex offender intends to reside or the district in which the sex offender last attended school, whichever is appropriate. The secretary shall send a similar notice to any approved private school the juvenile will attend, if known, or if unknown, to the approved private schools within the district the juvenile resides or intends to reside.

(6) For purposes of this section the following terms have the following meanings:

(a) "Violent offense" means a violent offense under RCW 9.94A.030;

(b) "Sex offense" means a sex offense under RCW 9.94A.030;

(c) "Stalking" means the crime of stalking as defined in RCW 9A.46.110;

(d) "Next of kin" means a person's spouse, parents, siblings, and children.

[1999 c 198 § 1; 1997 c 265 § 2; 1995 c 324 § 1. Prior: 1994 c 129 § 6; 1994 c 78 § 1; 1993 c 27 § 1; 1990 c 3 § 101.]

NOTES:

Severability—1997 c 265: See note following RCW 13.40.160.

Findings—Intent—1994 c 129: See note following RCW 4.24.550.

Index, part headings not law—Severability—Effective dates—Application—1990 c 3: See RCW 18.155.900 through 18.155.902.

13.40.217
Juveniles adjudicated of sex offenses—Release of information authorized.

(1) In addition to any other information required to be released under this chapter, the department is authorized, pursuant to RCW 4.24.550, to release relevant information that is necessary to protect the public concerning juveniles adjudicated of sex offenses.

(2) In order for public agencies to have the information necessary for notifying the public about sex offenders as authorized in RCW 4.24.550, the secretary shall issue to appropriate law enforcement agencies narrative notices regarding the pending release of sex offenders from the department's juvenile rehabilitation facilities. The narrative notices shall, at a minimum, describe the identity and criminal history behavior of the offender and shall include the department's risk level classification for the offender. For sex offenders classified as either risk level II or III, the narrative notices shall also include the reasons underlying the classification.

(3) For the purposes of this section, the department shall classify as risk level I those offenders whose risk assessments indicate a low risk of reoffense within the community at large. The department shall classify as risk level II those offenders whose risk assessments indicate a moderate risk of reoffense within the community at large. The department shall classify as risk level III those offenders whose risk assessments indicate a high risk of reoffense within the community at large.

[1997 c 364 § 2; 1990 c 3 § 102.]

NOTES:

  Severability—1997 c 364: See note following RCW 4.24.550.

  Index, part headings not law—Severability—Effective dates—Application—1990 c 3: See RCW 18.155.900 through 18.155.902.

13.40.219

Arrest for prostitution or prostitution loitering—Alleged offender—Victim of severe form of trafficking, commercial sex abuse of a minor.

In any proceeding under this chapter related to an arrest for prostitution or prostitution loitering, there is a presumption that the alleged offender meets the criteria for a certification as a victim of a severe form of trafficking in persons as defined in section 7105 of Title 22 of the United States code, and that the alleged offender is also a victim of commercial sex abuse of a minor.
[2010 c 289 § 9.]

13.40.220

Costs of support, treatment, and confinement—Order—Contempt of court.

(1) Whenever legal custody of a child is vested in someone other than his or her parents, under this chapter, and not vested in the department of social and health services, after due notice to the parents or other persons legally obligated to care for and support the child, and after a hearing, the court may order and decree that the parent or other legally obligated person shall pay in such a manner as the court may direct a reasonable sum representing in whole or in part the costs of support, treatment, and confinement of the child after the decree is entered.

(2) If the parent or other legally obligated person willfully fails or refuses to pay such sum, the court may proceed against such person for contempt.

(3) Whenever legal custody of a child is vested in the department under this chapter, the parents or other persons legally obligated to care for and support the child shall be liable for the costs of support, treatment, and confinement of the child, in accordance with the department's reimbursement of cost schedule. The department shall adopt a reimbursement of cost schedule based on the costs of providing such services, and shall determine an obligation based on the responsible parents' or other legally obligated person's ability to pay. The department is authorized to adopt additional rules as appropriate to enforce this section.

(4) To enforce subsection (3) of this section, the department shall serve on the parents or other person legally obligated to care for and support the child a notice and finding of financial responsibility requiring the parents or other legally obligated person to appear and show cause in an adjudicative proceeding why the finding of responsibility and/or the amount thereof is

incorrect and should not be ordered. This notice and finding shall relate to the costs of support, treatment, and confinement of the child in accordance with the department's reimbursement of cost schedule adopted under this section, including periodic payments to be made in the future. The hearing shall be held pursuant to chapter 34.05 RCW, the Administrative Procedure Act, and the rules of the department.

(5) The notice and finding of financial responsibility shall be served in the same manner prescribed for the service of a summons in a civil action or may be served on the parent or legally obligated person by certified mail, return receipt requested. The receipt shall be prima facie evidence of service.

(6) If the parents or other legally obligated person objects to the notice and finding of financial responsibility, then an application for an adjudicative hearing may be filed within twenty days of the date of service of the notice. If an application for an adjudicative proceeding is filed, the presiding or reviewing officer shall determine the past liability and responsibility, if any, of the parents or other legally obligated person and shall also determine the amount of periodic payments to be made in the future. If the parents or other legally responsible person fails to file an application within twenty days, the notice and finding of financial responsibility shall become a final administrative order.

(7) Debts determined pursuant to this section are subject to collection action without further necessity of action by a presiding or reviewing officer. The department may collect the debt in accordance with RCW 43.20B.635, 43.20B.640, 74.20A.060, and 74.20A.070. The department shall exempt from payment parents receiving adoption support under *RCW 74.13.100 through 74.13.145, parents eligible to receive adoption support under *RCW 74.13.150, and a parent or other legally obligated person when the parent or other legally obligated person, or such person's child, spouse, or spouse's child, was the victim of the offense for which the child was committed.

(8) An administrative order entered pursuant to this section shall supersede any court order entered prior to June 13, 1994.

(9) The department shall be subrogated to the right of the child and his or her parents or other legally responsible person to receive support payments for the benefit of the child from any parent or legally obligated person pursuant to a support order established by a superior court or pursuant to RCW 74.20A.055. The department's right of subrogation under this section is limited to the liability established in accordance with its cost schedule for support, treatment, and confinement, except as addressed in subsection (10) of this section.

(10) Nothing in this section precludes the department from recouping such additional support payments from the child's parents or other legally obligated person as required to qualify for receipt of federal funds. The department may adopt such rules dealing with liability for recoupment of support, treatment, or confinement costs as may become necessary to entitle the state to participate in federal funds unless such rules would be expressly prohibited by law. If any law dealing with liability for recoupment of support, treatment, or confinement costs is ruled to be in conflict with federal requirements which are a prescribed condition of the allocation of federal funds, such conflicting law is declared to be inoperative solely to the extent of the conflict.

[1995 c 300 § 1; 1994 sp.s. c 7 § 529; 1993 c 466 § 1; 1977 ex.s. c 291 § 76.]

NOTES:

   ***Reviser's note:** RCW 74.13.100 through 74.13.145 and 74.13.150 were recodified as RCW 74.13A.005 through 74.13A.080 and 74.13A.085 pursuant to 2009 c 520 § 95.

   Effective date—1995 c 300: "This act is necessary for the immediate preservation of the public peace, health, or safety, or support of the state government and its existing public institutions, and shall take effect immediately [May 9, 1995]." [1995 c 300 § 2.]

   Finding—Intent—Severability—1994 sp.s. c 7: See notes following RCW 43.70.540.

   Effective dates—Severability—1977 ex.s. c 291: See notes following RCW 13.04.005.

13.40.230
Appeal from order of disposition—Jurisdiction—Procedure—Scope—Release pending appeal.

   (1) Dispositions reviewed pursuant to RCW 13.40.160 shall be reviewed in the appropriate division of the court of appeals.

   An appeal under this section shall be heard solely upon the record that was before the disposition court. No written briefs may be required, and the appeal shall be heard within thirty days following the date of sentencing and a decision rendered within fifteen days following the argument. The supreme court shall promulgate any necessary rules to effectuate the purposes of this section.

   (2) To uphold a disposition outside the standard range, the court of appeals must find (a) that the reasons supplied by the disposition judge are supported by the record which was before the judge and that those reasons clearly and convincingly support the conclusion that a disposition within the range would constitute a manifest injustice, and (b) that the sentence imposed was neither clearly excessive nor clearly too lenient.

   (3) If the court does not find subsection (2)(a) of this section it shall remand the case for disposition within the standard range.

   (4) If the court finds subsection (2)(a) but not subsection (2)(b) of this section it shall remand the case with instructions for further proceedings consistent with the provisions of this chapter.

   (5) The disposition court may impose conditions on release pending appeal as provided in RCW * 13.40.040(4) and 13.40.050(6).

   (6) Appeal of a disposition under this section does not affect the finality or appeal of the underlying adjudication of guilt.
[1997 c 338 § 35; 1981 c 299 § 16; 1979 c 155 § 72; 1977 ex.s. c 291 § 77.]

NOTES:

   ***Reviser's note:** RCW 13.40.040 was amended by 2002 c 171 § 2, changing subsection (4) to subsection (5).

   Finding—Evaluation—Report—1997 c 338: See note following RCW 13.40.0357.

   Severability—Effective dates—1997 c 338: See notes following RCW 5.60.060.

   Effective date—Severability—1979 c 155: See notes following RCW 13.04.011.

   Effective dates—Severability—1977 ex.s. c 291: See notes following RCW 13.04.005.

13.40.240
Construction of RCW references to juvenile delinquents or juvenile delinquency.

All references to juvenile delinquents or juvenile delinquency in other chapters of the Revised Code of Washington shall be construed as meaning juvenile offenders or the commitment of an offense by juveniles as defined by this chapter.
[1977 ex.s. c 291 § 78.]
NOTES:
    Effective dates—Severability—1977 ex.s. c 291: See notes following RCW 13.04.005.

13.40.250
Traffic and civil infraction cases.

A traffic or civil infraction case involving a juvenile under the age of sixteen may be diverted in accordance with the provisions of this chapter or filed in juvenile court.
    (1) If a notice of a traffic or civil infraction is filed in juvenile court, the juvenile named in the notice shall be afforded the same due process afforded to adult defendants in traffic infraction cases.
    (2) A monetary penalty imposed upon a juvenile under the age of sixteen who is found to have committed a traffic or civil infraction may not exceed one hundred dollars. At the juvenile's request, the court may order performance of a number of hours of community restitution in lieu of a monetary penalty, at the rate of the prevailing state minimum wage per hour.
    (3) A diversion agreement entered into by a juvenile referred pursuant to this section shall be limited to thirty hours of community restitution, or educational or informational sessions.
    (4) Traffic or civil infractions referred to a youth court pursuant to this section are subject to the conditions imposed by RCW 13.40.630.
    (5) If a case involving the commission of a traffic or civil infraction or offense by a juvenile under the age of sixteen has been referred to a diversion unit, an abstract of the action taken by the diversion unit may be forwarded to the department of licensing in the manner provided for in RCW 46.20.270(2).
[2002 c 237 § 19; 2002 c 175 § 28; 1997 c 338 § 36; 1980 c 128 § 16.]
NOTES:
    Reviser's note: This section was amended by 2002 c 175 § 28 and by 2002 c 237 § 19, each without reference to the other. Both amendments are incorporated in the publication of this section under RCW 1.12.025(2). For rule of construction, see RCW 1.12.025(1).
    Effective date—2002 c 175: See note following RCW 7.80.130.
    Finding—Evaluation—Report—1997 c 338: See note following RCW 13.40.0357.
    Severability—Effective dates—1997 c 338: See notes following RCW 5.60.060.
    Effective date—Severability—1980 c 128: See notes following RCW 46.63.060.

13.40.265
Firearm, alcohol, and drug violations.

(1) If a juvenile thirteen years of age or older is found by juvenile court to have committed an offense while armed with a firearm or an offense that is a violation of RCW 9.41.040(2)(a)(iv) or chapter 66.44, 69.41, 69.50, or 69.52 RCW, the court shall notify the department of licensing within twenty-four hours after entry of the judgment, unless the offense is the juvenile's first offense while armed with a firearm, first unlawful possession of a firearm offense, or first offense in violation of chapter 66.44, 69.41, 69.50, or 69.52 RCW.

(2) Except as otherwise provided in subsection (3) of this section, upon petition of a juvenile who has been found by the court to have committed an offense that is a violation of chapter 66.44, 69.41, 69.50, or 69.52 RCW, the court may at any time the court deems appropriate notify the department of licensing that the juvenile's driving privileges should be reinstated.

(3) If the offense is the juvenile's second or subsequent violation of chapter 66.44, 69.41, 69.50, or 69.52 RCW, the juvenile may not petition the court for reinstatement of the juvenile's privilege to drive revoked pursuant to RCW 46.20.265 until the date the juvenile turns seventeen or one year after the date judgment was entered, whichever is later.
[2016 c 136 § 6; 2003 c 53 § 101; 1997 c 338 § 37; 1994 sp.s. c 7 § 435; 1989 c 271 § 116; 1988 c 148 § 2.]
NOTES:
> **Intent—Effective date—2003 c 53:** See notes following RCW 2.48.180.
> **Finding—Evaluation—Report—1997 c 338:** See note following RCW 13.40.0357.
> **Severability—Effective dates—1997 c 338:** See notes following RCW 5.60.060.
> **Finding—Intent—Severability—1994 sp.s. c 7:** See notes following RCW 43.70.540.
> **Effective date—1994 sp.s. c 7 §§ 401-410, 413-416, 418-437, and 439-460:** See note following RCW 9.41.010.
> **Severability—1989 c 271:** See note following RCW 9.94A.510.
> **Legislative finding—1988 c 148:** "The legislature finds that many persons under the age of eighteen unlawfully use intoxicating liquor and controlled substances. The use of these substances by juveniles can cause serious damage to their physical, mental, and emotional well-being, and in some instances results in lifelong disabilities.

The legislature also finds that juveniles who unlawfully use alcohol and controlled substances frequently operate motor vehicles while under the influence of and impaired by alcohol or drugs. Juveniles who use these substances often have seriously impaired judgment and motor skills and pose an unduly high risk of causing injury or death to themselves or other persons on the public highways.

The legislature also finds that juveniles will be deterred from the unlawful use of alcohol and controlled substances if their driving privileges are suspended or revoked for using illegal drugs or alcohol." [1988 c 148 § 1.]
> **Severability—1988 c 148:** "If any provision of this act or its application to any person or circumstance is held invalid, the remainder of the act or the application of the provision to other persons or circumstances is not affected." [1988 c 148 § 10.]

13.40.280
Transfer of juvenile to department of corrections facility—Grounds—Hearing—Term—Retransfer to a facility for juveniles.

(1) The secretary, with the consent of the secretary of the department of corrections, has the authority to transfer a juvenile presently or hereafter committed to the department of social and health services to the department of corrections for appropriate institutional placement in accordance with this section.

(2) The secretary of the department of social and health services may, with the consent of the secretary of the department of corrections, transfer a juvenile offender to the department of corrections if it is established at a hearing before a review board that continued placement of the juvenile offender in an institution for juvenile offenders presents a continuing and serious threat to the safety of others in the institution. The department of social and health services shall establish rules for the conduct of the hearing, including provision of counsel for the juvenile offender.

(3) Assaults made against any staff member at a juvenile corrections institution that are reported to a local law enforcement agency shall require a hearing held by the department of social and health services review board within ten judicial working days. The board shall determine whether the accused juvenile offender represents a continuing and serious threat to the safety of others in the institution.

(4) Upon conviction in a court of law for custodial assault as defined in RCW 9A.36.100, the department of social and health services review board shall conduct a second hearing, within five judicial working days, to recommend to the secretary of the department of social and health services that the convicted juvenile be transferred to an adult correctional facility if the review board has determined the juvenile offender represents a continuing and serious threat to the safety of others in the institution.

The juvenile has the burden to show cause why the transfer to an adult correctional facility should not occur.

(5) A juvenile offender transferred to an institution operated by the department of corrections shall not remain in such an institution beyond the maximum term of confinement imposed by the juvenile court.

(6) A juvenile offender who has been transferred to the department of corrections under this section may, in the discretion of the secretary of the department of social and health services and with the consent of the secretary of the department of corrections, be transferred from an institution operated by the department of corrections to a facility for juvenile offenders deemed appropriate by the secretary.

[1989 c 410 § 2; 1989 c 407 § 8; 1983 c 191 § 22.]
NOTES:

      Reviser's note: This section was amended by 1989 c 407 § 8 and by 1989 c 410 § 2, each without reference to the other. Both amendments are incorporated in the publication of this section pursuant to RCW 1.12.025(2). For rule of construction, see RCW 1.12.025(1).

Purpose—1989 c 410: "The legislature recognizes the ever-increasing severity of offenses committed by juvenile offenders residing in this state's juvenile detention facilities and the increasing aggressive nature of detained juveniles due to drugs and gang-related violence. The purpose of this act is to provide necessary protection to state employees and juvenile residents of these institutions from assaults committed against them by juvenile detainees." [1989 c 410 § 1.]

13.40.285
Juvenile offender sentenced to terms in juvenile and adult facilities—Transfer to department of corrections—Term of confinement.

A juvenile offender ordered to serve a term of confinement with the department of social and health services who is subsequently sentenced to the department of corrections may, with the consent of the department of corrections, be transferred by the secretary of social and health services to the department of corrections to serve the balance of the term of confinement ordered by the juvenile court. The juvenile and adult sentences shall be served consecutively. In no case shall the secretary credit time served as a result of an adult conviction against the term of confinement ordered by the juvenile court.
[1983 c 191 § 23.]

13.40.300
Commitment of juvenile beyond age twenty-one prohibited—Jurisdiction of juvenile court after juvenile's eighteenth birthday.

(1) In no case may a juvenile offender be committed by the juvenile court to the department of social and health services for placement in a juvenile correctional institution beyond the juvenile offender's twenty-first birthday. A juvenile may be under the jurisdiction of the juvenile court or the authority of the department of social and health services beyond the juvenile's eighteenth birthday only if prior to the juvenile's eighteenth birthday:

(a) Proceedings are pending seeking the adjudication of a juvenile offense and the court by written order setting forth its reasons extends jurisdiction of juvenile court over the juvenile beyond his or her eighteenth birthday;

(b) The juvenile has been found guilty after a fact finding or after a plea of guilty and an automatic extension is necessary to allow for the imposition of disposition;

(c) Disposition has been held and an automatic extension is necessary to allow for the execution and enforcement of the court's order of disposition. If an order of disposition imposes commitment to the department, then jurisdiction is automatically extended to include a period of up to twelve months of parole, in no case extending beyond the offender's twenty-first birthday; or

(d) While proceedings are pending in a case in which jurisdiction has been transferred to the adult criminal court pursuant to RCW 13.04.030, the juvenile turns eighteen years of age and is subsequently found not guilty of the charge for which he or she was transferred, or is convicted in the adult criminal court of a lesser included offense, and an automatic extension is necessary to impose the disposition as required by RCW 13.04.030(1)(e)(v)(E).

(2) If the juvenile court previously has extended jurisdiction beyond the juvenile offender's eighteenth birthday and that period of extension has not expired, the court may further extend jurisdiction by written order setting forth its reasons.

(3) In no event may the juvenile court have authority to extend jurisdiction over any juvenile offender beyond the juvenile offender's twenty-first birthday except for the purpose of enforcing an order of restitution or penalty assessment.

(4) Notwithstanding any extension of jurisdiction over a person pursuant to this section, the juvenile court has no jurisdiction over any offenses alleged to have been committed by a person eighteen years of age or older.

[2005 c 238 § 2; 2000 c 71 § 2; 1994 sp.s. c 7 § 530; 1986 c 288 § 6; 1983 c 191 § 17; 1981 c 299 § 17; 1979 c 155 § 73; 1975 1st ex.s. c 170 § 1. Formerly RCW 13.04.260.]

NOTES:

 Effective date—2000 c 71: See note following RCW 13.40.198.

 Finding—Intent—Severability—1994 sp.s. c 7: See notes following RCW 43.70.540.

 Severability—1986 c 288: See note following RCW 43.185C.260.

 Effective date—Severability—1979 c 155: See notes following RCW 13.04.011.

13.40.305

Juvenile offender adjudicated of theft of motor vehicle, possession of stolen vehicle, taking motor vehicle without permission in the first degree, taking motor vehicle without permission in the second degree—Local sanctions—Evaluation.

If a juvenile is adjudicated of theft of a motor vehicle under RCW 9A.56.065, possession of a stolen vehicle under RCW 9A.56.068, taking a motor vehicle without permission in the first degree as defined in RCW 9A.56.070(1), or taking a motor vehicle without permission in the second degree as defined in RCW 9A.56.075(1) and is sentenced to local sanctions, the juvenile's disposition shall include an evaluation to determine whether the juvenile is in need of community-based rehabilitation services and to complete any treatment recommended by the evaluation.

[2007 c 199 § 12.]

NOTES:

 Findings—Intent—Short title—2007 c 199: See notes following RCW 9A.56.065.

13.40.308
Juvenile offender adjudicated of taking motor vehicle without permission in the first degree, theft of motor vehicle, possession of a stolen vehicle, taking motor vehicle without permission in the second degree—Minimum sentences.

(1) If a respondent is adjudicated of taking a motor vehicle without permission in the first degree as defined in RCW 9A.56.070, the court shall impose the following minimum sentence, in addition to any restitution the court may order payable to the victim:

(a) Juveniles with a prior criminal history score of zero to one-half points shall be sentenced to a standard range sentence that includes no less than three months of community supervision, forty-five hours of community restitution, and a requirement that the juvenile remain at home such that the juvenile is confined to a private residence for no less than five days. The juvenile may be subject to electronic monitoring where available. If the juvenile is enrolled in school, the confinement shall be served on nonschool days;

(b) Juveniles with a prior criminal history score of three-quarters to one and one-half points shall be sentenced to a standard range sentence that includes six months of community supervision, no less than ten days of detention, and ninety hours of community restitution; and

(c) Juveniles with a prior criminal history score of two or more points shall be sentenced to no less than fifteen to thirty-six weeks commitment to the juvenile rehabilitation administration, four months of parole supervision, and ninety hours of community restitution.

(2) If a respondent is adjudicated of theft of a motor vehicle as defined under RCW 9A.56.065, or possession of a stolen vehicle as defined under RCW 9A.56.068, the court shall impose the following minimum sentence, in addition to any restitution the court may order payable to the victim:

(a) Juveniles with a prior criminal history score of zero to one-half points shall be sentenced to a standard range sentence that includes no less than three months of community supervision and either ninety hours of community restitution or a requirement that the juvenile remain at home such that the juvenile is confined in a private residence for no less than five days, or a combination thereof that includes a minimum of three days home confinement and a minimum of forty hours of community restitution. The juvenile may be subject to electronic monitoring where available;

(b) Juveniles with a prior criminal history score of three-quarters to one and one-half points shall be sentenced to a standard range sentence that includes no less than six months of community supervision, no less than ten days of detention, and ninety hours of community restitution; and

(c) Juveniles with a prior criminal history score of two or more points shall be sentenced to no less than fifteen to thirty-six weeks commitment to the juvenile rehabilitation administration, four months of parole supervision, and ninety hours of community restitution.

(3) If a respondent is adjudicated of taking a motor vehicle without permission in the second degree as defined in RCW 9A.56.075, the court shall impose a standard range as follows:

(a) Juveniles with a prior criminal history score of zero to one-half points shall be sentenced to a standard range sentence that includes three months of community supervision, fifteen hours of community restitution, and a requirement that the juvenile remain at home such that the juvenile is confined in a private residence for no less than one day. If the juvenile is enrolled in school, the confinement shall be served on nonschool days. The juvenile may be subject to electronic monitoring where available;

(b) Juveniles with a prior criminal history score of three-quarters to one and one-half points shall be sentenced to a standard range sentence that includes no less than one day of detention, three months of community supervision, thirty hours of community restitution, and a requirement that the juvenile remain at home such that the juvenile is confined in a private residence for no less than two days. If the juvenile is enrolled in school, the confinement shall be served on nonschool days. The juvenile may be subject to electronic monitoring where available; and

(c) Juveniles with a prior criminal history score of two or more points shall be sentenced to no less than three days of detention, six months of community supervision, forty-five hours of community restitution, and a requirement that the juvenile remain at home such that the juvenile is confined in a private residence for no less than seven days. If the juvenile is enrolled in school, the confinement shall be served on nonschool days. The juvenile may be subject to electronic monitoring where available.

[2016 c 136 § 4; 2009 c 454 § 4; 2007 c 199 § 15.]
NOTES:
>**Findings—Intent—Short title—2007 c 199:** See notes following RCW 9A.56.065.

13.40.310
Transitional treatment program for gang and drug-involved juvenile offenders.

(1) The department of social and health services may contract with a community-based nonprofit organization to establish a three-step transitional treatment program for gang and drug-involved juvenile offenders committed to the custody of the department under chapter 13.40 RCW. Any such program shall provide six to twenty-four months of treatment. The program shall emphasize the principles of self-determination, unity, collective work and responsibility, cooperative economics, and creativity. The program shall be culturally relevant and appropriate and shall include:

(a) A culturally relevant and appropriate institution-based program that provides comprehensive drug and alcohol services, individual and family counseling, and a wilderness experience of constructive group living, rigorous physical exercise, and academic studies;

(b) A culturally relevant and appropriate community-based structured group living program that focuses on individual goals, positive community involvement, coordinated drug and alcohol treatment, coordinated individual and family counseling, academic and vocational training, and employment in apprenticeship, internship, and entrepreneurial programs; and

(c) A culturally relevant and appropriate transitional group living program that provides support services, academic services, and coordinated individual and family counseling.

(2) Participation in any such program shall be on a voluntary basis.

(3) The department shall adopt rules as necessary to implement any such program.

[1991 c 326 § 4.]
NOTES:

Finding—1991 c 326: "The legislature finds that a destructive lifestyle of drug and street gang activity is rapidly becoming prevalent among some of the state's youths. Gang and drug activity may be a culturally influenced phenomenon which the legislature intends public and private agencies to consider and address in prevention and treatment programs. Gang and drug-involved youths are more likely to become addicted to drugs or alcohol, live in poverty, experience high unemployment, be incarcerated, and die of violence than other youths." [1991 c 326 § 3.]

13.40.320
Juvenile offender basic training camp program.

(1) The department of social and health services may establish a medium security juvenile offender basic training camp program. This program for juvenile offenders serving a term of confinement under the supervision of the department is exempt from the licensing requirements of chapter 74.15 RCW.

(2) The department may contract under this chapter with private companies, the national guard, or other federal, state, or local agencies to operate the juvenile offender basic training camp.

(3) The juvenile offender basic training camp shall be a structured and regimented model emphasizing the building up of an offender's self-esteem, confidence, and discipline. The juvenile offender basic training camp program shall provide participants with basic education, prevocational training, work-based learning, work experience, work ethic skills, conflict resolution counseling, substance abuse intervention, anger management counseling, and structured intensive physical training. The juvenile offender basic training camp program shall have a curriculum training and work schedule that incorporates a balanced assignment of these or other rehabilitation and training components for no less than sixteen hours per day, six days a week.

The department shall develop standards for the safe and effective operation of the juvenile offender basic training camp program, for an offender's successful program completion, and for the continued after-care supervision of offenders who have successfully completed the program.

(4) Offenders eligible for the juvenile offender basic training camp option shall be those with a disposition of not more than sixty-five weeks. Violent and sex offenders shall not be eligible for the juvenile offender basic training camp program.

(5) If the court determines that the offender is eligible for the juvenile offender basic training camp option, the court may recommend that the department place the offender in the program. The department shall evaluate the offender and may place the offender in the program. The evaluation shall include, at a minimum, a risk assessment developed by the department and designed to determine the offender's suitability for the program. No juvenile who is assessed as a high risk offender or suffers from any mental or physical problems that could endanger his or her

health or drastically affect his or her performance in the program shall be admitted to or retained in the juvenile offender basic training camp program.

(6) All juvenile offenders eligible for the juvenile offender basic training camp sentencing option shall spend one hundred twenty days of their disposition in a juvenile offender basic training camp. This period may be extended for up to forty days by the secretary if a juvenile offender requires additional time to successfully complete the basic training camp program. If the juvenile offender's activities while in the juvenile offender basic training camp are so disruptive to the juvenile offender basic training camp program, as determined by the secretary according to standards developed by the department, as to result in the removal of the juvenile offender from the juvenile offender basic training camp program, or if the offender cannot complete the juvenile offender basic training camp program due to medical problems, the secretary shall require that the offender be committed to a juvenile institution to serve the entire remainder of his or her disposition, less the amount of time already served in the juvenile offender basic training camp program.

(7) All offenders who successfully graduate from the juvenile offender basic training camp program shall spend the remainder of their disposition on parole in a juvenile rehabilitation administration intensive aftercare program in the local community. Violation of the conditions of parole is subject to sanctions specified in RCW 13.40.210(4). The program shall provide for the needs of the offender based on his or her progress in the aftercare program as indicated by ongoing assessment of those needs and progress. The intensive aftercare program shall monitor postprogram juvenile offenders and assist them to successfully reintegrate into the community. In addition, the program shall develop a process for closely monitoring and assessing public safety risks. The intensive aftercare program shall be designed and funded by the department of social and health services.

(8) The department shall also develop and maintain a database to measure recidivism rates specific to this incarceration program. The database shall maintain data on all juvenile offenders who complete the juvenile offender basic training camp program for a period of two years after they have completed the program. The database shall also maintain data on the criminal activity, educational progress, and employment activities of all juvenile offenders who participated in the program.
[2015 3rd sp.s. c 23 § 1; 2002 c 354 § 234; 2001 c 137 § 1; 1997 c 338 § 38; 1995 c 40 § 1; 1994 sp.s. c 7 § 532.]

NOTES:

      Short title—Headings, captions not law—Severability—Effective dates—2002 c 354: See RCW 41.80.907 through 41.80.910.

      Finding—Evaluation—Report—1997 c 338: See note following RCW 13.40.0357.

      Severability—Effective dates—1997 c 338: See notes following RCW 5.60.060.

      Findings and intent—Juvenile basic training camps—1994 sp.s. c 7: "The legislature finds that the number of juvenile offenders and the severity of their crimes is increasing rapidly statewide. In addition, many juvenile offenders continue to reoffend after they are released from the juvenile justice system causing disproportionately high and expensive rates of recidivism.

      The legislature further finds that juvenile criminal behavior is often the result of a lack of self-discipline, the lack of systematic work habits and ethics, the inability to deal with authority figures, and an unstable or unstructured living environment. The legislature further finds that the department of social and health services currently operates an insufficient number of confinement beds to meet the rapidly growing juvenile offender population. Together these factors are combining to produce a serious public safety hazard and the need to develop more effective and stringent juvenile punishment and rehabilitation options.

The legislature intends that juvenile offenders who enter the state rehabilitation system have the opportunity and are given the responsibility to become more effective participants in society by enhancing their personal development, work ethics, and life skills. The legislature recognizes that structured incarceration programs for juvenile offenders such as juvenile offender basic training camps, can instill the self-discipline, accountability, self-esteem, and work ethic skills that could discourage many offenders from returning to the criminal justice system. Juvenile offender basic training camp incarceration programs generally emphasize life skills training, prevocational work skills training, anger management, dealing with difficult at-home family problems and/or abuses, discipline, physical training, structured and intensive work activities, and educational classes. The legislature further recognizes that juvenile offenders can benefit from a highly structured basic training camp environment and the public can also benefit through increased public protection and reduced cost due to lowered rates of recidivism." [1994 sp.s. c 7 § 531.]

Finding—Intent—Severability—1994 sp.s. c 7: See notes following RCW 43.70.540.

13.40.400
Applicability of RCW 10.01.040 to chapter.

The provisions of RCW 10.01.040 apply to chapter 13.40 RCW.
[1979 c 155 § 74.]
NOTES:
Effective date—Severability—1979 c 155: See notes following RCW 13.04.011.

13.40.430
Disparity in disposition of juvenile offenders—Data collection.

The administrative office of the courts shall collect such data as may be necessary to monitor any disparity in processing or disposing of cases involving juvenile offenders due to economic, gender, geographic, or racial factors that may result from implementation of section 1, chapter 373, Laws of 1993. The administrative office of the courts may, in consultation with juvenile courts, determine a format for the collection of such data and a schedule for the reporting of such data and shall keep a minimum of five years of data at any given time.
[2005 c 282 § 27; 2003 c 207 § 13; 1993 c 373 § 2.]

NOTES:

      Severability—1993 c 373: See note following RCW 13.40.020.

13.40.460
Juvenile rehabilitation programs—Administration.

The secretary, assistant secretary, or the secretary's designee shall manage and administer the department's juvenile rehabilitation responsibilities, including but not limited to the operation of all state institutions or facilities used for juvenile rehabilitation.

The secretary or assistant secretary shall:

(1) Prepare a biennial budget request sufficient to meet the confinement and rehabilitative needs of the juvenile rehabilitation program, as forecast by the office of financial management;

(2) Create by rule a formal system for inmate classification. This classification system shall consider:

(a) Public safety;

(b) Internal security and staff safety;

(c) Rehabilitative resources both within and outside the department;

(d) An assessment of each offender's risk of sexually aggressive behavior as provided in RCW 13.40.470; and

(e) An assessment of each offender's vulnerability to sexually aggressive behavior as provided in RCW 13.40.470;

(3) Develop agreements with local jurisdictions to develop regional facilities with a variety of custody levels;

(4) Adopt rules establishing effective disciplinary policies to maintain order within institutions;

(5) Develop a comprehensive diagnostic evaluation process to be used at intake, including but not limited to evaluation for substance addiction or abuse, literacy, learning disabilities, fetal alcohol syndrome or effect, attention deficit disorder, and mental health;

(6) Develop placement criteria:

(a) To avoid assigning youth who present a moderate or high risk of sexually aggressive behavior to the same sleeping quarters as youth assessed as vulnerable to sexual victimization under RCW 13.40.470(1)(c); and

(b) To avoid placing a juvenile offender on parole status who has been assessed as a moderate to high risk for sexually aggressive behavior in a department community residential program with another child who is: (i) Dependent under chapter 13.34 RCW, or an at-risk youth or child in need of services under chapter 13.32A RCW; and (ii) not also a juvenile offender on parole status;

(7) Develop a plan to implement, by July 1, 1995:

(a) Substance abuse treatment programs for all state juvenile rehabilitation facilities and institutions;

(b) Vocational education and instruction programs at all state juvenile rehabilitation facilities and institutions; and

(c) An educational program to establish self-worth and responsibility in juvenile offenders. This educational program shall emphasize instruction in character-building principles such as: Respect for self, others, and authority; victim awareness; accountability; work ethics; good citizenship; and life skills; and

(8)(a) The juvenile rehabilitation administration shall develop uniform policies related to custodial assaults consistent with RCW 72.01.045 and 9A.36.100 that are to be followed in all juvenile rehabilitation administration facilities; and

(b) The juvenile rehabilitation administration will report assaults in accordance with the policies developed in (a) of this subsection.

[2003 c 229 § 1; 1999 c 372 § 2; 1997 c 386 § 54; 1994 sp.s. c 7 § 516.]

NOTES:

   Implementation deadline—1997 c 386 § 54: "The policy developed under RCW 13.40.460(6)(b) shall be implemented within the juvenile rehabilitation administration and the division of children and family services by July 1, 1998." [1997 c 386 § 55.]

   Finding—Intent—1997 c 386 §§ 50-55: See note following RCW 13.40.470.

   Finding—Intent—Severability—1994 sp.s. c 7: See notes following RCW 43.70.540.

13.40.462
Reinvesting in youth program.

(1) The department of social and health services juvenile rehabilitation administration shall establish a reinvesting in youth program that awards grants to counties for implementing research-based early intervention services that target juvenile justice-involved youth and reduce crime, subject to the availability of amounts appropriated for this specific purpose.

(2) Effective July 1, 2007, any county or group of counties may apply for participation in the reinvesting in youth program.

(3) Counties that participate in the reinvesting in youth program shall have a portion of their costs of serving youth through the research-based intervention service models paid for with moneys from the reinvesting in youth account established pursuant to RCW 13.40.466.

(4) The department of social and health services juvenile rehabilitation administration shall review county applications for funding through the reinvesting in youth program and shall select the counties that will be awarded grants with funds appropriated to implement this program. The department, in consultation with the Washington state institute for public policy, shall develop guidelines to determine which counties will be awarded funding in accordance with the reinvesting in youth program. At a minimum, counties must meet the following criteria in order to participate in the reinvesting in youth program:

(a) Counties must match state moneys awarded for research-based early intervention services with nonstate resources that are at least proportional to the expected local government share of state and local government cost avoidance that would result from the implementation of such services;

(b) Counties must demonstrate that state funds allocated pursuant to this section are used only for the intervention service models authorized pursuant to RCW 13.40.464;

(c) Counties must participate fully in the state quality assurance program established in RCW 13.40.468 to ensure fidelity of program implementation. If no state quality assurance program is in effect for a particular selected research-based service, the county must submit a quality assurance plan for state approval with its grant application. Failure to demonstrate continuing compliance with quality assurance plans shall be grounds for termination of state funding; and

(d) Counties that submit joint applications must submit for approval by the department of social and health services juvenile rehabilitation administration multicounty plans for efficient program delivery.

[2011 1st sp.s. c 32 § 4; 2006 c 304 § 2.]

NOTES:

> **Transition plan—Report to the legislature—2011 1st sp.s. c 32:** See note following RCW 70.305.005.

> **Finding—Intent—2006 c 304:** "The legislature finds that there are youth and family-focused intervention services that have been proven through rigorous evaluation in the state of Washington and elsewhere to significantly reduce violence and crime while saving more public safety dollars than they cost. Under current state laws, no local government acting alone has the financial incentive to invest in these cost-effective services because the savings accrue to multiple levels of government with the largest savings going to the state. It is the intent of the legislature to create incentives for local government to invest in cost-effective intervention services that reduce crime by reimbursing local governments with a portion of the cost savings that accrue to the state as the result of local investments in such services." [2006 c 304 § 1.]

> **Entitlement not created—2006 c 304:** "Nothing in this act creates an entitlement for a county or group of counties to receive funding under the program in sections 2 and 3 of this act." [2006 c 304 § 8.]

> **Effective date—2006 c 304:** "This act takes effect July 1, 2006." [2006 c 304 § 9.]

13.40.464
Reinvesting in youth program—Guidelines.

(1)(a) In order to receive funding through the reinvesting in youth program established pursuant to RCW 13.40.462, intervention service models must meet the following minimum criteria:

(i) There must be scientific evidence from at least one rigorous evaluation study of the specific service model that measures recidivism reduction;

(ii) There must be evidence that the specific service model's results can be replicated outside of an academic research environment;

(iii) The evaluation or evaluations of the service model must permit dollar cost estimates of both benefits and costs so that the benefit-cost ratio of the model can be calculated; and

(iv) The public taxpayer benefits to all levels of state and local government must exceed the service model costs.

(b) In calendar year 2006, for use beginning in fiscal year 2008, the Washington state institute for public policy shall publish a list of service models that are eligible for reimbursement through the investing in youth program. As authorized by the board of the institute and to the extent necessary to respond to new research and information, the institute shall periodically update the list of service models. The institute shall use the technical advisory committee established in *RCW 13.40.462(5) to review and provide comments on the list of service models that are eligible for reimbursement.

(2) In calendar year 2006, for use beginning in fiscal year 2008, the Washington state institute for public policy shall review and update the methodology for calculating cost savings resulting from implementation of this program. As authorized by the board of the institute and to the extent necessary to respond to new research and information, the institute shall periodically further review and update the methodology. As authorized by the board of the institute, when the institute reviews and updates the methodology for calculating cost savings, the institute shall provide an estimate of savings and avoided costs resulting from this program, along with a projection of future savings and avoided costs, to the appropriate committees of the legislature. The institute shall use the technical advisory committee established in *RCW 13.40.462(5) to review and provide comments on its methodology and cost calculations.

(3) In calendar year 2006, for use beginning in fiscal year 2008, the department of social and health services' juvenile rehabilitation administration shall establish a distribution formula to provide funding to local governments that implement research-based intervention services pursuant to this program. The department shall periodically update the distribution formula. The distribution formula shall require that the state allocation to local governments be proportional to the expected state government share of state and local government cost avoidance that would result from the implementation of such services based on the methodology maintained by the Washington state institute for public policy pursuant to subsection (2) of this section. The department shall use the technical advisory committee established in *RCW 13.40.462(5) to review and provide comments on its proposed distribution formula.

(4) The department of social and health services juvenile rehabilitation administration shall provide a report to the legislature on the initial cost savings calculation methodology and distribution formula by October 1, 2006.
[2006 c 304 § 3.]
NOTES:

   ***Reviser's note:** RCW 13.40.462 was amended by 2011 1st sp.s. c 32 § 4, deleting subsection (5).

   Finding—Intent—Entitlement not created—Effective date—2006 c 304: See notes following RCW 13.40.462.

13.40.466
Reinvesting in youth account.

(1) The reinvesting in youth account is created in the state treasury. Moneys in the account shall be spent only after appropriation. Expenditures from the account may be used to reimburse local governments for the implementation of the reinvesting in youth program established in RCW 13.40.462 and 13.40.464. During the 2013-2015 fiscal biennium, the legislature may appropriate moneys from the reinvesting in youth account for juvenile rehabilitation purposes.

(2) Revenues to the reinvesting in youth account consist of revenues appropriated to or deposited in the account.

(3) The department of social and health services juvenile rehabilitation administration shall review and monitor the expenditures made by any county or group of counties that is funded, in whole or in part, with funds provided through the reinvesting in youth account. Counties shall repay any funds that are not spent in accordance with RCW 13.40.462 and 13.40.464.
[2013 2nd sp.s. c 4 § 953; 2006 c 304 § 4.]
NOTES:
   Effective dates—2013 2nd sp.s. c 4: See note following RCW 2.68.020.
   Finding—Intent—Entitlement not created—Effective date—2006 c 304: See notes following RCW 13.40.462.

13.40.468
Juvenile rehabilitation administration—State quality assurance program.

The department of social and health services juvenile rehabilitation administration shall establish a state quality assurance program. The juvenile rehabilitation administration shall monitor the implementation of intervention services funded pursuant to RCW 13.40.466 and shall evaluate adherence to service model design and service completion rate.
[2006 c 304 § 6.]
NOTES:
   Finding—Intent—Entitlement not created—Effective date—2006 c 304: See notes following RCW 13.40.462.

13.40.470
Vulnerable youth committed to residential facilities—Protection from sexually aggressive youth—Assessment process.

(1) The department shall implement a policy for protecting youth committed to state-operated or state-funded residential facilities under this chapter who are vulnerable to sexual victimization

by other youth committed to those facilities who are sexually aggressive. The policy shall include, at a minimum, the following elements:

(a) Development and use of an assessment process for identifying youth, within thirty days of commitment to the department, who present a moderate or high risk of sexually aggressive behavior for the purposes of this section. The assessment process need not require that every youth who is adjudicated or convicted of a sex offense as defined in RCW 9.94A.030 be determined to be sexually aggressive, nor shall a sex offense adjudication or conviction be required in order to determine a youth is sexually aggressive. Instead, the assessment process shall consider the individual circumstances of the youth, including his or her age, physical size, sexual abuse history, mental and emotional condition, and other factors relevant to sexual aggressiveness. The definition of "sexually aggressive youth" in RCW 74.13.075 does not apply to this section to the extent that it conflicts with this section;

(b) Development and use of an assessment process for identifying youth, within thirty days of commitment to the department, who may be vulnerable to victimization by youth identified under (a) of this subsection as presenting a moderate or high risk of sexually aggressive behavior. The assessment process shall consider the individual circumstances of the youth, including his or her age, physical size, sexual abuse history, mental and emotional condition, and other factors relevant to vulnerability;

(c) Development and use of placement criteria to avoid assigning youth who present a moderate or high risk of sexually aggressive behavior to the same sleeping quarters as youth assessed as vulnerable to sexual victimization, except that they may be assigned to the same multiple-person sleeping quarters if those sleeping quarters are regularly monitored by visual surveillance equipment or staff checks;

(d) Development and use of procedures for minimizing, within available funds, unsupervised contact in state-operated or state-funded residential facilities between youth presenting moderate to high risk of sexually aggressive behavior and youth assessed as vulnerable to sexual victimization. The procedures shall include taking reasonable steps to prohibit any youth committed under this chapter who present a moderate to high risk of sexually aggressive behavior from entering any sleeping quarters other than the one to which they are assigned, unless accompanied by an authorized adult.

(2) For the purposes of this section, the following terms have the following meanings:

(a) "Sleeping quarters" means the bedrooms or other rooms within a residential facility where youth are assigned to sleep.

(b) "Unsupervised contact" means contact occurring outside the sight or hearing of a responsible adult for more than a reasonable period of time under the circumstances.
[1997 c 386 § 50.]
NOTES:

Finding—Intent—1997 c 386 §§ 50-55: "The legislature finds that the placement of children and youth in state-operated or state-funded residential facilities must be done in such a manner as to protect children who are vulnerable to sexual victimization from youth who are sexually aggressive. To achieve this purpose, the legislature intends the department of social and health services to develop a policy for assessing sexual aggressiveness and vulnerability to sexual victimization of children and youth who are placed in state-operated or state-funded residential facilities." [1997 c 386 § 49.]

13.40.480
Student records and information—Reasons for release—Who may request.

(1) Pursuant to RCW 28A.600.475, and to the extent permitted by the family educational and privacy rights act of 1974, 20 U.S.C. Sec. 1232g(b), and in order to serve the juvenile while in detention and to prepare any postconviction services, schools shall make all student records and information necessary for risk assessment, security classification, and placement available to court personnel and the department within three working days of a request under this section.

(2)(a) When a juvenile has one or more prior convictions, a request for records shall be made by the county prosecuting attorney, or probation department if available, to the school not more than ten days following the juvenile's arrest or detention, whichever occurs later, and prior to trial. The request may be made by subpoena.

(b) Where a juvenile has no prior conviction, a request to release records shall be made by subpoena upon the juvenile's conviction. When the request for a juvenile's student records and information is made by subpoena following conviction, the court or other issuing agency shall order the school on which the subpoena is served not to disclose to any person the existence or contents of the subpoena or any information furnished in response to the subpoena. When the court or issuing agency so orders, the school shall not provide notice to the juvenile or his or her parents.

[1998 c 269 § 12.]

NOTES:

Intent—Finding—Effective date—1998 c 269: See notes following RCW 72.05.020.

13.40.500
Community juvenile accountability programs—Findings—Purpose.

The legislature finds that meaningful community involvement is vital to the juvenile justice system's ability to respond to the serious problem of juvenile crime. Citizens and crime victims need to be active partners in responding to crime, in the management of resources, and in the disposition decisions regarding juvenile offenders in their community. Involvement of citizens and crime victims increase offender accountability and build healthier communities, which will reduce recidivism and crime rates in Washington state.

The legislature also finds that local governments are in the best position to develop, coordinate, and manage local community prevention, intervention, and corrections programs for juvenile offenders, and to determine local resource priorities. Local community management will build upon local values and increase local control of resources, encourage the use of a comprehensive range of community-based intervention strategies.

The primary purpose of RCW 13.40.500 through 13.40.540, the community juvenile accountability act, is to provide a continuum of community-based programs that emphasize the juvenile offender's accountability for his or her actions while assisting him or her in the development of skills necessary to function effectively and positively in the community in a manner consistent with public safety.
[1997 c 338 § 60.]
NOTES:

      Evaluation—Report—1997 c 338 §§ 60-64: "The Washington state institute for public policy shall evaluate the costs and benefits of the programs funded in sections 60 through 64 of this act. The evaluation must measure whether the programs cost-effectively reduce recidivism and crime rates in Washington state. The institute shall submit reports to the governor and the legislature by December 1, 1998, and December 1, 2000." [1997 c 338 § 65.]

      Finding—Evaluation—Report—1997 c 338: See note following RCW 13.40.0357.

      Severability—Effective dates—1997 c 338: See notes following RCW 5.60.060.

13.40.510
Community juvenile accountability programs—Establishment—Proposals—Guidelines.

(1) In order to receive funds under RCW 13.40.500 through 13.40.540, local governments may, through their respective agencies that administer funding for consolidated juvenile services, submit proposals that establish community juvenile accountability programs within their communities. These proposals must be submitted to the juvenile rehabilitation administration of the department of social and health services for certification.

(2) The proposals must:

(a) Demonstrate that the proposals were developed with the input of the local law and justice councils established under RCW 72.09.300;

(b) Describe how local community groups or members are involved in the implementation of the programs funded under RCW 13.40.500 through 13.40.540;

(c) Include a description of how the grant funds will contribute to the expected outcomes of the program and the reduction of youth violence and juvenile crime in their community. Data approaches are not required to be replicated if the networks have information that addresses risks in the community for juvenile offenders.

(3) A local government receiving a grant under this section shall agree that any funds received must be used efficiently to encourage the use of community-based programs that reduce the reliance on secure confinement as the sole means of holding juvenile offenders accountable for their crimes. The local government shall also agree to account for the expenditure of all funds received under the grant and to submit to audits for compliance with the grant criteria developed under RCW 13.40.520.

(4) The juvenile rehabilitation administration, in consultation with the Washington association of juvenile court administrators and the state law and justice advisory council, shall

establish guidelines for programs that may be funded under RCW 13.40.500 through 13.40.540. The guidelines must:

(a) Target diverted and adjudicated juvenile offenders;

(b) Include assessment methods to determine services, programs, and intervention strategies most likely to change behaviors and norms of juvenile offenders;

(c) Provide maximum structured supervision in the community. Programs should use natural surveillance and community guardians such as employers, relatives, teachers, clergy, and community mentors to the greatest extent possible;

(d) Promote good work ethic values and educational skills and competencies necessary for the juvenile offender to function effectively and positively in the community;

(e) Maximize the efficient delivery of treatment services aimed at reducing risk factors associated with the commission of juvenile offenses;

(f) Maximize the reintegration of the juvenile offender into the community upon release from confinement;

(g) Maximize the juvenile offender's opportunities to make full restitution to the victims and amends to the community;

(h) Support and encourage increased court discretion in imposing community-based intervention strategies;

(i) Be compatible with research that shows which prevention and early intervention strategies work with juvenile offenders;

(j) Be outcome-based in that it describes what outcomes will be achieved or what outcomes have already been achieved;

(k) Include an evaluation component; and

(l) Recognize the diversity of local needs.

(5) The state law and justice advisory council may provide support and technical assistance to local governments for training and education regarding community-based prevention and intervention strategies.

[2010 1st sp.s. c 7 § 62; 1997 c 338 § 61.]

NOTES:

Effective date—2010 1st sp.s. c 26; 2010 1st sp.s. c 7: See note following RCW 43.03.027.

Finding—Evaluation—Report—1997 c 338: See note following RCW 13.40.0357.

Evaluation—Report—1997 c 338 §§ 60-64: See note following RCW 13.40.500.

Severability—Effective dates—1997 c 338: See notes following RCW 5.60.060.

13.40.520
Community juvenile accountability programs—Grants.

(1) The state may make grants to local governments for the provision of community-based programs for juvenile offenders. The grants must be made under a grant formula developed by

the juvenile rehabilitation administration, in consultation with the Washington association of juvenile court administrators.

(2) Upon certification by the juvenile rehabilitation administration that a proposal satisfies the application and selection criteria, grant funds will be distributed to the local government agency that administers funding for consolidated juvenile services.

[1997 c 338 § 62.]

NOTES:

> **Finding—Evaluation—Report—1997 c 338:** See note following RCW 13.40.0357.
> **Evaluation—Report—1997 c 338 §§ 60-64:** See note following RCW 13.40.500.
> **Severability—Effective dates—1997 c 338:** See notes following RCW 5.60.060.

13.40.530
Community juvenile accountability programs—Effectiveness standards.

The legislature recognizes the importance of evaluation and outcome measurements of programs serving juvenile offenders in order to ensure cost-effective use of public funds.

The Washington state institute for public policy shall develop standards for measuring the effectiveness of juvenile accountability programs established and approved under RCW 13.40.510. The standards must be developed and presented to the governor and legislature not later than January 1, 1998. The standards must include methods for measuring success factors following intervention. Success factors include, but are not limited to, continued use of alcohol or controlled substances, arrests, violations of terms of community supervision, convictions for subsequent offenses, and restitution to victims.

[1997 c 338 § 63.]

NOTES:

> **Finding—Evaluation—Report—1997 c 338:** See note following RCW 13.40.0357.
> **Evaluation—Report—1997 c 338 §§ 60-64:** See note following RCW 13.40.500.
> **Severability—Effective dates—1997 c 338:** See notes following RCW 5.60.060.

13.40.540
Community juvenile accountability programs—Information collection—Report.

(1) Each community juvenile accountability program approved and funded under RCW 13.40.500 through 13.40.540 shall comply with the information collection requirements in subsection (2) of this section and the reporting requirements in subsection (3) of this section.

(2) The information collected by each community juvenile accountability program must include, at a minimum for each juvenile participant: (a) The name, date of birth, gender, social security number, and, when available, the juvenile information system (JUVIS) control number;

(b) an initial intake assessment of each juvenile participating in the program; (c) a list of all juveniles who completed the program; and (d) an assessment upon completion or termination of each juvenile, including outcomes and, where applicable, reasons for termination.

(3) The juvenile rehabilitation administration shall annually compile the data and report to the legislature on: (a) The programs funded under RCW 13.40.500 through 13.40.540; (b) the total cost for each funded program and cost per juvenile; and (c) the essential elements of the program.

[1997 c 338 § 64.]

NOTES:

> **Finding—Evaluation—Report—1997 c 338:** See note following RCW 13.40.0357.
> **Evaluation—Report—1997 c 338 §§ 60-64:** See note following RCW 13.40.500.
> **Severability—Effective dates—1997 c 338:** See notes following RCW 5.60.060.

13.40.550
Community juvenile accountability programs—Short title.

RCW 13.40.500 through 13.40.540 may be known as the community juvenile accountability act.

[1997 c 338 § 66.]

NOTES:

> **Finding—Evaluation—Report—1997 c 338:** See note following RCW 13.40.0357.
> **Severability—Effective dates—1997 c 338:** See notes following RCW 5.60.060.

13.40.560
Juvenile accountability incentive account.

The juvenile accountability incentive account is created in the custody of the state treasurer. Federal awards for juvenile accountability incentives received by the secretary of the department of social and health services shall be deposited into the account. Interest earned from the inception of the trust account shall be deposited in the account. Expenditures from the account may be used only for the purposes specified in the federal award or awards. Moneys in the account may be spent only after appropriation.

[1999 c 182 § 1.]

13.40.570
Sexual misconduct by state employees, contractors.

(1) When the secretary has reasonable cause to believe that sexual intercourse or sexual contact between an employee and an offender has occurred, notwithstanding any rule adopted under chapter 41.06 RCW the secretary shall immediately suspend the employee.

(2) The secretary shall immediately institute proceedings to terminate the employment of any person:

(a) Who is found by the department, based on a preponderance of the evidence, to have had sexual intercourse or sexual contact with the offender; or

(b) Upon a guilty plea or conviction for any crime specified in chapter 9A.44 RCW when the victim was an offender.

(3) When the secretary has reasonable cause to believe that sexual intercourse or sexual contact between the employee of a contractor and an offender has occurred, the secretary shall require the employee of a contractor to be immediately removed from any employment position which would permit the employee to have any access to any offender.

(4) The secretary shall disqualify for employment with a contractor in any position with access to an offender, any person:

(a) Who is found by the department, based on a preponderance of the evidence, to have had sexual intercourse or sexual contact with the offender; or

(b) Upon a guilty plea or conviction for any crime specified in chapter 9A.44 RCW when the victim was an offender.

(5) The secretary, when considering the renewal of a contract with a contractor who has taken action under subsection (3) or (4) of this section, shall require the contractor to demonstrate that there has been significant progress made in reducing the likelihood that any of its employees will have sexual intercourse or sexual contact with an offender. The secretary shall examine whether the contractor has taken steps to improve hiring, training, and monitoring practices and whether the employee remains with the contractor. The secretary shall not renew a contract unless he or she determines that significant progress has been made.

(6)(a) For the purposes of RCW 50.20.060, a person terminated under this section shall be considered discharged for misconduct.

(b)(i) The department may, within its discretion or upon request of any member of the public, release information to an individual or to the public regarding any person or contract terminated under this section.

(ii) An appointed or elected public official, public employee, or public agency as defined in RCW 4.24.470 is immune from civil liability for damages for any discretionary release of relevant and necessary information, unless it is shown that the official, employee, or agency acted with gross negligence or in bad faith. The immunity provided under this section applies to the release of relevant and necessary information to other public officials, public employees, or public agencies, and to the public.

(iii) Except as provided in chapter 42.56 RCW, or elsewhere, nothing in this section shall impose any liability upon a public official, public employee, or public agency for failing to release information authorized under this section. Nothing in this section implies that information regarding persons designated in subsection (2) of this section is confidential except as may otherwise be provided by law.

(7) The department shall adopt rules to implement this section. The rules shall reflect the legislative intent that this section prohibits individuals who are employed by the department or a contractor of the department from having sexual intercourse or sexual contact with offenders. The rules shall also reflect the legislative intent that when a person is employed by the department or a contractor of the department, and has sexual intercourse or sexual contact with an offender against the employed person's will, the termination provisions of this section shall not be invoked.

(8) As used in this section:

(a) "Contractor" includes all subcontractors of a contractor;

(b) "Offender" means a person under the jurisdiction or supervision of the department; and

(c) "Sexual intercourse" and "sexual contact" have the meanings provided in RCW 9A.44.010.

[2005 c 274 § 210; 1999 c 72 § 1.]

NOTES:

> **Part headings not law—Effective date—2005 c 274:** See RCW 42.56.901 and 42.56.902.

> **Application—1999 c 72:** "Nothing in section 1 or 2 of this act affects any collective bargaining agreement in place on July 25, 1999." [1999 c 72 § 3.]

13.40.580
Youth courts—Diversion.

Youth courts provide a diversion for cases involving juvenile offenders, in which participants, under the supervision of an adult coordinator, may serve in various capacities within the program, acting in the role of jurors, lawyers, bailiffs, clerks, and judges. Youths who appear before youth courts are youths eligible for diversion pursuant to *RCW 13.40.070 (6) and (7). Youth courts have no jurisdiction except as provided for in chapter 237, Laws of 2002. Youth courts are diversion units and not courts established under Article IV of the state Constitution.

[2002 c 237 § 9.]

NOTES:

> ***Reviser's note:** RCW 13.40.070 was amended by 2010 c 289 § 7, changing subsection (7) to subsection (8).

13.40.590
Youth court programs.

(1) The administrative office of the courts shall encourage the juvenile courts to work with cities and counties to implement, expand, or use youth court programs for juveniles who commit diversion-eligible offenses, civil, or traffic infractions. Program operations of youth court programs may be funded by government and private grants. Youth court programs are limited to those that:

(a) Are developed using the guidelines for creating and operating youth court programs developed by nationally recognized experts in youth court projects;

(b) Target offenders age eight through seventeen; and

(c) Emphasize the following principles:

(i) Youth must be held accountable for their problem behavior;

(ii) Youth must be educated about the impact their actions have on themselves and others including their victims, their families, and their community;

(iii) Youth must develop skills to resolve problems with their peers more effectively; and

(iv) Youth should be provided a meaningful forum to practice and enhance newly developed skills.

(2) Youth court programs under this section may be established by private nonprofit organizations and schools, upon prior approval and under the supervision of juvenile court. [2002 c 237 § 10.]

13.40.600
Youth court jurisdiction.

(1) Youth courts have authority over juveniles ages eight through seventeen who:

(a) Along with their parent, guardian, or legal custodian, voluntarily and in writing request youth court involvement;

(b) Admit they have committed the offense they are referred for;

(c) Along with their parent, guardian, or legal custodian, waive any privilege against self-incrimination concerning the offense; and

(d) Along with their parent, guardian, or legal custodian, agree to comply with the youth court disposition of the case.

(2) Youth courts shall not exercise authority over youth who are under the continuing jurisdiction of the juvenile court for law violations, including a youth with a matter pending before the juvenile court but which has not yet been adjudicated.

(3) Youth courts may decline to accept a youth for youth court disposition for any reason and may terminate a youth from youth court participation at any time.

(4) A youth or his or her parent, guardian, or legal custodian may withdraw from the youth court process at any time.

---

(5) Youth courts shall give any victims of a juvenile the opportunity to be notified, present, and heard in any youth court proceeding.
[2002 c 237 § 11.]

13.40.610
Youth court notification of satisfaction of conditions.

Youth court may not notify the juvenile court of satisfaction of conditions until all ordered restitution has been paid.
[2002 c 237 § 12.]

13.40.620
Appearance before youth court with parent, guardian, or legal custodian.

Every youth appearing before a youth court shall be accompanied by his or her parent, guardian, or legal custodian.
[2002 c 237 § 13.]

13.40.630
Youth court dispositions.

(1) Youth court dispositional options include those delineated in RCW 13.40.080, and may also include:
(a) Participating in law-related education classes, appropriate counseling, treatment, or other education [educational] programs;
(b) Providing periodic reports to the youth court;
(c) Participating in mentoring programs;
(d) Serving as a participant in future youth court proceedings;
(e) Writing apology letters; or
(f) Writing essays.
(2) Youth courts shall not impose a term of confinement or detention. Youth courts may require that the youth pay reasonable fees to participate in youth court and in classes, counseling, treatment, or other educational programs that are the disposition of the youth court.
(3) A youth court disposition shall be completed within one hundred eighty days from the date of referral.

(4) Pursuant to RCW 13.40.080(1), a youth court disposition shall be reduced to writing and signed by the youth and his or her parent, guardian, or legal custodian accepting the disposition terms.

(5) [A] youth court shall notify the juvenile court upon successful or unsuccessful completion of the disposition.

(6) [A] youth court shall notify the prosecutor or probation counselor of a failure to successfully complete the youth court disposition.

[2002 c 237 § 14.]

13.40.640
Youth court nonrefundable fee.

A youth court may require that a youth pay a nonrefundable fee, not exceeding thirty dollars, to cover the costs of administering the program. The fee may be reduced or waived for a participant. Fees shall be paid to and accounted for by the youth court.

[2002 c 237 § 15.]

13.40.650
Use of restraints on pregnant youth in custody—Allowed in extraordinary circumstances.

(1) Except in extraordinary circumstances, no restraints of any kind may be used on any pregnant youth in an institution or detention facility covered by this chapter during transportation to and from visits to medical providers and court proceedings during the third trimester of her pregnancy, or during postpartum recovery. For purposes of this section, "extraordinary circumstances" exist where an employee at an institution or detention facility makes an individualized determination that restraints are necessary to prevent an incarcerated pregnant youth from escaping, or from injuring herself, medical or correctional personnel, or others. In the event the employee of the institution or detention facility determines that extraordinary circumstances exist and restraints are used, the employee of the institution or detention facility must fully document in writing the reasons that he or she determined such extraordinary circumstances existed such that restraints were used. As part of this documentation, the employee of the institution or detention facility must also include the kind of restraints used and the reasons those restraints were considered the least restrictive available and the most reasonable under the circumstances.

(2) While the pregnant youth is in labor or in childbirth no restraints of any kind may be used. Nothing in this section affects the use of hospital restraints requested for the medical safety of a patient by treating physicians licensed under Title 18 RCW.

(3) Anytime restraints are permitted to be used on a pregnant youth, the restraints must be the least restrictive available and the most reasonable under the circumstances, but in no case shall leg irons or waist chains be used on any youth known to be pregnant.

(4) No employee of the institution or detention facility shall be present in the room during the pregnant youth's labor or childbirth, unless specifically requested by medical personnel. If the employee's presence is requested by medical personnel, the employee should be female, if practicable.

(5) If the doctor, nurse, or other health professional treating the pregnant youth requests that restraints not be used, the employee of the institution or detention facility accompanying the pregnant youth shall immediately remove all restraints.
[2010 c 181 § 11.]

13.40.651
Use of restraints on pregnant youth in custody—Provision of information to staff and pregnant youth in custody.

(1) The director of the juvenile detention facility shall provide an informational packet about the requirements of chapter 181, Laws of 2010 to all medical staff and nonmedical staff who are involved in the transportation of youth who are pregnant, as well as such other staff as appropriate. The informational packet provided to staff under this section shall be developed as provided in RCW 70.48.800.

(2) The director shall cause the requirements of chapter 181, Laws of 2010 to be provided to all youth who are pregnant, at the time the facility assumes custody of the person. In addition, the facility shall cause a notice containing the requirements of chapter 181, Laws of 2010 to be posted in conspicuous locations in the detention facilities, including but not limited to the locations in which medical care is provided within the facilities.
[2010 c 181 § 12.]

13.40.720
Imposition of legal financial obligations—City, town, or county authority.

Cities, towns, and counties may not impose any legal financial obligations, fees, fines, or costs associated with juvenile offenses unless there is express statutory authority for those legal financial obligations, fees, fines, or costs.
[2015 c 265 § 5.]
NOTES:
      Finding—Intent—2015 c 265: See note following RCW 13.50.010.

13.40.800
Juvenile offenses with firearms—Data—Reports.

(1)(a) The juvenile rehabilitation administration of the department of social and health services must compile and analyze data regarding juvenile offenders who have been found to have committed the offense of unlawful possession of a firearm under RCW 9.41.040 and made their initial contact with the criminal justice system between January 1, 2005, and December 31, 2013. Information compiled and analyzed must include:

(i) Previous and subsequent criminal offenses committed by the offenders as juveniles or adults;

(ii) Where applicable, treatment interventions provided to the offenders as juveniles, including the nature of provided interventions and whether the offenders completed the interventions, if known; and

(iii) Gang association of the offenders, if known.

(b) The department of corrections and the caseload forecast council must provide any information necessary to assist the juvenile rehabilitation administration in compiling the data required for this purpose. Information provided may include individual identifier level data, however such data must remain confidential and must not be disseminated for purposes other than as identified in this section or otherwise permitted by law.

(2) The juvenile rehabilitation administration shall report its findings to the appropriate committees of the legislature no later than October 1, 2014.

[2014 c 117 § 4.]

13.40.900
Construction—Chapter applicable to state registered domestic partnerships—2009 c 521.

For the purposes of this chapter, the terms spouse, marriage, marital, husband, wife, widow, widower, next of kin, and family shall be interpreted as applying equally to state registered domestic partnerships or individuals in state registered domestic partnerships as well as to marital relationships and married persons, and references to dissolution of marriage shall apply equally to state registered domestic partnerships that have been terminated, dissolved, or invalidated, to the extent that such interpretation does not conflict with federal law. Where necessary to implement chapter 521, Laws of 2009, gender-specific terms such as husband and wife used in any statute, rule, or other law shall be construed to be gender neutral, and applicable to individuals in state registered domestic partnerships.

[2009 c 521 § 43.]

SECTION 5

Chapter 13.50 RCW: KEEPING AND RELEASE OF RECORDS BY JUVENILE JUSTICE OR CARE AGENCIES

13.50.010
Definitions—Conditions when filing petition or information—Duties to maintain accurate records and access—Confidential child welfare records.

(1) For purposes of this chapter:

(a) "Good faith effort to pay" means a juvenile offender has either (i) paid the principal amount in full; (ii) made at least eighty percent of the value of full monthly payments within the period from disposition or deferred disposition until the time the amount of restitution owed is under review; or (iii) can show good cause why he or she paid an amount less than eighty percent of the value of full monthly payments;

(b) "Juvenile justice or care agency" means any of the following: Police, diversion units, court, prosecuting attorney, defense attorney, detention center, attorney general, the legislative children's oversight committee, the office of the family and children's ombuds, the department of social and health services and its contracting agencies, schools; persons or public or private agencies having children committed to their custody; and any placement oversight committee created under RCW 72.05.415;

(c) "Official juvenile court file" means the legal file of the juvenile court containing the petition or information, motions, memorandums, briefs, notices of hearing or appearance, service documents, witness and exhibit lists, findings of the court and court orders, agreements, judgments, decrees, notices of appeal, as well as documents prepared by the clerk, including court minutes, letters, warrants, waivers, affidavits, declarations, invoices, and the index to clerk papers;

(d) "Records" means the official juvenile court file, the social file, and records of any other juvenile justice or care agency in the case;

(e) "Social file" means the juvenile court file containing the records and reports of the probation counselor.

(2) Each petition or information filed with the court may include only one juvenile and each petition or information shall be filed under a separate docket number. The social file shall be filed separately from the official juvenile court file.

(3) It is the duty of any juvenile justice or care agency to maintain accurate records. To this end:

(a) The agency may never knowingly record inaccurate information. Any information in records maintained by the department of social and health services relating to a petition filed pursuant to chapter 13.34 RCW that is found by the court to be false or inaccurate shall be corrected or expunged from such records by the agency;

(b) An agency shall take reasonable steps to assure the security of its records and prevent tampering with them; and

(c) An agency shall make reasonable efforts to insure the completeness of its records, including action taken by other agencies with respect to matters in its files.

(4) Each juvenile justice or care agency shall implement procedures consistent with the provisions of this chapter to facilitate inquiries concerning records.

(5) Any person who has reasonable cause to believe information concerning that person is included in the records of a juvenile justice or care agency and who has been denied access to those records by the agency may make a motion to the court for an order authorizing that person to inspect the juvenile justice or care agency record concerning that person. The court shall grant the motion to examine records unless it finds that in the interests of justice or in the best interests of the juvenile the records or parts of them should remain confidential.

(6) A juvenile, or his or her parents, or any person who has reasonable cause to believe information concerning that person is included in the records of a juvenile justice or care agency may make a motion to the court challenging the accuracy of any information concerning the moving party in the record or challenging the continued possession of the record by the agency. If the court grants the motion, it shall order the record or information to be corrected or destroyed.

(7) The person making a motion under subsection (5) or (6) of this section shall give reasonable notice of the motion to all parties to the original action and to any agency whose records will be affected by the motion.

(8) The court may permit inspection of records by, or release of information to, any clinic, hospital, or agency which has the subject person under care or treatment. The court may also permit inspection by or release to individuals or agencies, including juvenile justice advisory committees of county law and justice councils, engaged in legitimate research for educational, scientific, or public purposes. Each person granted permission to inspect juvenile justice or care agency records for research purposes shall present a notarized statement to the court stating that the names of juveniles and parents will remain confidential.

(9) The court shall release to the caseload forecast council the records needed for its research and data-gathering functions. Access to caseload forecast data may be permitted by the council for research purposes only if the anonymity of all persons mentioned in the records or information will be preserved.

(10) Juvenile detention facilities shall release records to the caseload forecast council upon request. The commission shall not disclose the names of any juveniles or parents mentioned in the records without the named individual's written permission.

(11) Requirements in this chapter relating to the court's authority to compel disclosure shall not apply to the legislative children's oversight committee or the office of the family and children's ombuds.

(12) For the purpose of research only, the administrative office of the courts shall maintain an electronic research copy of all records in the judicial information system related to juveniles. Access to the research copy is restricted to the administrative office of the courts for research

purposes as authorized by the supreme court or by state statute. The administrative office of the courts shall maintain the confidentiality of all confidential records and shall preserve the anonymity of all persons identified in the research copy. Data contained in the research copy may be shared with other governmental agencies as authorized by state statute, pursuant to data-sharing and research agreements, and consistent with applicable security and confidentiality requirements. The research copy may not be subject to any records retention schedule and must include records destroyed or removed from the judicial information system pursuant to RCW 13.50.270 and 13.50.100(3).

(13) The court shall release to the Washington state office of public defense records needed to implement the agency's oversight, technical assistance, and other functions as required by RCW 2.70.020. Access to the records used as a basis for oversight, technical assistance, or other agency functions is restricted to the Washington state office of public defense. The Washington state office of public defense shall maintain the confidentiality of all confidential information included in the records.

(14) The court shall release to the Washington state office of civil legal aid records needed to implement the agency's oversight, technical assistance, and other functions as required by RCW 2.53.045. Access to the records used as a basis for oversight, technical assistance, or other agency functions is restricted to the Washington state office of civil legal aid. The Washington state office of civil legal aid shall maintain the confidentiality of all confidential information included in the records, and shall, as soon as possible, destroy any retained notes or records obtained under this section that are not necessary for its functions related to RCW 2.53.045.

(15) For purposes of providing for the educational success of youth in foster care, the department of social and health services may disclose only those confidential child welfare records that pertain to or may assist with meeting the educational needs of foster youth to another state agency or state agency's contracted provider responsible under state law or contract for assisting foster youth to attain educational success. The records retain their confidentiality pursuant to this chapter and federal law and cannot be further disclosed except as allowed under this chapter and federal law.

[2016 c 93 § 2; 2016 c 72 § 109; 2016 c 71 § 2. Prior: 2015 c 265 § 2; 2015 c 262 § 1; prior: 2014 c 175 § 2; 2014 c 117 § 5; 2013 c 23 § 6; 2011 1st sp.s. c 40 § 30; 2010 c 150 § 3; 2009 c 440 § 1; 1998 c 269 § 4; prior: 1997 c 386 § 21; 1997 c 338 § 39; 1996 c 232 § 6; 1994 sp.s. c 7 § 541; 1993 c 374 § 1; 1990 c 246 § 8; 1986 c 288 § 11; 1979 c 155 § 8.]

NOTES:

Reviser's note: This section was amended by 2016 c 71 § 2, 2016 c 72 § 109, and by 2016 c 93 § 2, each without reference to the other. All amendments are incorporated in the publication of this section under RCW 1.12.025(2). For rule of construction, see RCW 1.12.025(1).

Finding—Intent—2016 c 72: See note following RCW 28A.600.015.

Intent—2016 c 71: See note following RCW 28A.300.590.

Finding—Intent—2015 c 265: "The legislature finds that requiring juvenile offenders to pay all legal financial obligations before being eligible to have a juvenile record administratively sealed disproportionately affects youth based on their socioeconomic status. Juveniles who cannot afford to pay their legal financial obligations cannot seal their juvenile records once they turn eighteen and oftentimes struggle to find employment. By eliminating most nonrestitution legal financial obligations for juveniles convicted of less serious crimes, juvenile offenders will be better able to find employment and focus on making restitution payments first to the actual victim. This legislation is intended to help juveniles understand the consequences of their actions and the harm that those actions have caused others without placing insurmountable burdens on juveniles attempting to become productive members of society. Depending on the juvenile's ability to pay, and upon the consent of the victim, courts should also strongly consider ordering community restitution in lieu of paying restitution where appropriate." [2015 c 265 § 1.]

Findings—Intent—2014 c 175: "The legislature finds that:

(1) The primary goal of the Washington state juvenile justice system is the rehabilitation and reintegration of former juvenile offenders. The public has a compelling interest in the rehabilitation of former juvenile offenders and their successful reintegration into society as active, law-abiding, and contributing members of their communities. When juvenile court records are publicly available, former juvenile offenders face substantial barriers to reintegration, as they are denied housing, employment, and education opportunities on the basis of these records.

(2) The legislature declares it is the policy of the state of Washington that the interest in juvenile rehabilitation and reintegration constitutes compelling circumstances that outweigh the public interest in continued availability of juvenile court records. The legislature intends that juvenile court proceedings be openly administered but, except in limited circumstances, the records of these proceedings be closed when the juvenile has reached the age of eighteen and completed the terms of disposition." [2014 c 175 § 1.]

Application—Recalculation of community custody terms—2011 1st sp.s. c 40: See note following RCW 9.94A.501.

Alphabetization—1998 c 269: "The code reviser shall alphabetize the definitions in RCW 13.50.010 and 74.15.020 and correct any references." [1998 c 269 § 18.]

Intent—Finding—Effective date—1998 c 269: See notes following RCW 72.05.020.

Application—1997 c 386: "Sections 8 through 14 and 17 through 34 of this act apply only to incidents occurring on or after January 1, 1998." [1997 c 386 § 67.]

Effective date—1997 c 386: "Sections 8 through 13 and 21 through 34 of this act take effect January 1, 1998." [1997 c 386 § 68.]

Finding—Evaluation—Report—1997 c 338: See note following RCW 13.40.0357.

Severability—Effective dates—1997 c 338: See notes following RCW 5.60.060.

Effective dates—1996 c 232: See note following RCW 13.40.030.

Application—1994 sp.s. c 7 §§ 540-545: "Sections 540 through 545 of this act shall apply to offenses committed on or after July 1, 1994." [1994 sp.s. c 7 § 917.]

Finding—Intent—Severability—1994 sp.s. c 7: See notes following RCW 43.70.540.

Severability—1990 c 246: See note following RCW 13.34.060.

Severability—1986 c 288: See note following RCW 43.185C.260.

Effective date—Severability—1979 c 155: See notes following RCW 13.04.011.

13.50.050
Records relating to commission of juvenile offenses—Maintenance of, access to, and destruction.

(1) This section and RCW 13.50.260 and 13.50.270 govern records relating to the commission of juvenile offenses, including records relating to diversions.

(2) The official juvenile court file of any alleged or proven juvenile offender shall be open to public inspection, unless sealed pursuant to RCW 13.50.260.

(3) All records other than the official juvenile court file are confidential and may be released only as provided in this chapter, RCW 13.40.215 and 4.24.550.

(4) Except as otherwise provided in this chapter, records retained or produced by any juvenile justice or care agency may be released to other participants in the juvenile justice or care system only when an investigation or case involving the juvenile in question is being pursued by the other participant or when that other participant is assigned the responsibility for supervising the juvenile.

(5) Except as provided in RCW 4.24.550, information not in an official juvenile court file concerning a juvenile or a juvenile's family may be released to the public only when that information could not reasonably be expected to identify the juvenile or the juvenile's family.

(6) Notwithstanding any other provision of this chapter, the release, to the juvenile or his or her attorney, of law enforcement and prosecuting attorneys' records pertaining to investigation, diversion, and prosecution of juvenile offenses shall be governed by the rules of discovery and other rules of law applicable in adult criminal investigations and prosecutions.

(7) Upon the decision to arrest or the arrest, law enforcement and prosecuting attorneys may cooperate with schools in releasing information to a school pertaining to the investigation, diversion, and prosecution of a juvenile attending the school. Upon the decision to arrest or the arrest, incident reports may be released unless releasing the records would jeopardize the investigation or prosecution or endanger witnesses. If release of incident reports would jeopardize the investigation or prosecution or endanger witnesses, law enforcement and prosecuting attorneys may release information to the maximum extent possible to assist schools in protecting other students, staff, and school property.

(8) The juvenile court and the prosecutor may set up and maintain a central recordkeeping system which may receive information on all alleged juvenile offenders against whom a complaint has been filed pursuant to RCW 13.40.070 whether or not their cases are currently pending before the court. The central recordkeeping system may be computerized. If a complaint has been referred to a diversion unit, the diversion unit shall promptly report to the juvenile court or the prosecuting attorney when the juvenile has agreed to diversion. An offense shall not be reported as criminal history in any central recordkeeping system without notification by the diversion unit of the date on which the offender agreed to diversion.

(9) Upon request of the victim of a crime or the victim's immediate family, the identity of an alleged or proven juvenile offender alleged or found to have committed a crime against the victim and the identity of the alleged or proven juvenile offender's parent, guardian, or custodian

and the circumstance of the alleged or proven crime shall be released to the victim of the crime or the victim's immediate family.

(10) Subject to the rules of discovery applicable in adult criminal prosecutions, the juvenile offense records of an adult criminal defendant or witness in an adult criminal proceeding shall be released upon request to prosecution and defense counsel after a charge has actually been filed. The juvenile offense records of any adult convicted of a crime and placed under the supervision of the adult corrections system shall be released upon request to the adult corrections system.

(11) Any juvenile to whom the provisions of this section or RCW 13.50.260 or 13.50.270 may apply shall be given written notice of his or her rights under this section at the time of his or her disposition hearing or during the diversion process.

(12) Nothing in this section or RCW 13.50.260 or 13.50.270 may be construed to prevent a crime victim or a member of the victim's family from divulging the identity of the alleged or proven juvenile offender or his or her family when necessary in a civil proceeding.

(13) Except as provided in RCW 13.50.270(2), no identifying information held by the Washington state patrol in accordance with chapter 43.43 RCW is subject to destruction or sealing under this section. For the purposes of this subsection, identifying information includes photographs, fingerprints, palmprints, soleprints, toeprints and any other data that identifies a person by physical characteristics, name, birthdate or address, but does not include information regarding criminal activity, arrest, charging, diversion, conviction or other information about a person's treatment by the criminal justice system or about the person's behavior.

(14) Information identifying child victims under age eighteen who are victims of sexual assaults by juvenile offenders is confidential and not subject to release to the press or public without the permission of the child victim or the child's legal guardian. Identifying information includes the child victim's name, addresses, location, photographs, and in cases in which the child victim is a relative of the alleged perpetrator, identification of the relationship between the child and the alleged perpetrator. Information identifying a child victim of sexual assault may be released to law enforcement, prosecutors, judges, defense attorneys, or private or governmental agencies that provide services to the child victim of sexual assault.

[2014 c 175 § 3; 2012 c 177 § 2. Prior: 2011 c 338 § 4; 2011 c 333 § 4; 2010 c 150 § 2; 2008 c 221 § 1; 2004 c 42 § 1; prior: 2001 c 175 § 1; 2001 c 174 § 1; 2001 c 49 § 2; 1999 c 198 § 4; 1997 c 338 § 40; 1992 c 188 § 7; 1990 c 3 § 125; 1987 c 450 § 8; 1986 c 257 § 33; 1984 c 43 § 1; 1983 c 191 § 19; 1981 c 299 § 19; 1979 c 155 § 9.]

NOTES:

Rules of court: *Superior Court Criminal Rules (CrR), generally. Discovery: CrR 4.7.*

   Findings—Intent—2014 c 175: See note following RCW 13.50.010.

   Application—2011 c 333: "RCW 13.50.050 (14)(b) and (17)(b) apply to all records of a full and unconditional pardon and should be applied retroactively as well as prospectively." [2011 c 333 § 5.]

   Findings—Intent—2011 c 333: See note following RCW 19.182.040.

   Intent—2001 c 49: "The legislature intends to change the results of the holding of *State v. T. K.*, 139 Wn. 2d 320 (1999), and have any motion made after July 1, 1997, to seal juvenile records be determined by the provisions of RCW 13.50.050 in effect after July 1, 1997." [2001 c 49 § 1.]

Finding—Evaluation—Report—1997 c 338: See note following RCW 13.40.0357.

Severability—Effective dates—1997 c 338: See notes following RCW 5.60.060.

Findings—Intent—Severability—1992 c 188: See notes following RCW 7.69A.020.

Index, part headings not law—Severability—Effective dates—Application—1990 c 3: See RCW 18.155.900 through 18.155.902.

Severability—1986 c 257: See note following RCW 9A.56.010.

Effective date—1986 c 257 §§ 17-35: See note following RCW 9.94A.030.

Effective date—Severability—1979 c 155: See notes following RCW 13.04.011.

13.50.100

Records not relating to commission of juvenile offenses—Maintenance and access—Release of information for child custody hearings—Disclosure of unfounded allegations prohibited.

(1) This section governs records not covered by RCW 13.50.050, 13.50.260, and 13.50.270.

(2) Records covered by this section shall be confidential and shall be released only pursuant to this section and RCW 13.50.010.

(3) Records retained or produced by any juvenile justice or care agency may be released to other participants in the juvenile justice or care system only when an investigation or case involving the juvenile in question is being pursued by the other participant or when that other participant is assigned the responsibility of supervising the juvenile. Records covered under this section and maintained by the juvenile courts which relate to the official actions of the agency may be entered in the statewide judicial information system. However, truancy records associated with a juvenile who has no other case history, and records of a juvenile's parents who have no other case history, shall be removed from the judicial information system when the juvenile is no longer subject to the compulsory attendance laws in chapter 28A.225 RCW. A county clerk is not liable for unauthorized release of this data by persons or agencies not in his or her employ or otherwise subject to his or her control, nor is the county clerk liable for inaccurate or incomplete information collected from litigants or other persons required to provide identifying data pursuant to this section.

(4) Subject to (a) of this subsection, the department of social and health services may release information retained in the course of conducting child protective services investigations to a family or juvenile court hearing a petition for custody under chapter 26.10 RCW.

(a) Information that may be released shall be limited to information regarding investigations in which: (i) The juvenile was an alleged victim of abandonment or abuse or neglect; or (ii) the petitioner for custody of the juvenile, or any individual aged sixteen or older residing in the petitioner's household, is the subject of a founded or currently pending child protective services investigation made by the department subsequent to October 1, 1998.

(b) Additional information may only be released with the written consent of the subject of the investigation and the juvenile alleged to be the victim of abandonment or abuse and neglect, or the parent, custodian, guardian, or personal representative of the juvenile, or by court order obtained with notice to all interested parties.

(5) Any disclosure of records or information by the department of social and health services pursuant to this section shall not be deemed a waiver of any confidentiality or privilege attached to the records or information by operation of any state or federal statute or regulation, and any recipient of such records or information shall maintain it in such a manner as to comply with such state and federal statutes and regulations and to protect against unauthorized disclosure.

(6) A contracting agency or service provider of the department of social and health services that provides counseling, psychological, psychiatric, or medical services may release to the office of the family and children's ombuds information or records relating to services provided to a juvenile who is dependent under chapter 13.34 RCW without the consent of the parent or guardian of the juvenile, or of the juvenile if the juvenile is under the age of thirteen years, unless such release is otherwise specifically prohibited by law.

(7) A juvenile, his or her parents, the juvenile's attorney, and the juvenile's parent's attorney, shall, upon request, be given access to all records and information collected or retained by a juvenile justice or care agency which pertain to the juvenile except:

(a) If it is determined by the agency that release of this information is likely to cause severe psychological or physical harm to the juvenile or his or her parents the agency may withhold the information subject to other order of the court: PROVIDED, That if the court determines that limited release of the information is appropriate, the court may specify terms and conditions for the release of the information; or

(b) If the information or record has been obtained by a juvenile justice or care agency in connection with the provision of counseling, psychological, psychiatric, or medical services to the juvenile, when the services have been sought voluntarily by the juvenile, and the juvenile has a legal right to receive those services without the consent of any person or agency, then the information or record may not be disclosed to the juvenile's parents without the informed consent of the juvenile unless otherwise authorized by law; or

(c) That the department of social and health services may delete the name and identifying information regarding persons or organizations who have reported alleged child abuse or neglect.

(8) A juvenile or his or her parent denied access to any records following an agency determination under subsection (7) of this section may file a motion in juvenile court requesting access to the records. The court shall grant the motion unless it finds access may not be permitted according to the standards found in subsection (7)(a) and (b) of this section.

(9) The person making a motion under subsection (8) of this section shall give reasonable notice of the motion to all parties to the original action and to any agency whose records will be affected by the motion.

(10) Subject to the rules of discovery in civil cases, any party to a proceeding seeking a declaration of dependency or a termination of the parent-child relationship and any party's counsel and the guardian ad litem of any party, shall have access to the records of any natural or adoptive child of the parent, subject to the limitations in subsection (7) of this section. A party denied access to records may request judicial review of the denial. If the party prevails, he or she

shall be awarded attorneys' fees, costs, and an amount not less than five dollars and not more than one hundred dollars for each day the records were wrongfully denied.

(11) No unfounded allegation of child abuse or neglect as defined in RCW 26.44.020(1) may be disclosed to a child-placing agency, private adoption agency, or any other licensed provider. [2014 c 175 § 8; 2013 c 23 § 7; 2003 c 105 § 2; 2001 c 162 § 2; 2000 c 162 § 18; 1999 c 390 § 3; 1997 c 386 § 22; 1995 c 311 § 16; 1990 c 246 § 9; 1983 c 191 § 20; 1979 c 155 § 10.]

NOTES:
  Findings—Intent—2014 c 175: See note following RCW 13.50.010.
  Application—Effective date—1997 c 386: See notes following RCW 13.50.010.
  Severability—1990 c 246: See note following RCW 13.34.060.
  Effective date—Severability—1979 c 155: See notes following RCW 13.04.011.

13.50.140
Disclosure of privileged information to office of the family and children's ombuds—Privilege not waived as to others.

Any communication or advice privileged under RCW 5.60.060 that is disclosed by the office of the attorney general or the department of social and health services to the office of the family and children's ombuds may not be deemed to be a waiver of the privilege as to others. [2013 c 23 § 8; 1999 c 390 § 8.]

13.50.150
Confidential records—Expungement to protect due process rights.

Nothing in this chapter shall be construed to prevent the expungement of any juvenile record ordered expunged by a court to preserve the due process rights of its subject. [1977 ex.s. c 291 § 13. Formerly RCW 13.04.276, see 1979 c 155 § 12.]

NOTES:
  Effective date—Severability—1979 c 155: See notes following RCW 13.04.011.
  Effective date—Severability—1977 ex.s. c 291: See notes following RCW 13.04.005.

13.50.160
Disposition records—Provision to schools.

Records of disposition for a juvenile offense must be provided to schools as provided in RCW 13.04.155.
[1997 c 266 § 8.]
NOTES:

> **Findings—Intent—Severability—1997 c 266:** See notes following RCW 28A.600.455.

13.50.200
Records of motor vehicle operation violation forwarded.

Notwithstanding any other provision of this chapter, whenever a child is arrested for a violation of any law, including municipal ordinances, regulating the operation of vehicles on the public highways, a copy of the traffic citation and a record of the action taken by the court shall be forwarded by the juvenile court to the department of licensing in the same manner as provided in RCW 46.20.270.
[1979 c 155 § 13; 1977 ex.s. c 291 § 14. Formerly RCW 13.04.278.]
NOTES:

> **Effective date—Severability—1979 c 155:** See notes following RCW 13.04.011.
> **Effective date—Severability—1977 ex.s. c 291:** See notes following RCW 13.04.005.

13.50.250
Records chapter applicable to.

This chapter applies to all juvenile justice or care agency records created on or after July 1, 1978.
[1979 c 155 § 11.]
NOTES:

> **Effective date—Severability—1979 c 155:** See notes following RCW 13.04.011.

13.50.260
Sealing hearings—Sealing of records.

(1)(a) The court shall hold regular sealing hearings. During these regular sealing hearings, the court shall administratively seal an individual's juvenile record pursuant to the requirements of this subsection unless the court receives an objection to sealing or the court notes a compelling reason not to seal, in which case, the court shall set a contested hearing to be conducted on the record to address sealing. Although the juvenile record shall be sealed, the social file may be available to any juvenile justice or care agency when an investigation or case involving the juvenile subject of the records is being prosecuted by the juvenile justice or care agency or when the juvenile justice or care agency is assigned the responsibility of supervising the juvenile. The contested hearing shall be set no sooner than eighteen days after notice of the hearing and the opportunity to object has been sent to the juvenile, the victim, and juvenile's attorney. The juvenile respondent's presence is not required at a sealing hearing pursuant to this subsection.

(b) At the disposition hearing of a juvenile offender, the court shall schedule an administrative sealing hearing to take place during the first regularly scheduled sealing hearing after the latest of the following events that apply:

(i) The respondent's eighteenth birthday;

(ii) Anticipated completion of a respondent's probation, if ordered;

(iii) Anticipated release from confinement at the juvenile rehabilitation administration, or the completion of parole, if the respondent is transferred to the juvenile rehabilitation administration.

(c) A court shall enter a written order sealing an individual's juvenile court record pursuant to this subsection if:

(i) One of the offenses for which the court has entered a disposition is not at the time of commission of the offense:

(A) A most serious offense, as defined in RCW 9.94A.030;

(B) A sex offense under chapter 9A.44 RCW; or

(C) A drug offense, as defined in RCW 9.94A.030; and

(ii) The respondent has completed the terms and conditions of disposition, including affirmative conditions and has paid the full amount of restitution owing to the individual victim named in the restitution order, excluding restitution owed to any insurance provider authorized under Title 48 RCW.

(d) Following a contested sealing hearing on the record after an objection is made pursuant to (a) of this subsection, the court shall enter a written order sealing the juvenile court record unless the court determines that sealing is not appropriate.

(2) The court shall enter a written order immediately sealing the official juvenile court record upon the acquittal after a fact finding or upon the dismissal of charges with prejudice, subject to the state's right, if any, to appeal the dismissal.

(3) If a juvenile court record has not already been sealed pursuant to this section, in any case in which information has been filed pursuant to RCW 13.40.100 or a complaint has been filed with the prosecutor and referred for diversion pursuant to RCW 13.40.070, the person who is the subject of the information or complaint may file a motion with the court to have the court vacate

its order and findings, if any, and, subject to RCW 13.50.050(13), order the sealing of the official juvenile court record, the social file, and records of the court and of any other agency in the case.

(4)(a) The court shall grant any motion to seal records for class A offenses made pursuant to subsection (3) of this section if:

(i) Since the last date of release from confinement, including full-time residential treatment, if any, or entry of disposition, the person has spent five consecutive years in the community without committing any offense or crime that subsequently results in an adjudication or conviction;

(ii) No proceeding is pending against the moving party seeking the conviction of a juvenile offense or a criminal offense;

(iii) No proceeding is pending seeking the formation of a diversion agreement with that person;

(iv) The person is no longer required to register as a sex offender under RCW 9A.44.130 or has been relieved of the duty to register under RCW 9A.44.143 if the person was convicted of a sex offense;

(v) The person has not been convicted of rape in the first degree, rape in the second degree, or indecent liberties that was actually committed with forcible compulsion; and

(vi) The person has paid the full amount of restitution owing to the individual victim named in the restitution order, excluding restitution owed to any insurance provider authorized under Title 48 RCW.

(b) The court shall grant any motion to seal records for class B, class C, gross misdemeanor, and misdemeanor offenses and diversions made under subsection (3) of this section if:

(i) Since the date of last release from confinement, including full-time residential treatment, if any, entry of disposition, or completion of the diversion agreement, the person has spent two consecutive years in the community without being convicted of any offense or crime;

(ii) No proceeding is pending against the moving party seeking the conviction of a juvenile offense or a criminal offense;

(iii) No proceeding is pending seeking the formation of a diversion agreement with that person;

(iv) The person is no longer required to register as a sex offender under RCW 9A.44.130 or has been relieved of the duty to register under RCW 9A.44.143 if the person was convicted of a sex offense; and

(v) The person has paid the full amount of restitution owing to the individual victim named in the restitution order, excluding restitution owed to any insurance provider authorized under Title 48 RCW.

(c) Notwithstanding the requirements in (a) or (b) of this subsection, the court shall grant any motion to seal records of any deferred disposition vacated under RCW 13.40.127(9) prior to June 7, 2012, if restitution has been paid and the person is eighteen years of age or older at the time of the motion.

(5) The person making a motion pursuant to subsection (3) of this section shall give reasonable notice of the motion to the prosecution and to any person or agency whose records are sought to be sealed.

(6)(a) If the court enters a written order sealing the juvenile court record pursuant to this section, it shall, subject to RCW 13.50.050(13), order sealed the official juvenile court record, the social file, and other records relating to the case as are named in the order. Thereafter, the proceedings in the case shall be treated as if they never occurred, and the subject of the records may reply accordingly to any inquiry about the events, records of which are sealed. Any agency shall reply to any inquiry concerning confidential or sealed records that records are confidential, and no information can be given about the existence or nonexistence of records concerning an individual.

(b) In the event the subject of the juvenile records receives a full and unconditional pardon, the proceedings in the matter upon which the pardon has been granted shall be treated as if they never occurred, and the subject of the records may reply accordingly to any inquiry about the events upon which the pardon was received. Any agency shall reply to any inquiry concerning the records pertaining to the events for which the subject received a pardon that records are confidential, and no information can be given about the existence or nonexistence of records concerning an individual.

(c) Effective July 1, 2019, the department of licensing may release information related to records the court has ordered sealed only to the extent necessary to comply with federal law and regulation.

(7) Inspection of the files and records included in the order to seal may thereafter be permitted only by order of the court upon motion made by the person who is the subject of the information or complaint, except as otherwise provided in RCW 13.50.010(8) and 13.50.050(13).

(8)(a) Any adjudication of a juvenile offense or a crime subsequent to sealing has the effect of nullifying a sealing order; however, the court may order the juvenile court record resealed upon disposition of the subsequent matter if the case meets the sealing criteria under this section and the court record has not previously been resealed.

(b) Any charging of an adult felony subsequent to the sealing has the effect of nullifying the sealing order.

(c) The administrative office of the courts shall ensure that the superior court judicial information system provides prosecutors access to information on the existence of sealed juvenile records.

(d) The Washington state patrol shall ensure that the Washington state identification system provides criminal justice agencies access to sealed juvenile records information.

(9) If the juvenile court record has been sealed pursuant to this section, the record of an employee is not admissible in an action for liability against the employer based on the former juvenile offender's conduct to show that the employer knew or should have known of the juvenile record of the employee. The record may be admissible, however, if a background check conducted or authorized by the employer contained the information in the sealed record.

(10) County clerks may interact or correspond with the respondent, his or her parents, and any holders of potential assets or wages of the respondent for the purposes of collecting an outstanding legal financial obligation after juvenile court records have been sealed pursuant to this section.

(11) Persons and agencies that obtain sealed juvenile records information pursuant to this section may communicate about this information with the respondent, but may not disseminate or be compelled to release the information to any person or agency not specifically granted access to sealed juvenile records in this section.

[2015 c 265 § 3; 2014 c 175 § 4.]

NOTES:

        Finding—Intent—2015 c 265: See note following RCW 13.50.010.
        Findings—Intent—2014 c 175: See note following RCW 13.50.010.

13.50.270
Destruction of records.

(1)(a) Subject to RCW 13.50.050(13), all records maintained by any court or law enforcement agency, including the juvenile court, local law enforcement, the Washington state patrol, and the prosecutor's office, shall be automatically destroyed within ninety days of becoming eligible for destruction. Juvenile records are eligible for destruction when:

(i) The person who is the subject of the information or complaint is at least eighteen years of age;

(ii) The person's criminal history consists entirely of one diversion agreement or counsel and release entered on or after June 12, 2008;

(iii) Two years have elapsed since completion of the agreement or counsel and release;

(iv) No proceeding is pending against the person seeking the conviction of a criminal offense; and

(v) There is no restitution owing in the case.

(b) No less than quarterly, the administrative office of the courts shall provide a report to the juvenile courts of those individuals whose records may be eligible for destruction. The juvenile court shall verify eligibility and notify the Washington state patrol and the appropriate local law enforcement agency and prosecutor's office of the records to be destroyed. The requirement to destroy records under this subsection is not dependent on a court hearing or the issuance of a court order to destroy records.

(c) The state and local governments and their officers and employees are not liable for civil damages for the failure to destroy records pursuant to this section.

(2) All records maintained by any court or law enforcement agency, including the juvenile court, local law enforcement, the Washington state patrol, and the prosecutor's office, shall be automatically destroyed within thirty days of being notified by the governor's office that the subject of those records received a full and unconditional pardon by the governor.

(3)(a) A person may request that the court order the records in his or her case destroyed as follows:

(i) A person eighteen years of age or older whose criminal history consists entirely of one diversion agreement or counsel and release entered prior to June 12, 2008. The request shall be granted if the court finds that two years have elapsed since completion of the agreement or counsel and release.

(ii) A person twenty-three years of age or older whose criminal history consists of only referrals for diversion. The request shall be granted if the court finds that all diversion agreements have been successfully completed and no proceeding is pending against the person seeking the conviction of a criminal offense.

(b) If the court grants the motion to destroy records made pursuant to this subsection, it shall, subject to RCW 13.50.050(13), order the official juvenile court record, the social file, and any other records named in the order to be destroyed.

(c) The person making the motion pursuant to this subsection must give reasonable notice of the motion to the prosecuting attorney and to any agency whose records are sought to be destroyed.

(4) Any juvenile justice or care agency may, subject to the limitations in RCW 13.50.050(13) and this section, develop procedures for the routine destruction of records relating to juvenile offenses and diversions.

(a) Records may be routinely destroyed only when the person the subject of the information or complaint has attained twenty-three years of age or older or pursuant to subsection (1) of this section.

(b) The court may not routinely destroy the official juvenile court record or recordings or transcripts of any proceedings.
[2014 c 175 § 5.]
NOTES:
>   **Findings—Intent—2014 c 175:** See note following RCW 13.50.010.

13.50.280
Court and judicial agency records—Use for research or data gathering purposes.

(1) Courts and judicial agencies that maintain a database of juvenile records may provide those records, whether sealed or not, to government agencies for the purpose of carrying out research or data gathering functions. This data may also be linked with records from other agencies or research organizations, provided that any agency receiving or using records under this subsection maintain strict confidentiality of the identity of the juveniles who are the subjects of such records.

(2) Juvenile records, whether sealed or not, can be provided without personal identifiers to researchers conducting legitimate research for educational, scientific, or public purposes, so long as the data is not used by the recipients of the records to identify an individual with a juvenile record.
[2015 c 265 § 9.]
NOTES:
>   **Finding—Intent—2015 c 265:** See note following RCW 13.50.010.

SECTION 6

JUVENILE REHABILITATION
SENTENCING WORKSHEET

Sentencing Worksheet Instructions

These instructions describe the use of the Juvenile Rehabilitation (JR) Sentencing Worksheet DSHS 20-198.

Purpose

The Sentencing Worksheet is used to report information pertinent to the disposition of each juvenile admitted to JR or those sentenced to community supervision through the Special Sex Offender Disposition Alternative (SSODA) or Option C (Chemical Dependency/MHDA Disposition Alternative (CDMHDA)). The form serves as a worksheet for determining the minimum and maximum length of the standard range of confinement for each offense. The structure of the form conforms to and facilitates the application of the disposition standards developed by the Sentencing Guidelines Commission, as required by RCW 13.40.030.

A single disposition grid will establish standard ranges to be imposed, unless the court chooses Option C (CDMHDA) or Option D (Manifest Injustice).

If a Manifest Injustice is invoked or the 300% or 150% rule is in effect, the length of the actual sentence ordered by the court should be entered on the Sentencing Worksheet in lieu of the standard range.

Data from the Sentencing Worksheet will be processed and stored in the Juvenile Rehabilitation's computer files in Olympia. For youths admitted to JR the data will be used by JR facilities for setting minimum and maximum release dates. Data about offenders assigned to the community through SSODA and Option C (CDMHDA) will be used to track offenders in those programs. Data extracted from the system will be used by JR to study the impact of the implementation of the Juvenile Justice Act.

General Instructions

A JR Sentencing Worksheet is completed for each juvenile admitted to the Juvenile Rehabilitation and each juvenile sentenced to community supervision through either SSODA or Option B (suspended disposition).

The juvenile sentencing guidelines are subject to modification by the state legislature. It is the responsibility of the sentencing court to ensure that the appropriate standards are being used for a specific offender.

Questions regarding the use of the **Juvenile Disposition Guidelines Manual** should be referred to:

> Caseload Forecast Council
> P.O. Box 40962
> Olympia, WA 98504-0962
> (360) 664-9380

Questions regarding the use or completion of the **Juvenile Rehabilitation's Sentencing Worksheet** should be referred to:

> Juvenile Rehabilitation
> P.O. Box 45720
> Olympia, WA 98504-5720
> (360) 902-8085

Personnel designated by the juvenile court administrators are responsible for the accuracy of the information provided to JR. Please read the detailed instructions on the following pages before completing the worksheet. If you have any questions regarding the worksheet or these instructions, please contact the JR Information Services Manager.

For juveniles admitted to JR, the court should place the white copy of the Sentencing Worksheet in the case file, send the yellow copy to JR and retain the pink copy. The yellow copy of the worksheet should be sent to JR, along with any other admittance documents, in time to <u>precede or coincide</u> with the juvenile's arrival.

For offenders sentenced to community supervision through SSODA or Option C (CDMHDA), the court should send a copy of the Sentencing Worksheet to the JR regional office. The worksheet should be sent as soon as possible after the juvenile's disposition.

Up to three current offenses can be put on a worksheet. If there are more than four offenses, attach a second sheet.

If there are more than sixteen prior offenses, compute the total score of the additional prior offenses not listed and place it in the appropriate box.

Supply of forms:

Requests for blank forms should be directed to your local JR regional office.

Instructions for completing each item:

The following definitions and procedures are to be used for completing the individual items. (The numbers correspond to the numbers on the attached sample worksheet).

**Washington State
Department of Social
& Health Services**
Transforming lives

JUVENILE REHABILITATION (JR)

Sentencing Worksheet

1. NAME (LAST, FIRST, MIDDLE INITIAL)	

2. BIRTHDATE (MM/DD/YYYY)	3. SEX ☐ Male ☐ Female	4. RACE
5. HISPANIC ORIGIN	6. JRA NUMBER	7. DETENTION CREDIT DAYS
8. JUVIS NUMBER		9. NAME OF COUNTY COURT

A. Current Offense Information

10. Current offense number _____ of _____ total current offenses.

11. COURT ORDER NUMBER

12. SENTENCE START DATE (MM/DD/YYYY)	13. DISPOSITION DATE (MM/DD/YYYY)	14. ADJUDICATION DATE (MM/DD/YYYY)	15. OFFENSE DATE (MM/DD/YYYY)

16. JR OFFENSE CODE	17. ANTICIPATORY TYPE ☐ COMPLETED ☐ CONSPIRACY ☐ ATTEMPTED ☐ SOLICITATION	18. JR OFFENSE CATEGORY	19. FINDING OF SEXUAL MOTIVATION ☐ Yes ☐ No	20. FINDING OF FIREARM ENHANCEMENT ☐ Yes ☐ No

21. TYPE OF PLACEMENT
☐ JR Direct
☐ Suspended Disposition Alternative (SDA)
☐ Special Sex Offender Disposition Alternative (SSODA)
☐ Chemical Dependency / Mental Health Disposition Alternative (CDMHDA)
Please check one of the following boxes for CDMHDA:
☐ Chemical Dependency ☐ Mental Health ☐ Co-Occurring

☐ SDA Revoke
☐ SSODA Revoke
☐ CDMHDA Revoke

B. Prior Offense Information

22. ADJUDICATION DATE (MM/DD/YYYY)	23. OFFENSE DATE (MM/DD/YYYY)	24. JR OFFENSE CODE	25. ANTICIPATORY TYPE	26. SEXUAL MOTIVATION	27. CRIMINAL CLASS	28. PRIOR SCORE
			☐ COMPLETED ☐ CONSPIRACY ☐ ATTEMPTED ☐ SOLICITATION	☐ YES ☐ NO		
			☐ COMPLETED ☐ CONSPIRACY ☐ ATTEMPTED ☐ SOLICITATION	☐ YES ☐ NO		
			☐ COMPLETED ☐ CONSPIRACY ☐ ATTEMPTED ☐ SOLICITATION	☐ YES ☐ NO		
			☐ COMPLETED ☐ CONSPIRACY ☐ ATTEMPTED ☐ SOLICITATION	☐ YES ☐ NO		
			☐ COMPLETED ☐ CONSPIRACY ☐ ATTEMPTED ☐ SOLICITATION	☐ YES ☐ NO		
			☐ COMPLETED ☐ CONSPIRACY ☐ ATTEMPTED ☐ SOLICITATION	☐ YES ☐ NO		
			☐ COMPLETED ☐ CONSPIRACY ☐ ATTEMPTED ☐ SOLICITATION	☐ YES ☐ NO		
			☐ COMPLETED ☐ CONSPIRACY ☐ ATTEMPTED ☐ SOLICITATION	☐ YES ☐ NO		
			☐ COMPLETED ☐ CONSPIRACY ☐ ATTEMPTED ☐ SOLICITATION	☐ YES ☐ NO		
			☐ COMPLETED ☐ CONSPIRACY ☐ ATTEMPTED ☐ SOLICITATION	☐ YES ☐ NO		
			☐ COMPLETED ☐ CONSPIRACY ☐ ATTEMPTED ☐ SOLICITATION	☐ YES ☐ NO		
			☐ COMPLETED ☐ CONSPIRACY ☐ ATTEMPTED ☐ SOLICITATION	☐ YES ☐ NO		
			☐ COMPLETED ☐ CONSPIRACY ☐ ATTEMPTED ☐ SOLICITATION	☐ YES ☐ NO		
			☐ COMPLETED ☐ CONSPIRACY ☐ ATTEMPTED ☐ SOLICITATION	☐ YES ☐ NO		

C. Sentencing Information

29. TOTAL PRIOR OFFENSE SCORE	30. SENTENCE ADJUSTMENT ☐ None (Standard Range) ☐ Manifest Injustice ☐ 150% Rule ☐ 300% Rule

31. THIS SENTENCE IS IN: ☐ Days ☐ Weeks	32. TOTAL MINIMUM EXCLUDING FIREARM ENHANCEMENT	33. TOTAL MAXIMUM EXCLUDING FIREARM ENHANCEMENT	34. TOTAL MINIMUM INCLUDING FIREARM ENHANCEMENT	35. TOTAL MAXIMUM INCLUDING FIREARM ENHANCEMENT

36. NAME OF PERSON COMPLETING THIS FORM FOR THE COURT	37. DATE COMPLETED (MM/DD/YYYY)	38. TELEPHONE NUMBER (INCLUDE AREA CODE)

SENTENCING WORKSHEET
DSHS 20-198 (REV. 08/2016)

The Caseload Forecast Council is not liable for errors or omissions in the manual, for sentences that may be inappropriately calculated as a result of a practitioner's or court's reliance on the manual, or for any other written or verbal information related to adult or juvenile sentencing. The scoring sheets are intended to provide assistance in most cases but does not cover all permutations of the scoring rules. If you find any errors or omissions, we encourage you to report them to the Caseload Forecast Council.

SECTION 6: JUVENILE REHABILITATIONADMINISTRATION WORKSHEET

SENTENCING WORKSHEET INSTRUCTIONS

1. **NAME:** Enter the youth's last name, first name, and middle initial as they appear on the court order.
2. **BIRTHDATE:** Enter the month, day, and year of the youth's birth. For example, enter 09/01/1986 for a youth born on September 1, 1986.
3. **SEX:** Check the box indicating whether the youth is male or female.
4. **RACE:** Using Appendix A of the Juvenile Disposition Manual, indicate the code for the youth's reported race.
5. **HISPANIC ORIGIN:** Using Appendix A of the Juvenile Disposition Manual, indicate the code for the youth's reported Hispanic origin.
6. **JR NUMBER:** Enter the youth's JR number for this youth if the youth has had a previous admission to a JR facility. Leave blank if unknown.
7. **DETENTION CREDIT DAYS:** If the youth has detention credit, enter the days to be taken off the sentence. Detention credit is time in detention or jail prior to the court hearing at which an admittance to JR is ordered and is listed on the court order. Any additional "pre-admission" detention credit, i.e., credit for time served after adjudication or disposition but prior to admission, will be determined separately by the JR admitting agency.
8. **JUVIS NUMBER:** Enter the youth's JUVIS number.
9. **COUNTY COURT:** Enter the name of the Juvenile Court, e.g., Benton/ Franklin, etc.

A. CURRENT OFFENSE INFORMATION

10. **CURRENT OFFENSE NUMBER:** Use one worksheet for each offense. Mark here which current offense this is and the total number of current offenses for this commitment. Staple all sheets together.
11. **COURT ORDER NUMBER:** Enter the court order number that has been assigned by the court for the sentence for this current offense.
12. **SENTENCE START DATE:** Enter the month, day, and year of the date that the youth's sentence actually began. This is the date that the "clock" technically began for youths committed to JR.
13. **DISPOSITION DATE:** Enter the month, day, and year of the date of the court order establishing the youth's sentence for this offense.
14. **ADJUDICATION DATE:** Enter the date that the youth was found guilty for this current offense.
15. **OFFENSE DATE:** Enter the month, day, and year that the youth's current offense occurred, e.g. 07/15/2002.
16. **JR OFFENSE CODE:** Enter the ten character JR Offense Code from the JR Code, Description, and Offense Category table in Section 2 of the Juvenile Disposition Manual. Use one sheet for each current offense.
17. **ANTICIPATORY TYPE:** Check one appropriate box to indicate whether the court charged the youth with completion, attempt, conspiracy, or solicitation of the crime.
18. **JUVENILE OFFENSE CATEGORY:** Enter the two character offense category from the JR Code, Description, and Offense Category table in Section 2 of the Juvenile Disposition Manual. Seriousness is indicated by the offense category, an A+ offense being the most serious and E offense being the least serious. If the offense cannot be found in the Code, Description, and Offense Category table, use one of the generic codes at the end of the table to determine category. If the offense is a new one and expected to occur frequently, contact JR in Olympia to determine if a new code can be assigned to the offense.
19. **FINDING OF SEXUAL MOTIVATION:** Check yes if the court order includes a finding of sexual motivation. Check no if there was no finding of sexual motivation in the court order.
20. **FINDING OF FIREARM ENHANCEMENT:** The court may apply an enhancement when an offender, or an accomplice, was armed with a firearm. The enhancement will apply to all felonies except those where the use of a firearm is an element of the offense definition (possession of a machine gun, possession of a stolen firearm, drive-by shooting, theft of a firearm, unlawful possession of a firearm 1 or 2, or use of a machine gun in a felony). The enhancement must be served consecutively to the base sentence. Check yes or no.
21. **TYPE OF PLACEMENT:** Indicate one type of placement for this current offense / sentence:

    JR Direct: Check if the youth is being directly committed to JR.

    SSODA Revoke: Check if the youth is being committed to JR because a SSODA sentence has been revoked.

    Chemical Dependency / Mental Health Disposition Alternative (CDMHDA): Check if the youth is being assigned to community supervision through the Chemical Dependency / Mental Health Disposition Alternative. Please check Chemical Dependency, Mental Health or the Co-occurring box.

    CDMHDA Revoke: Check if the youth is being committed to JR because a Chemical Dependency/Mental Health Disposition Alternative sentence has been revoked.

    SSODA: Check if the youth is being assigned to community supervision through the Special Sex Offender Disposition Alternative (SSODA).

    SDA: Check if youth is being assigned to community supervision through the suspended disposition alternative.

    SDA Revoked: Check if the youth is being committed to JR because a JR SDA sentence has been revoked.

B. PRIOR OFFENSE INFORMATION

22. **ADJUDICATION DATE:** Enter the date that the youth was adjudicated, i.e. found guilty, for this prior.
23. **OFFENSE DATE:** Enter the month, day, and year that the youth's prior offense occurred.
24. **JR OFFENSE CODE:** Enter the JR Offense Code from the JR Code, Description, and Offense Category table in Section 2 of the Juvenile Disposition Manual.
25. **ANTICIPATORY TYPE:** Check the appropriate box to indicate whether the court charged the youth with completion, attempt, conspiracy, or solicitation of the offense.
26. **SEXUAL MOTIVATION:** Check yes if the court order for this prior offense included a finding of sexual motivation. Check no if the court order did not include a finding of sexual motivation.
27. **CRIMINAL CLASS:** Enter "A" if the offense was a Class A felony, "B" if it was a Class B felony, or "C" if it was a Class C felony. Enter "GM" if it was a gross misdemeanor, "M" if it was a misdemeanor, or "V" if it was a violation.
28. **PRIOR SCORE:** Each prior felony adjudication counts as one point. Each prior violation, misdemeanor, and gross misdemeanor adjudication counts as one-fourth point. Indicate the score for each prior offense.

C. SENTENCING INFORMATION

29. **PRIOR OFFENSE SCORE:** Add prior points and enter the total here. Fractional points are rounded down to the nearest whole number.
30. **SENTENCE ADJUSTMENT:** Check the appropriate box to indicate disposition:

    None (Standard Range): Check if there was no adjustment to the youth's standard range sentence.

    Manifest Injustice: Check if manifest injustice was invoked.

    150% Rule: Check if the 150% rule has been invoked, limiting the length of the youth's sentence. The 150% rule is intended to limit the amount of sanction (to 150% of the sanction for the most serious offense) that an offender may receive for offenses committed through a single act or omission.

    300% Rule: Check if the 300% rule has been invoked, limiting the length of the youth's sentence. The 300% rule has been invoked, limiting the amount of sanction (to 300% of the sanction for the most serious offense) that an offender may receive for multiple offenses which are disposed of during a court appearance. (See RCW 13.40.180 for an explanation.)
30. **DAYS OR WEEKS:** Check whether this sentence is listed in days or weeks.
31. **TOTAL MINIMUM SENTENCE EXCLUDING FIREARM ENHANCEMENT:** Indicate here the total of the minimum sentence.
32. **TOTAL MAXIMUM SENTENCE EXCLUDING FIREARM ENHANCEMENT:** Indicate here the total of the maximum sentence.
33. **TOTAL MINIMUM SENTENCE INCLUDING FIREARM ENHANCEMENT:** Indicate here the total of the minimum sentence including any firearm enhancement.
34. **TOTAL MAXIMUM SENTENCE INCLUDING FIREARM ENHANCEMENT:** Indicate here the total of the maximum sentence including any firearm enhancement. .
35. **PRINT NAME OF PERSON COMPLETING THIS FORM FOR THE COURT:** Print the name of the person completing this form.
36. **DATE COMPLETED:** Record the date the form was filled out.
37. **TELEPHONE NUMBER:** Record the telephone number of the person who filled out this form.

DSHS 20-198 (REV. 08/2016) INSTRUCTIONS

JUVENILE OFFENDER SENTENCING GRID (OPTION A)

STANDARD RANGE

CURRENT OFFENSE CATEGORY	0	1	2	3	4 or more
A+	180 weeks to age 21 for all category A+ offenses				
A	103 - 129 weeks for all category A offenses				
A-	15 - 36 weeks Except 30 – 40 weeks for 15 to 17 year olds	52 - 65 weeks	80 - 100 weeks	103 - 129 weeks	103 - 129 weeks
B+	15 - 36 weeks	15 – 36 weeks	52 - 65 weeks	80 - 100 weeks	103 - 129 weeks
B	LS	LS	15 - 36 weeks	15 - 36 weeks	52 - 65 weeks
C+	LS	LS	LS	15 - 36 weeks	15 - 36 weeks
C	LS	LS	LS	LS	15 - 36 weeks
D+	LS	LS	LS	LS	LS
D	LS	LS	LS	LS	LS
E	LS	LS	LS	LS	LS

PRIOR ADJUDICATIONS

NOTE: References in the grid to days or weeks mean periods of confinement. "LS" means "local sanctions" as defined in RCW 13.40.020.

(1) The vertical axis of the grid is the current offense category. The current offense category is determined by the offense of adjudication.

(2) The horizontal axis of the grid is the number of prior adjudications included in the juvenile's criminal history. Each prior felony adjudication shall count as one point. Each prior violation, misdemeanor, and gross misdemeanor adjudication shall count as 1/4 point. Fractional points shall be rounded down.

(3) The standard range disposition for each offense is determined by the intersection of the column defined by the prior adjudications and the row defined by the current offense category.

(4) RCW 13.40.180 applies if the offender is being sentenced for more than one offense.

(5) A current offense that is a violation is equivalent to an offense category of E. However, a disposition for a violation shall not include confinement.

LS = Local Sanctions: 0 - 30 days of confinement, and/or
0 - 12 months of community supervision, and/or
0 - 150 hours of community restitution, and/or
$0 - $500 fine.

APPENDIX A

APPENDIX A:

RACE CODES		HISPANIC ORIGIN CODES	
597	INDIAN-AMERICAN	709	YES, CUBAN
600	ASIAN-INDIAN	722	YES, MEXICAN-AMER
604	CAMBODIAN	727	YES, PUERTO RICAN
605	CHINESE	799	YES, OTHER SPANISH
608	FILIPINO	000	NOT REPORTED
611	JAPANESE	999	NO
612	KOREAN		
613	LAOTIAN		
618	THAI		
619	VIETNAMESE		
653	HAWAIIAN		
655	SAMOAN		
660	GUAMANIAN		
699	OTHER-ASIAN		
799	OTHER RACE		
800	WHITE		
870	BLK-AFR-AMR		
935	ESKIMO		
941	ALEUT		
999	UNREPORTED		

COURT CODE	COURT NAME
001	ADAMS
002	ASOTIN/GARFIELD
003	BENTON/FRANKLIN
004	CHELAN
005	CLALLAM
006	CLARK
007	COLUMBIA/WALLA WALLA
008	COWLITZ
009	DOUGLAS
026	PEND OR/STEVENS/FERRY
003	BENTON/FRANKLIN
002	ASOTIN/GARFIELD
013	GRANT
014	GRAYS HARBOR
015	ISLAND
016	JEFFERSON
017	KING
018	KITSAP
019	KITTITAS
020	KLICKITAT
021	LEWIS
022	LINCOLN
023	MASON
024	OKANOGAN
025	PACIFIC/WAHKIAKUM
026	PEND OR/STEVENS/FERRY
027	PIERCE
028	SAN JUAN
029	SKAGIT
030	SKAMANIA
031	SNOHOMISH
032	SPOKANE
026	PEND OR/STEVENS/FERRY
034	THURSTON
025	PACIFIC/WAHKIAKUM
007	COLUMBIA/WALLA WALLA
037	WHATCOM
038	WHITMAN
039	YAKIMA

APPENDIX B

Note: Appendix B provides a list of JRA offenses code as a courtesy. These codes are used by JRA in its client tracking system. New codes are added as needed by JRA.

NOTE to all offense tables: The state legislature occasionally amends the title, definition, or (juvenile) seriousness level of crimes/offenses. Typically, when this happens, the change is effective on or after the effective date of the statute passed by the legislature. We have opted to retain the original as well as the updated listing for such offenses in our offense tables, even when the underlying crime no longer exists. For example, the crime Reckless Endangerment has been replaced by two classes of crime, Reckless Endangerment 1 and Reckless Endangerment 2. We retain the original crime as well as the two new classes. In referring to these offense lists, manual users should verify that the offense information they are using is appropriate given the date of the offense.

APPENDIX B: JRA OFFENSE CODES BY OFFENSE TITLE

OFFENSE TITLE	CATEGORY	RCW	JRA CODE
AIMING OR DISCHARGING FIREARMS, DANGEROUS WEAPONS	D	941230	DANWEAPAD
AIMING OR DISCHARGING FIREARMS, DANGEROUS WEAPONS ATTEMPTED	E	941230	DANWEAPAD
AIMING OR DISCHARGING FIREARMS, DANGEROUS WEAPONS CONSPIRACY	E	941230	DANWEAPAD
AIMING OR DISCHARGING FIREARMS, DANGEROUS WEAPONS SOLICITATION	E	941230	DANWEAPAD
ALIEN POSSESSION OF FIREARMS	C	941171	POSFIRARMA
ALIEN POSSESSION OF FIREARMS ATTEMPTED	D	941171	POSFIRARMA
ALIEN POSSESSION OF FIREARMS CONSPIRACY	D	941171	POSFIRARMA
ALIEN POSSESSION OF FIREARMS SOLICITATION	D	941171	POSFIRARMA
ALTERATION OF IDENTIFYING MARKS ON FIREARM	E	941140	FIRARMALT
ALTERATION OF IDENTIFYING MARKS ON FIREARM ATTEMPTED	E	941140	FIRARMALT
ALTERATION OF IDENTIFYING MARKS ON FIREARM CONSPIRACY	E	941140	FIRARMALT
ALTERATION OF IDENTIFYING MARKS ON FIREARM SOLICITATION	E	941140	FIRARMALT
ANIMAL CRUELTY 1	B	1652205	ANIMCRUEL1
ANIMAL CRUELTY 1 ATTEMPT	D	1652205	ANIMCRUEL1
ANIMAL CRUELTY 1 CONSPIRACY	D	1652205	ANIMCRUEL1
ANIMAL CRUELTY 1 SOLICITATION	D	1652205	ANIMCRUEL1
ANIMAL CRUELTY 2	E	1652207	ANIMCRUEL2
ARSON 1	A	9A48020	ARSON1

The Caseload Forecast Council is not liable for errors or omissions in the manual, for sentences that may be inappropriately calculated as a result of a practitioner's or court's reliance on the manual, or for any other written or verbal information related to adult or juvenile sentencing. The scoring sheets are intended to provide assistance in most cases but does not cover all permutations of the scoring rules. If you find any errors or omissions, we encourage you to report them to the Caseload Forecast Council.

OFFENSE TITLE	CATEGORY	RCW	JRA CODE
ARSON 1 ATTEMPT	B+	9A48020	ARSON1
ARSON 1 CONSPIRACY	B+	9A48020	ARSON1
ARSON 1 SOLICITATION	B+	9A48020	ARSON1
ARSON 2	B	9A48030	ARSON2
ARSON 2 ATTEMPT	C	9A48030	ARSON2
ARSON 2 CONSPIRACY	C	9A48030	ARSON2
ARSON 2 SOLICITATION	C	9A48030	ARSON2
ASSAULT 1	A	9A36011	ASSAULT1
ASSAULT 1 ATTEMPT	B+	9A36011	ASSAULT1
ASSAULT 1 CONSPIRACY	B+	9A36011	ASSAULT1
ASSAULT 1 SOLICITATION	B+	9A36011	ASSAULT1
ASSAULT 2	B+	9A36021	ASSAULT2
ASSAULT 2 ACCOMPLICE	B+	9A36021	ASSAULT2AC
ASSAULT 2 ACCOMPLICE ATTEMPTED	C+	9A36021	ASSAULT2AC
ASSAULT 2 ACCOMPLICE CONSPIRACY	C+	9A36021	ASSAULT2AC
ASSAULT 2 ACCOMPLICE SOLICITATION	C+	9A36021	ASSAULT2AC
ASSAULT 2 ATTEMPT	C+	9A36021	ASSAULT2
ASSAULT 2 CONSPIRACY	C+	9A36021	ASSAULT2
ASSAULT 2 SOLICITATION	C+	9A36021	ASSAULT2
ASSAULT 2 WITH SM	A	9A36021	ASSAULT2SM
ASSAULT 2 WITH SM ATTEMPT	B+	9A36021	ASSAULT2SM
ASSAULT 2 WITH SM CONSPIRACY	B+	9A36021	ASSAULT2SM
ASSAULT 2 WITH SM SOLICITATION	B+	9A36021	ASSAULT2SM
ASSAULT 3	C+	9A36031	ASSAULT3
ASSAULT 3 ATTEMPT	D+	9A36031	ASSAULT3
ASSAULT 3 CONSPIRACY	D+	9A36031	ASSAULT3
ASSAULT 3 SOLICITATION	D+	9A36031	ASSAULT3
ASSAULT 4	D+	9A36041	ASSAULT4
ASSAULT 4 ATTEMPT	E	9A36041	ASSAULT4
ASSAULT 4 CONSPIRACY	E	9A36041	ASSAULT4
ASSAULT 4 SOLICITATION	E	9A36041	ASSAULT4
ASSAULT BY WATERCRAFT	B	79A6060	ASSAULTWC
ASSAULT BY WATERCRAFT ATTEMPT	C	79A6060	ASSAULTWC
ASSAULT BY WATERCRAFT CONSPIRACY	C	79A6060	ASSAULTWC
ASSAULT BY WATERCRAFT SOLICITATION	C	79A6060	ASSAULTWC
ASSAULT OF CHILD 1	A	9A36120	ASSAULTCH1
ASSAULT OF CHILD 1 ATTEMPT	B	9A36120	ASSAULTCH1
ASSAULT OF CHILD 1 CONSPIRACY	B	9A36120	ASSAULTCH1
ASSAULT OF CHILD 1 SOLICITATION	B	9A36120	ASSAULTCH1
ASSAULT OF CHILD 2	B	9A36130	ASSAULTCH2
ASSAULT OF CHILD 2 ATTEMPT	C	9A36130	ASSAULTCH2
ASSAULT OF CHILD 2 CONSPIRACY	C	9A36130	ASSAULTCH2
ASSAULT OF CHILD 2 SOLICITATION	C	9A36130	ASSAULTCH2
ATTEMPTING TO ELUDE A POLICE VEHICLE	C	4661024	ELUDEPV
ATTEMPTING TO ELUDE A POLICE VEHICLE ATTEMPT	D	4661024	ELUDEPV
ATTEMPTING TO ELUDE A POLICE VEHICLE CONSPIRACY	D	4661024	ELUDEPV

The Caseload Forecast Council is not liable for errors or omissions in the manual, for sentences that may be inappropriately calculated as a result of a practitioner's or court's reliance on the manual, or for any other written or verbal information related to adult or juvenile sentencing. The scoring sheets are intended to provide assistance in most cases but does not cover all permutations of the scoring rules. If you find any errors or omissions, we encourage you to report them to the Caseload Forecast Council.

OFFENSE TITLE	CATEGORY	RCW	JRA CODE
ATTEMPTING TO ELUDE A POLICE VEHICLE SOLICITATION	D	4661024	ELUDEPV
AUTO THEFT TOOLS (MAKING OR POSSESSING)	D	9A56063	AUTOTOOLS
AUTO THEFT TOOLS (MAKING OR POSSESSING) ATTEMPTED	E	9A56063	AUTOTOOLS
AUTO THEFT TOOLS (MAKING OR POSSESSING) CONSPIRACY	E	9A56063	AUTOTOOLS
AUTO THEFT TOOLS (MAKING OR POSSESSING) SOLICITATION	E	9A56063	AUTOTOOLS
BOMB THREAT	B	961160	BOMBTHREAT
BOMB THREAT ATTEMPT	C	961160	BOMBTHREAT
BOMB THREAT CONSPIRACY	C	961160	BOMBTHREAT
BOMB THREAT SOLICITATION	C	961160	BOMBTHREAT
BURG TOOLS (POSSESSION OF)	D	9A52060	BURGTOOLS
BURG TOOLS (POSSESSION OF) ATTEMPT	E	9A52060	BURGTOOLS
BURG TOOLS (POSSESSION OF) CONSPIRACY	E	9A52060	BURGTOOLS
BURG TOOLS (POSSESSION OF) SOLICITIATION	E	9A52060	BURGTOOLS
BURGLARY 1	B+	9A52020	BURG1
BURGLARY 1 ATTEMPT	C+	9A52020	BURG1
BURGLARY 1 CONSPIRACY	C+	9A52020	BURG1
BURGLARY 1 SOLICITATION	C+	9A52020	BURG1
BURGLARY 2	B	9A52030	BURG2
BURGLARY 2 ATTEMPT	C	9A52030	BURG2
BURGLARY 2 CONSPIRACY	C	9A52030	BURG2
BURGLARY 2 SOLICITATION	C	9A52030	BURG2
CARRY WEAPON TO SCHOOL	D	941280	CARWEAPSCH
CARRY WEAPON TO SCHOOL ATTEMPT	E	941280	CARWEAPSCH
CARRY WEAPON TO SCHOOL CONSPIRACY	E	941280	CARWEAPSCH
CARRY WEAPON TO SCHOOL SOLICITATION	E	941280	CARWEAPSCH
CHILD MOLESTATION 1	A-	9A44083	CHILDMOL1
CHILD MOLESTATION 1 ATTEMPT	B+	9A44083	CHILDMOL1
CHILD MOLESTATION 1 CONSPIRACY	B+	9A44083	CHILDMOL1
CHILD MOLESTATION 1 SOLICITATION	B+	9A44083	CHILDMOL1
CHILD MOLESTATION 2	B	9A44086	CHILDMOL2
CHILD MOLESTATION 2 ATTEMPT	C+	9A44086	CHILDMOL2
CHILD MOLESTATION 2 CONSPIRACY	C+	9A44086	CHILDMOL2
CHILD MOLESTATION 2 SOLICITATION	C+	9A44086	CHILDMOL2
CHILD MOLESTATION 3	C	9A44089	CHILDMOL3
CHILD MOLESTATION 3 ATTEMPTED	D	9A44089	CHILDMOL3
CHILD MOLESTATION 3 CONSPIRACY	D	9A44089	CHILDMOL3
CHILD MOLESTATION 3 SOLICITATION	D	9A44089	CHILDMOL3
COERCION	D+	9A36070	COERCION
COERCION ATTEMPT	E	9A36070	COERCION
COERCION CONSPIRACY	E	9A36070	COERCION
COERCION SOLICITATION	E	9A36070	COERCION
COMMERCIAL SEXUAL ABUSE OF A MINOR	B	968A100	SEXABUSEMI
COMMERCIAL SEXUAL ABUSE OF A MINOR	C	968A100	SEXABUSEMI

OFFENSE TITLE	CATEGORY	RCW	JRA CODE
ATTEMPTED			
COMMERCIAL SEXUAL ABUSE OF A MINOR CONSPIRACY	C	968A100	SEXABUSEMI
COMMERCIAL SEXUAL ABUSE OF A MINOR SOLICITATION	C	968A100	SEXABUSEMI
COMMUNICATING WITH A MINOR FOR IMMORAL PURPOSE	D	968A090	COMMINOR
COMMUNICATING WITH A MINOR FOR IMMORAL PURPOSE - SUBSEQUENT SEX OFFENSE	C	968A090	COMMINORSS
COMMUNICATING WITH A MINOR FOR IMMORAL PURPOSE - SUBSEQUENT SEX OFFENSE ATTEMPT	D	968A090	COMMINORSS
COMMUNICATING WITH A MINOR FOR IMMORAL PURPOSE - SUBSEQUENT SEX OFFENSE CONSPIRACY	D	968A090	COMMINORSS
COMMUNICATING WITH A MINOR FOR IMMORAL PURPOSE - SUBSEQUENT SEX OFFENSE SOLICITATION	D	968A090	COMMINORSS
COMMUNICATING WITH A MINOR FOR IMMORAL PURPOSE ATTEMPT	E	968A090	COMMINOR
COMMUNICATING WITH A MINOR FOR IMMORAL PURPOSE CONSPIRACY	E	968A090	COMMINOR
COMMUNICATING WITH A MINOR FOR IMMORAL PURPOSE SOLICITATION	E	968A090	COMMINOR
CONTEMPT	D	721040	CONTEMPT
CONTROLLED SUBSTANCES HOMICIDE	B	6950415	HOMICIDECS
CONTROLLED SUBSTANCES HOMICIDE ATTEMPT	C	6950415	HOMICIDECS
CONTROLLED SUBSTANCES HOMICIDE CONSPIRACY	C	6950415	HOMICIDECS
CONTROLLED SUBSTANCES HOMICIDE SOLICITATION	C	6950415	HOMICIDECS
CRIMINAL IMPERSONATION 1	C	9A60040	IMPERSON1
CRIMINAL IMPERSONATION 1 ATTEMPT	D	9A60040	IMPERSON1
CRIMINAL IMPERSONATION 1 CONSPIRACY	D	9A60040	IMPERSON1
CRIMINAL IMPERSONATION 1 SOLICITATION	D	9A60040	IMPERSON1
CRIMINAL IMPERSONATION 2	D	9A60045	IMPERSON2
CRIMINAL IMPERSONATION 2 ATTEMPT	E	9A60045	IMPERSON2
CRIMINAL IMPERSONATION 2 CONSPIRACY	E	9A60045	IMPERSON2
CRIMINAL IMPERSONATION 2 SOLICITATION	E	9A60045	IMPERSON2
CRIMINAL TRESPASS 1	D	9A52070	CRIMTRES1
CRIMINAL TRESPASS 1 ATTEMPT	E	9A52070	CRIMTRES1
CRIMINAL TRESPASS 1 CONSPIRACY	E	9A52070	CRIMTRES1
CRIMINAL TRESPASS 1 SOLICITATION	E	9A52070	CRIMTRES1
CRIMINAL TRESPASS 2	E	9A52080	CRIMTRES2
CRIMINAL TRESPASS 2 ATTEMPT	E	9A52080	CRIMTRES2
CRIMINAL TRESPASS 2 CONSPIRACY	E	9A52080	CRIMTRES2
CRIMINAL TRESPASS 2 SOLICITATION	E	9A52080	CRIMTRES2
CUSTODIAL ASSAULT	C+	9A36100	CUSASSAULT
CUSTODIAL ASSAULT ATTEMPT	D+	9A36100	CUSASSAULT
CUSTODIAL ASSAULT CONSPIRACY	D+	9A36100	CUSASSAULT
CUSTODIAL ASSAULT SOLICITATION	D+	9A36100	CUSASSAULT
CUSTODIAL INTERFERENCE 1	C	9A40060	CUSINTER1

OFFENSE TITLE	CATEGORY	RCW	JRA CODE
CUSTODIAL INTERFERENCE 1 ATTEMPT	D	9A40060	CUSINTER1
CUSTODIAL INTERFERENCE 1 CONSPIRACY	D	9A40060	CUSINTER1
CUSTODIAL INTERFERENCE 1 SOLICITATION	D	9A40060	CUSINTER1
CUSTODIAL INTERFERENCE 2	D	9A40070	CUSINTER2
CUSTODIAL INTERFERENCE 2 ATTEMPT	D	9A40070	CUSINTER2
CUSTODIAL INTERFERENCE 2 CONSPIRACY	D	9A40070	CUSINTER2
CUSTODIAL INTERFERENCE 2 SOLICITATION	D	9A40070	CUSINTER2
CUSTODIAL INTERFERENCE 2 SUBSEQUEENT SOLICITATION	D	9A40070	CUSINTER2S
CUSTODIAL INTERFERENCE 2 SUBSEQUENT	C	9A40070	CUSINTER2S
CUSTODIAL INTERFERENCE 2 SUBSEQUENT ATTEMPT	D	9A40070	CUSINTER2S
CUSTODIAL INTERFERENCE 2 SUBSEQUENT CONSPIRACY	D	9A40070	CUSINTER2S
CYBERSTALKING	D	961260	CYBSTALK
CYBERSTALKING ATTEMPTED	E	961260	CYBSTALK
CYBERSTALKING C FELONY W PREVIOUS HARASSMENT	C	961260	CYBSTALKC
CYBERSTALKING CONSPIRACY	E	961260	CYBSTALK
CYBERSTALKING SOLICITATION	E	961260	CYBSTALK
CYBERSTALKING W PREVIOUS HARASSMENT ATTEMPTED	D	961260	CYBSTALK
CYBERSTALKING W PREVIOUS HARASSMENT CONSPIRACY	D	961260	CYBSTALK
CYBERSTALKING W PREVIOUS HARASSMENT SOLICITATION	D	961260	CYBSTALK
DEALING IN DEPICTIONS OF MINOR ENGAGED IN SEXUALLY EXPLICIT CONDUCT 1	B	968A050	DELCHPORN1
DEALING IN DEPICTIONS OF MINOR ENGAGED IN SEXUALLY EXPLICIT CONDUCT 1 ATTEMPT	C	968A050	DELCHPORN1
DEALING IN DEPICTIONS OF MINOR ENGAGED IN SEXUALLY EXPLICIT CONDUCT 1 CONSPIRACY	C	968A050	DELCHPORN1
DEALING IN DEPICTIONS OF MINOR ENGAGED IN SEXUALLY EXPLICIT CONDUCT 1 SOLICITATION	C	968A050	DELCHPORN1
DEALING IN DEPICTIONS OF MINOR ENGAGED IN SEXUALLY EXPLICIT CONDUCT 2	C	968A050	DELCHPORN2
DEALING IN DEPICTIONS OF MINOR ENGAGED IN SEXUALLY EXPLICIT CONDUCT 2 ATTEMPT	D	968A050	DELCHPORN2
DEALING IN DEPICTIONS OF MINOR ENGAGED IN SEXUALLY EXPLICIT CONDUCT 2 CONSPIRACY	D	968A050	DELCHPORN2
DEALING IN DEPICTIONS OF MINOR ENGAGED IN SEXUALLY EXPLICIT CONDUCT 2 SOLICITATION	D	968A050	DELCHPORN2
DIAGNOSTIC ONLY	UK	9973	DIAGNOSTIC
DISARMING LAW ENFORCEMENT OFFICER	C	9A76023	DISLAWOFF
DISARMING LAW ENFORCEMENT OFFICER ATTEMPTED	D	9A76023	DISLAWOFF
DISARMING LAW ENFORCEMENT OFFICER CONSPIRACY	D	9A76023	DISLAWOFF

The Caseload Forecast Council is not liable for errors or omissions in the manual, for sentences that may be inappropriately calculated as a result of a practitioner's or court's reliance on the manual, or for any other written or verbal information related to adult or juvenile sentencing. The scoring sheets are intended to provide assistance in most cases but does not cover all permutations of the scoring rules. If you find any errors or omissions, we encourage you to report them to the Caseload Forecast Council.

OFFENSE TITLE	CATEGORY	RCW	JRA CODE
DISARMING LAW ENFORCEMENT OFFICER SOLICITATION	D	9A76023	DISLAWOFF
DISORDERLY CONDUCT	E	9A84030	DISCONDUCT
DISORDERLY CONDUCT ATTEMPT	E	9A84030	DISCONDUCT
DISORDERLY CONDUCT CONSPIRACY	E	9A84030	DISCONDUCT
DISORDERLY CONDUCT SOLICITATION	E	9A84030	DISCONDUCT
DISTURBING SCHOOL, SCHOOL ACTIVITIES OR MEETINGS	E	28A6350	DISTRBSCHL
DRIVE BY SHOOTING	B+	9A36045	DBSHOOTING
DRIVE BY SHOOTING ATTEMPT	C+	9A36045	DBSHOOTING
DRIVE BY SHOOTING CONSPIRACY	C+	9A36045	DBSHOOTING
DRIVE BY SHOOTING SOLICITATION	C+	9A36045	DBSHOOTING
DRIVER UNDER TWENTY-ONE CONSUMING ALCOHOL OR MARIJUANA	E	4661503	DUI_U21
DRIVER UNDER TWENTY-ONE CONSUMING ALCOHOL OR MARIJUANA ATTEMPTED	E	4661503	DUI_U21
DRIVER UNDER TWENTY-ONE CONSUMING ALCOHOL OR MARIJUANA CONSPIRACY	E	4661503	DUI_U21
DRIVER UNDER TWENTY-ONE CONSUMING ALCOHOL OR MARIJUANA SOLICITATION	E	4661503	DUI_U21
DRIVING UNDER INFLUENCE	D	4661515	DUI
DRIVING UNDER INFLUENCE ATTEMPT	E	4661515	DUI
DRIVING UNDER INFLUENCE CONSPIRACY	E	4661515	DUI
DRIVING UNDER INFLUENCE SOLICITATION	E	4661515	DUI
DRIVING WHILE LICENSE INVALIDATED	D	4620342	DWIL
DRIVING WHILE LICENSE INVALIDATED 2	D	4620342	DWIL2
DRIVING WITHOUT A LICENSE	E	4620021	DWOL
DRUG PARAPHERNALIA	E	6950412	DRUGPARA
DRVING WHILE LICENSE INVALIDATED 3	E	4620342	DWIL3
DUTY ON STRIKING UNATTENDED CAR OR OTHER PROPERTY	E	4652010	DUTYUNVEH
DUTY ON STRIKING UNATTENDED CAR OR OTHER PROPERTY ATTEMPT	E	4652010	DUTYUNVEH
DUTY ON STRIKING UNATTENDED CAR OR OTHER PROPERTY CONSPIRACY	E	4652010	DUTYUNVEH
DUTY ON STRIKING UNATTENDED CAR OR OTHER PROPERTY SOLICITATION	E	4652010	DUTYUNVEH
DUTY TO ATTENDED VEHICLE OR OTHER PROPERTY IN CASE OF DEATH	B+	4652020	DUTYDEATH
DUTY TO ATTENDED VEHICLE OR OTHER PROPERTY IN CASE OF DEATH ATTEMPT	C	4652020	DUTYDEATH
DUTY TO ATTENDED VEHICLE OR OTHER PROPERTY IN CASE OF DEATH CONSPIRACY	C	4652020	DUTYDEATH
DUTY TO ATTENDED VEHICLE OR OTHER PROPERTY IN CASE OF DEATH SOLICITATION	C	4652020	DUTYDEATH
DUTY TO ATTENDED VEHICLE OR OTHER PROPERTY IN CASE OF INJURY	C	4652020	DUTYINJ

The Caseload Forecast Council is not liable for errors or omissions in the manual, for sentences that may be inappropriately calculated as a result of a practitioner's or court's reliance on the manual, or for any other written or verbal information related to adult or juvenile sentencing. The scoring sheets are intended to provide assistance in most cases but does not cover all permutations of the scoring rules. If you find any errors or omissions, we encourage you to report them to the Caseload Forecast Council.

OFFENSE TITLE	CATEGORY	RCW	JRA CODE
DUTY TO ATTENDED VEHICLE OR OTHER PROPERTY IN CASE OF INJURY ATTEMPT	D	4652020	DUTYINJ
DUTY TO ATTENDED VEHICLE OR OTHER PROPERTY IN CASE OF INJURY CONSPIRACY	D	4652020	DUTYINJ
DUTY TO ATTENDED VEHICLE OR OTHER PROPERTY IN CASE OF INJURY SOLICITATION	D	4652020	DUTYINJ
DUTY TO ATTENDED VEHICLE OR OTHER PROPERTY IN CASE OF STRIKING BODY OF DECEASED	D+	4652020	DUTYBODY
DUTY TO ATTENDED VEHICLE OR OTHER PROPERTY IN CASE OF STRIKING BODY OF DECEASED ATTEMPT	E	4652020	DUTYBODY
DUTY TO ATTENDED VEHICLE OR OTHER PROPERTY IN CASE OF STRIKING BODY OF DECEASED CONSPIRACY	E	4652020	DUTYBODY
DUTY TO ATTENDED VEHICLE OR OTHER PROPERTY IN CASE OF STRIKING BODY OF DECEASED SOLICITATION	E	4652020	DUTYBODY
ESCAPE 1	C	9A76110	ESCAPE1
ESCAPE 1 ATTEMPT	C	9A76110	ESCAPE1
ESCAPE 1 CONSPIRACY	C	9A76110	ESCAPE1
ESCAPE 1 SOLICITATION	C	9A76110	ESCAPE1
ESCAPE 2	C	9A76120	ESCAPE2
ESCAPE 2 ATTEMPT	C	9A76120	ESCAPE2
ESCAPE 2 CONSPIRACY	C	9A76120	ESCAPE2
ESCAPE 2 SOLICITATION	C	9A76120	ESCAPE2
ESCAPE 3	D	9A76130	ESCAPE3
ESCAPE 3 ATTEMPT	E	9A76130	ESCAPE3
ESCAPE 3 CONSPIRACY	E	9A76130	ESCAPE3
ESCAPE 3 SOLICITATION	E	9A76130	ESCAPE3
EXHIBITING EFFECTS/POSSESSION/CONSUMPTION OF ALCOHOL	E	6644270	POSCONSALC
EXTORTION 1	B+	9A56120	EXTORTION1
EXTORTION 1 ATTEMPT	C+	9A56120	EXTORTION1
EXTORTION 1 CONSPIRACY	C+	9A56120	EXTORTION1
EXTORTION 1 SOLICITATION	C+	9A56120	EXTORTION1
EXTORTION 2	C+	9A56130	EXTORTION2
EXTORTION 2 ATTEMPT	D+	9A56130	EXTORTION2
EXTORTION 2 CONSPIRACY	D+	9A56130	EXTORTION2
EXTORTION 2 SOLICITATION	D+	9A56130	EXTORTION2
FAIL TO REGISTER AS A KIDNAPPER	C	9A44132	FAILREGK
FAIL TO REGISTER AS A KIDNAPPER ATTEMPT	D	9A44132	FAILREGK
FAIL TO REGISTER AS A KIDNAPPER CONSPIRACY	D	9A44132	FAILREGK
FAIL TO REGISTER AS A KIDNAPPER SOLICITATION	D	9A44132	FAILREGK
FAIL TO REGISTER AS A SEX OFFENDER	C	9A44132	FAILREGS
FAIL TO REGISTER AS A SEX OFFENDER ATTEMPT	D	9A44132	FAILREGS
FAIL TO REGISTER AS A SEX OFFENDER CONSPIRACY	D	9A44132	FAILREGS
FAIL TO REGISTER AS A SEX OFFENDER SOLICITATION	D	9A44132	FAILREGS

OFFENSE TITLE	CATEGORY	RCW	JRA CODE
FAIL TO REGISTER AS A SEX OFFENDER TWO OR MORE PRIOR OCCASIONS	B	9A44132	FAILREGSx3
FAILURE TO DISPERSE	E	9A84020	FAILDISP
FALSE REPORTING	D	9A84040	FALSEREP
FALSE REPORTING ATTEMPT	E	9A84040	FALSEREP
FALSE REPORTING CONSPIRACY	E	9A84040	FALSEREP
FALSE REPORTING SOLICITATION	E	9A84040	FALSEREP
FORGERY	C	9A60020	FORGERY
FORGERY ATTEMPT	D	9A60020	FORGERY
FORGERY CONSPIRACY	D	9A60020	FORGERY
FORGERY SOLICITATION	D	9A60020	FORGERY
FRAUDULENTLY OBTAINING CONTROLLED SUBSTANCE	C	6950401	FRAUDOBTCS
GAME, TRAFFIC, TOBACCO AND OTHER VIOLATIONS	V	9972	VIOLATION
HARASSMENT	D	9A46020	HARASSD
HARASSMENT - MALICIOUS Disc against race,color,relig,ance,nat.origin,gender,sexualorient,ment,phys,or sensory handicap	D	9A36080	HARASSMAL
HARASSMENT - MALICIOUS Disc against race,color,relig,ance,nat.origin,gender,sexualorient,ment,phys,or sensory handicap	D	9A36080	HARASSMAL
HARASSMENT - MALICIOUS Disc against race,color,relig,ance,nat.origin,gender,sexualorient,ment,phys,or sensory handicap	D	9A36080	HARASSMAL
HARASSMENT - MALICIOUS Disc against race,color,relig,ance,nat.origin,gender,sexualorient,ment,phys,or sensory handicap	C	9A36080	HARASSMAL
HARASSMENT - WITH THREAT TO KILL	C	9A46020	HARASTHRTC
HARASSMENT ATTEMPTED	E	9A46020	HARASSD
HARASSMENT CONSPIRACY	E	9A46020	HARASSD
HARASSMENT SAME VICTIM OR VICTIMS FAMILY	C	9A46020	HARASSC
HARASSMENT SAME VICTIM OR VICTIMS FAMILY ATTEMPTED	D	9A46020	HARASSC
HARASSMENT SAME VICTIM OR VICTIMS FAMILY CONSPIRACY	D	9A46020	HARASSC
HARASSMENT SAME VICTIM OR VICTIMS FAMILY SOLICITATION	D	9A46020	HARASSC
HARASSMENT SOLICITATION	E	9A46020	HARASSD
HIT-RUN ATTENDED	D	4652022	HITRUNAT
HIT-RUN ATTENDED ATTEMPT	E	4652022	HITRUNAT
HIT-RUN ATTENDED CONSPIRACY	E	4652022	HITRUNAT
HIT-RUN ATTENDED SOLICITATION	E	4652022	HITRUNAT
HIT-RUN DEATH	B+	4652022	HITRUNDE
HIT-RUN DEATH ATTEMPT	C+	4652022	HITRUNDE
HIT-RUN DEATH CONSPIRACY	C+	4652022	HITRUNDE
HIT-RUN DEATH SOLICITATION	C+	4652022	HITRUNDE
HIT-RUN INJURY	C	4652021	HITRUNIN

The Caseload Forecast Council is not liable for errors or omissions in the manual, for sentences that may be inappropriately calculated as a result of a practitioner's or court's reliance on the manual, or for any other written or verbal information related to adult or juvenile sentencing. The scoring sheets are intended to provide assistance in most cases but does not cover all permutations of the scoring rules. If you find any errors or omissions, we encourage you to report them to the Caseload Forecast Council.

OFFENSE TITLE	CATEGORY	RCW	JRA CODE
HIT-RUN INJURY ATTEMPT	D	4652021	HITRUNIN
HIT-RUN INJURY CONSPIRACY	D	4652021	HITRUNIN
HIT-RUN INJURY SOLICITATION	D	4652021	HITRUNIN
HIT-RUN UNATTENDED	E	4652010	HITRUNUN
HOMICIDE BY WATERCRAFT, BY DISREGARD FOR THE SAFETY OF OTHERS	A	79A6050	HOMICIDEWD
HOMICIDE BY WATERCRAFT, BY DISREGARD FOR THE SAFETY OF OTHERS ATTEMPT	B	79A6050	HOMICIDEWD
HOMICIDE BY WATERCRAFT, BY DISREGARD FOR THE SAFETY OF OTHERS CONSPIRACY	B	79A6050	HOMICIDEWD
HOMICIDE BY WATERCRAFT, BY DISREGARD FOR THE SAFETY OF OTHERS SOLICITATION	B	79A6050	HOMICIDEWD
HOMICIDE BY WATERCRAFT, OPERATING ANY VESSEL IN A RECKLESS MANNER	A	79A605A	HOMICIDEWR
HOMICIDE BY WATERCRAFT, OPERATING ANY VESSEL IN A RECKLESS MANNER ATTEMPT	B	79A605A	HOMICIDEWR
HOMICIDE BY WATERCRAFT, OPERATING ANY VESSEL IN A RECKLESS MANNER CONSPIRACY	B	79A605A	HOMICIDEWR
HOMICIDE BY WATERCRAFT, OPERATING ANY VESSEL IN A RECKLESS MANNER SOLICITATION	B	79A605A	HOMICIDEWR
HOMICIDE BY WATERCRAFT, WHILE UNDER THE INFLUENCE OF INTOXICATING LIQUOR OR ANY DRUG	A	79A605B	HOMICIDEWI
HOMICIDE BY WATERCRAFT, WHILE UNDER THE INFLUENCE OF INTOXICATING LIQUOR OR ANY DRUG ATTEMPT	B	79A605B	HOMICIDEWI
HOMICIDE BY WATERCRAFT, WHILE UNDER THE INFLUENCE OF INTOXICATING LIQUOR OR ANY DRUG CONSPIRACY	B	79A605B	HOMICIDEWI
HOMICIDE BY WATERCRAFT, WHILE UNDER THE INFLUENCE OF INTOXICATING LIQUOR OR ANY DRUG SOLICITATION	B	79A605B	HOMICIDEWI
IDENTITY THEFT 1	C	9350200	IDENTITY1
IDENTITY THEFT 1 ATTEMPT	D	9350200	IDENTITY1
IDENTITY THEFT 1 CONSPIRACY	D	9350200	IDENTITY1
IDENTITY THEFT 1 SOLICITATION	D	9350200	IDENTITY1
IDENTITY THEFT 2	D	9350200	IDENTITY2
IDENTITY THEFT 2 ATTEMPT	E	9350200	IDENTITY2
IDENTITY THEFT 2 CONSPIRACY	E	9350200	IDENTITY2
IDENTITY THEFT 2 SOLICITATION	E	9350200	IDENTITY2
INCEST 1	B	9A64020	INCEST1
INCEST 1 ATTEMPT	C	9A64020	INCEST1
INCEST 1 CONSPIRACY	C	9A64020	INCEST1
INCEST 1 SOLICITATION	C	9A64020	INCEST1
INCEST 2	C	9A64020	INCEST2
INCEST 2 ATTEMPT	D	9A64020	INCEST2
INCEST 2 CONSPIRACY	D	9A64020	INCEST2
INCEST 2 SOLICITATION	D	9A64020	INCEST2

OFFENSE TITLE	CATEGORY	RCW	JRA CODE
INDECENT EXPOSURE (VICTIM <14)	D+	9A8801C	INDEXP<14
INDECENT EXPOSURE (VICTIM <14) ATTEMPT	E	9A8801C	INDEXP<14
INDECENT EXPOSURE (VICTIM <14) CONSPIRACY	E	9A8801C	INDEXP<14
INDECENT EXPOSURE (VICTIM <14) REPEAT	C	9A8801D	INDEXP<14R
INDECENT EXPOSURE (VICTIM <14) SOLICITATION	E	9A8801C	INDEXP<14
INDECENT EXPOSURE (VICTIM 14+)	E	9A8810A	INDEXP14+
INDECENT EXPOSURE (VICTIM 14+) REPEAT	C	9A88010	INDEXP14+R
INDECENT LIBERTIES WITH FORCIBLE COMPULSION	B+	9A44100	INDLIBFC
INDECENT LIBERTIES WITH FORCIBLE COMPULSION ATTEMPT	C+	9A44100	INDLIBFC
INDECENT LIBERTIES WITH FORCIBLE COMPULSION CONSPIRACY	C+	9A44100	INDLIBFC
INDECENT LIBERTIES WITH FORCIBLE COMPULSION SOLICITATION	C+	9A44100	INDLIBFC
INDECENT LIBERTIES WITHOUT FORCIBLE COMPULSION	B+	9A44100	INDLIB
INDECENT LIBERTIES WITHOUT FORCIBLE COMPULSION ATTEMPT	C+	9A44100	INDLIB
INDECENT LIBERTIES WITHOUT FORCIBLE COMPULSION CONSPIRACY	C+	9A44100	INDLIB
INDECENT LIBERTIES WITHOUT FORCIBLE COMPULSION SOLICITATION	C+	NULL	INDLIBWOC
INTERFERING WITH THE REPORTING OF DOMESTIC VIOLENCE	D	9A36150	DVREPINTER
INTERFERING WITH THE REPORTING OF DOMESTIC VIOLENCE ATTEMPTED	E	9A36150	DVREPINTER
INTERFERING WITH THE REPORTING OF DOMESTIC VIOLENCE CONSPIRACY	E	9A36150	DVREPINTER
INTERFERING WITH THE REPORTING OF DOMESTIC VIOLENCE SOLICITATION	E	9A36150	DVREPINTER
INTIMIDATING A PUBLIC SERVANT	B+	9A76180	INTPUBSERV
INTIMIDATING A PUBLIC SERVANT ATTEMPT	C+	9A76180	INTPUBSERV
INTIMIDATING A PUBLIC SERVANT CONSPIRACY	C+	9A76180	INTPUBSERV
INTIMIDATING A PUBLIC SERVANT SOLICITATION	C+	9A76180	INTPUBSERV
INTIMIDATING ANOTHER PERSON BY USE OF A WEAPON	D	941270	INTWWEAPON
INTIMIDATING ANOTHER PERSON BY USE OF A WEAPON ATTEMPT	E	941270	INTWWEAPON
INTIMIDATING ANOTHER PERSON BY USE OF A WEAPON CONSPIRACY	E	941270	INTWWEAPON
INTIMIDATING ANOTHER PERSON BY USE OF A WEAPON SOLICITATION	E	941270	INTWWEAPON
INTIMIDATING WITNESS	B+	9A72110	INTWITNESS
INTIMIDATING WITNESS ATTEMPT	C+	9A72110	INTWITNESS
INTIMIDATING WITNESS CONSPIRACY	C+	9A72110	INTWITNESS
INTIMIDATING WITNESS SOLICITATION	C+	9A72110	INTWITNESS
INTRODUCING CONTRABAND 1	B	9A76140	INTCONT1

OFFENSE TITLE	CATEGORY	RCW	JRA CODE
INTRODUCING CONTRABAND 1 ATTEMPT	C	9A76140	INTCONT1
INTRODUCING CONTRABAND 1 CONSPIRACY	C	9A76140	INTCONT1
INTRODUCING CONTRABAND 1 SOLICITATION	C	9A76140	INTCONT1
INTRODUCING CONTRABAND 2	C	9A76150	INTCONT2
INTRODUCING CONTRABAND 2 ATTEMPT	D	9A76150	INTCONT2
INTRODUCING CONTRABAND 2 CONSPIRACY	D	9A76150	INTCONT2
INTRODUCING CONTRABAND 2 SOLICITATION	D	9A76150	INTCONT2
INTRODUCING CONTRABAND 3	E	9A76160	INTCONT3
KIDNAP 1	A	9A40020	KIDNAP1
KIDNAP 1 ATTEMPT	B+	9A40020	KIDNAP1
KIDNAP 1 CONSPIRACY	B+	9A40020	KIDNAP1
KIDNAP 1 SOLICITATION	B+	9A40020	KIDNAP1
KIDNAP 2	B+	9A40030	KIDNAP2
KIDNAP 2 ATTEMPT	C+	9A40030	KIDNAP2
KIDNAP 2 CONSPIRACY	C+	9A40030	KIDNAP2
KIDNAP 2 SOLICITATION	C+	9A40030	KIDNAP2
LEGEND DRUG WITH INTENET TO DELIVER SOLICITATION	D+	694103A	LEGDRUGSAL
LEGEND DRUG WITH INTENT TO DELIVER	C+	694103A	LEGDRUGSAL
LEGEND DRUG WITH INTENT TO DELIVER CONSPIRACY	D+	694103A	LEGDRUGSAL
LEGEND DRUG WITH INTENT TO DELLIVER ATTEMPT	D+	694103A	LEGDRUGSAL
LICENSE REQUIRED TO MANUFACTURE, PURCHASE, SELL, USE, POSSESS, TRANSPORT, OR STORE EXPLOSIVES	C	7074022	EXPLLICREQ
LICENSE REQUIRED TO MANUFACTURE, PURCHASE, SELL, USE, POSSESS, TRANSPORT, OR STORE EXPLOSIVES ATTEMPTED	D	7074022	EXPLLICREQ
LICENSE REQUIRED TO MANUFACTURE, PURCHASE, SELL, USE, POSSESS, TRANSPORT, OR STORE EXPLOSIVES CONSPIRACY	D	7074022	EXPLLICREQ
LICENSE REQUIRED TO MANUFACTURE, PURCHASE, SELL, USE, POSSESS, TRANSPORT, OR STORE EXPLOSIVES SOLICITATION	D	7074022	EXPLLICREQ
MAINTAIN A DWELLING OR PLACE FOR CONTROLLED SUBSTANCE	C	6950402	MDCONTSUB
MAKING FALSE OR MISLEADING STATEMENT TO A PUBLIC SERVANT ATTEMPTED	E	9A76175	FALSESTATE
MAKING FALSE OR MISLEADING STATEMENT TO A PUBLIC SERVANT CONSPIRACY	E	9A76175	FALSESTATE
MAKING FALSE OR MISLEADING STATEMENT TO A PUBLIC SERVANT SOLICITATION	E	9A76175	FALSESTATE
MAKING FALSE OR MISLEADING STATEMENTS TO A PUBLIC SERVANT	D	9A76175	FALSESTATE
MALICIOUS MISCHIEF 1	B	9A48070	MALMIS1
MALICIOUS MISCHIEF 1 ATTEMPT	C	9A48070	MALMIS1
MALICIOUS MISCHIEF 1 CONSPIRACY	C	9A48070	MALMIS1

OFFENSE TITLE	CATEGORY	RCW	JRA CODE
MALICIOUS MISCHIEF 1 SOLICITATION	C	9A48070	MALMIS1
MALICIOUS MISCHIEF 2	C	9A48080	MALMIS2
MALICIOUS MISCHIEF 2 ATTEMPT	D	9A48080	MALMIS2
MALICIOUS MISCHIEF 2 CONSPIRACY	D	9A48080	MALMIS2
MALICIOUS MISCHIEF 2 SOLICITATION	D	9A48080	MALMIS2
MALICIOUS MISCHIEF 3	D	9A48090	MALMIS3
MALICIOUS MISCHIEF 3 (<$50)	E	9A4809A	MALMIS3<50
MALICIOUS MISCHIEF 3 ATTEMPT	E	9A48090	MALMIS3
MALICIOUS MISCHIEF 3 CONSPIRACY	E	9A48090	MALMIS3
MALICIOUS MISCHIEF 3 SOLICITATION	E	9A48090	MALMIS3
MANSLAUGHTER 1	B+	9A32060	MANSL1
MANSLAUGHTER 1 ATTEMPT	C+	9A32060	MANSL1
MANSLAUGHTER 1 CONSPIRACY	C+	9A32060	MANSL1
MANSLAUGHTER 1 SOLICITATION	C+	9A32060	MANSL1
MANSLAUGHTER 2	C+	9A32070	MANSL2
MANSLAUGHTER 2 ATTEMPT	D+	9A32070	MANSL2
MANSLAUGHTER 2 CONSPIRACY	D+	9A32070	MANSL2
MANSLAUGHTER 2 SOLICITATION	D+	9A32070	MANSL2
MULTIPLE DETENTION	V	9990000	MULTDET
MURDER 1	A+	9A32030	MURDER1
MURDER 1 ATTEMPT	A	9A32030	MURDER1
MURDER 1 CONSPIRACY	A	9A32030	MURDER1
MURDER 1 SOLICITATION	A	9A32030	MURDER1
MURDER 2	A+	9A32050	MURDER2
MURDER 2 ATTEMPT	B+	9A32050	MURDER2
MURDER 2 CONSPIRACY	B+	9A32050	MURDER2
MURDER 2 SOLICITATION	B+	9A32050	MURDER2
OBSCENE PHONE CALLS	E	961230	OBSCENEPC
OBSTRUCTING A PUBLIC SERVANT	D	9A76020	OBSPUBSERV
OBSTRUCTING A PUBLIC SERVANT ATTEMPT	E	9A76020	OBSPUBSERV
OBSTRUCTING A PUBLIC SERVANT CONSPIRACY	E	9A76020	OBSPUBSERV
OBSTRUCTING A PUBLIC SERVANT SOLICITATION	E	9A76020	OBSPUBSERV
OBSTRUCTING LAW ENFORCEMENT OFFICER	D	9A76020	OBSLAWOFF
OBSTRUCTING LAW ENFORCEMENT OFFICER ATTEMPT	E	9A76020	OBSLAWOFF
OBSTRUCTING LAW ENFORCEMENT OFFICER CONSPIRACY	E	9A76020	OBSLAWOFF
OBSTRUCTING LAW ENFORCEMENT OFFICER SOLICITATION	E	9A76020	OBSLAWOFF
OBTAIN LEGEND DRUG	C	6941020	OBTLEGDRUG
OBTAIN LEGEND DRUG ATTEMPT	D	6941020	OBTLEGDRUG
OBTAIN LEGEND DRUG CONSPIRACY	D	6941020	OBTLEGDRUG
OBTAIN LEGEND DRUG SOLICITATION	D	6941020	OBTLEGDRUG
OFFERING AND AGREEING (PROSTITUTION)	E	9A88030	O&APROST
ORGANIZED RETAIL THEFT 1	B	9A56350	THEFT1ORG
ORGANIZED RETAIL THEFT 1 ATTEMPTED	C	9A56350	THEFT1ORG
ORGANIZED RETAIL THEFT 1 CONSPIRACY	C	9A56350	THEFT1ORG

The Caseload Forecast Council is not liable for errors or omissions in the manual, for sentences that may be inappropriately calculated as a result of a practitioner's or court's reliance on the manual, or for any other written or verbal information related to adult or juvenile sentencing. The scoring sheets are intended to provide assistance in most cases but does not cover all permutations of the scoring rules. If you find any errors or omissions, we encourage you to report them to the Caseload Forecast Council.

OFFENSE TITLE	CATEGORY	RCW	JRA CODE
ORGANIZED RETAIL THEFT 1 SOLICITATION	C	9A56350	THEFT1ORG
ORGANIZED RETAIL THEFT 2	C	9A56350	THEFT2ORG
ORGANIZED RETAIL THEFT 2 ATTEMPTED	D	9A56350	THEFT2ORG
ORGANIZED RETAIL THEFT 2 CONSPIRACY	D	9A56350	THEFT2ORG
ORGANIZED RETAIL THEFT 2 SOLICITATION	D	9A56350	THEFT2ORG
OTHER A OFFENSE	A	1340357	OTHERAOFF
OTHER A OFFENSE ATTEMPT	B+	1340357	OTHERAOFF
OTHER A OFFENSE CONSPIRACY	B+	1340357	OTHERAOFF
OTHER A OFFENSE SOLICITATION	B+	1340357	OTHERAOFF
OTHER B OFFENSE	B	1340357	OTHERBOFF
OTHER B OFFENSE ATTEMPT	C	1340357	OTHERBOFF
OTHER B OFFENSE CONSPIRACY	C	1340357	OTHERBOFF
OTHER B OFFENSE SOLICITATION	C	1340357	OTHERBOFF
OTHER B+OFFENSE	B+	1340357	OTHERB+OFF
OTHER B+OFFENSE ATTEMPT	C+	1340357	OTHERB+OFF
OTHER B+OFFENSE CONSPIRACY	C+	1340357	OTHERB+OFF
OTHER B+OFFENSE SOLICITATION	C+	1340357	OTHERB+OFF
OTHER C OFFENSE	C	1340357	OTHERCOFF
OTHER C OFFENSE ATTEMPT	D	1340357	OTHERCOFF
OTHER C OFFENSE CONSPIRACY	D	1340357	OTHERCOFF
OTHER C OFFENSE SOLICITATION	D	1340357	OTHERCOFF
OTHER C+OFFENSE	C+	1340357	OTHERC+OFF
OTHER C+OFFENSE ATTEMPT	D+	1340357	OTHERC+OFF
OTHER C+OFFENSE CONSPIRACY	D+	1340357	OTHERC+OFF
OTHER C+OFFENSE SOLICITATION	D+	1340357	OTHERC+OFF
OTHER D+OFFENSE	D+	1340357	OTHERD+OFF
OTHER D+OFFENSE	E	1340357	OTHERD+OFF
OTHER D+OFFENSE	E	1340357	OTHERD+OFF
OTHER D+OFFENSE	E	1340357	OTHERD+OFF
OTHER OFFENSE EQUIVALENT TO ADULT GROSS MISDEMEANOR	D	1340357	OTHERDOFF
OTHER OFFENSE EQUIVALENT TO ADULT GROSS MISDEMEANOR ATTEMPT	E	1340357	OTHERDOFF
OTHER OFFENSE EQUIVALENT TO ADULT GROSS MISDEMEANOR CONSPIRACY	E	1340357	OTHERDOFF
OTHER OFFENSE EQUIVALENT TO ADULT GROSS MISDEMEANOR SOLICITATION	E	1340357	OTHERDOFF
OTHER OFFENSE EQUIVALENT TO ADULT MISDEMEANOR	E	1340357	OTHEREOFF
PATRONIZING A PROSTITUTE	E	9A88110	PATPROSTI
PATRONIZING A PROSTITUTE ATTEMPTED	E	9A88110	PATPROSTI
PATRONIZING A PROSTITUTE CONSPIRACY	E	9A88110	PATPROSTI
PATRONIZING A PROSTITUTE SOLICITATION	E	9A88110	PATPROSTI
POSSESSION OF A STOLEN VEHICLE	B	9A56068	POSSTOLVEH
POSSESSION OF A STOLEN VEHICLE ATTEMPTED	C	9A56068	POSSTOLVEH
POSSESSION OF A STOLEN VEHICLE ATTEMPTED CONSPIRACY	C	9A56068	POSSTOLVEH

The Caseload Forecast Council is not liable for errors or omissions in the manual, for sentences that may be inappropriately calculated as a result of a practitioner's or court's reliance on the manual, or for any other written or verbal information related to adult or juvenile sentencing. The scoring sheets are intended to provide assistance in most cases but does not cover all permutations of the scoring rules. If you find any errors or omissions, we encourage you to report them to the Caseload Forecast Council.

OFFENSE TITLE	CATEGORY	RCW	JRA CODE
POSSESSION OF A STOLEN VEHICLE SOLICITATION	C	9A56068	POSSTOLVEH
POSSESSION OF DANGEROUS WEAPON	D+	941250	POSDANGW
POSSESSION OF DANGEROUS WEAPON AT SCHOOL	D	941280	POSDANGWAS
POSSESSION OF DANGEROUS WEAPON AT SCHOOL ATTEMPT	E	941280	POSDANGWAS
POSSESSION OF DANGEROUS WEAPON AT SCHOOL CONSPIRACY	E	941280	POSDANGWAS
POSSESSION OF DANGEROUS WEAPON AT SCHOOL SOLICITATION	E	941280	POSDANGWAS
POSSESSION OF DANGEROUS WEAPON ATTEMPT	E	941250	POSDANGW
POSSESSION OF DANGEROUS WEAPON CONSPIRACY	E	941250	POSDANGW
POSSESSION OF DANGEROUS WEAPON SOLICITATION	E	941250	POSDANGW
POSSESSION OF DEPICTIONS OF MINOR ENGAGED IN SEXUALLY EXPLICIT CONDUCT	C	968A070	POSCHPORN2
POSSESSION OF DEPICTIONS OF MINOR ENGAGED IN SEXUALLY EXPLICIT CONDUCT 1	B	968A070	POSCHPORN1
POSSESSION OF DEPICTIONS OF MINOR ENGAGED IN SEXUALLY EXPLICIT CONDUCT 1 ATTEMPT	C	968A070	POSCHPORN1
POSSESSION OF DEPICTIONS OF MINOR ENGAGED IN SEXUALLY EXPLICIT CONDUCT 1 CONSPIRACY	C	968A070	POSCHPORN1
POSSESSION OF DEPICTIONS OF MINOR ENGAGED IN SEXUALLY EXPLICIT CONDUCT 1 SOLICITATION	C	968A070	POSCHPORN1
POSSESSION OF DEPICTIONS OF MINOR ENGAGED IN SEXUALLY EXPLICIT CONDUCT ATTEMPT	D	968A070	POSCHPORN2
POSSESSION OF DEPICTIONS OF MINOR ENGAGED IN SEXUALLY EXPLICIT CONDUCT CONSPIRACY	D	968A070	POSCHPORN2
POSSESSION OF DEPICTIONS OF MINOR ENGAGED IN SEXUALLY EXPLICIT CONDUCT SOLICITATION	D	968A070	POSCHPORN2
POSSESSION OF EXPLOSIVE DEVICES	A	7074180	POSEXPDEV
POSSESSION OF EXPLOSIVE DEVICES ATTEMPT	B+	7074180	POSEXPDEV
POSSESSION OF EXPLOSIVE DEVICES CONSPIRACY	B+	7074180	POSEXPDEV
POSSESSION OF EXPLOSIVE DEVICES SOLICITATION	B+	7074180	POSEXPDEV
POSSESSION OF FIREARM BY MINOR (<18 YEARS)	C	941040	PFIREARMM
POSSESSION OF FIREARM BY MINOR (<18 YEARS) ATTEMPT	C	941040	PFIREARMM
POSSESSION OF FIREARM BY MINOR (<18 YEARS) CONSPIRACY	C	941040	PFIREARMM
POSSESSION OF FIREARM BY MINOR (<18 YEARS) SOLICITATION	C	941040	PFIREARMM
POSSESSION OF ILLEGAL FWRKS	E	7077255	POSILLFWKS
POSSESSION OF INCENDIARY DEVICE	A	940120	POSINCEND
POSSESSION OF INCENDIARY DEVICE ATTEMPT	B+	940120	POSINCEND
POSSESSION OF INCENDIARY DEVICE CONSPIRACY	B+	940120	POSINCEND
POSSESSION OF INCENDIARY SOLICITATION	B+	940120	POSINCEND
POSSESSION OF LEGEND DRUG	E	694103B	POSLEGDRUG
POSSESSION OF MACHINE GUN OR SHORT-BARRELED SHOTGUN OR RIFLE	C	941190	POSMACHGUN

The Caseload Forecast Council is not liable for errors or omissions in the manual, for sentences that may be inappropriately calculated as a result of a practitioner's or court's reliance on the manual, or for any other written or verbal information related to adult or juvenile sentencing. The scoring sheets are intended to provide assistance in most cases but does not cover all permutations of the scoring rules. If you find any errors or omissions, we encourage you to report them to the Caseload Forecast Council.

OFFENSE TITLE	CATEGORY	RCW	JRA CODE
POSSESSION OF MACHINE GUN OR SHORT-BARRELED SHOTGUN OR RIFLE ATTEMPT	D	941190	POSMACHGUN
POSSESSION OF MACHINE GUN OR SHORT-BARRELED SHOTGUN OR RIFLE CONSPIRACY	D	941190	POSMACHGUN
POSSESSION OF MACHINE GUN OR SHORT-BARRELED SHOTGUN OR RIFLE SOLICITATION	D	941190	POSMACHGUN
POSSESSION OF MARIJUANA <40 GRAMS	E	695040J	POSPOT<40
POSSESSION OF STOLEN FIREARM	B	9A56310	PSFIREARM
POSSESSION OF STOLEN FIREARM ATTEMPT	C	9A56310	PSFIREARM
POSSESSION OF STOLEN FIREARM CONSPIRACY	C	9A56310	PSFIREARM
POSSESSION OF STOLEN FIREARM SOLICITATION	C	9A56310	PSFIREARM
POSSESSION OF STOLEN PROPERTY 1	B	9A56150	PSP1
POSSESSION OF STOLEN PROPERTY 1 ATTEMPT	C	9A56150	PSP1
POSSESSION OF STOLEN PROPERTY 1 CONSPIRACY	C	9A56150	PSP1
POSSESSION OF STOLEN PROPERTY 1 SOLICITATION	C	9A56150	PSP1
POSSESSION OF STOLEN PROPERTY 2	C	9A56160	PSP2
POSSESSION OF STOLEN PROPERTY 2 ATTEMPT	D	9A56160	PSP2
POSSESSION OF STOLEN PROPERTY 2 CONSPIRACY	D	9A56160	PSP2
POSSESSION OF STOLEN PROPERTY 2 SOLICITATION	D	9A56160	PSP2
POSSESSION OF STOLEN PROPERTY 3	D	9A56170	PSP3
POSSESSION OF STOLEN PROPERTY 3 ATTEMPT	E	9A56170	PSP3
POSSESSION OF STOLEN PROPERTY 3 CONSPIRACY	E	9A56170	PSP3
POSSESSION OF STOLEN PROPERTY 3 SOLICITATION	E	9A56170	PSP3
POSSESSION OF WEAPONS BY PRISONER COUNTY FACILITY	C	994040	POSWEAPONC
POSSESSION OF WEAPONS BY PRISONER COUNTY FACILITY ATTEMPTED	D	994040	POSWEAPON
POSSESSION OF WEAPONS BY PRISONER COUNTY FACILITY CONSPIRACY	D	994040	POSWEAPON
POSSESSION OF WEAPONS BY PRISONER COUNTY FACILITY SOLICITATION	D	994040	POSWEAPON
POSSESSION OF WEAPONS BY PRISONER STATE FACILITY	B	994040	POSWEAPONB
POSSESSION OF WEAPONS BY PRISONER STATE FACILITY ATTEMPTED	C	994040	POSWEAPONS
POSSESSION OF WEAPONS BY PRISONER STATE FACILITY CONSPIRACY	C	994040	POSWEAPONS
POSSESSION OF WEAPONS BY PRISONER STATE FACILITY SOLICITAITON	C	994040	POSWEAPONS
PROMOTE SUICIDE	C+	9A36060	PROSUICIDE
PROMOTE SUICIDE ATTEMPT	D+	9A36060	PROSUICIDE
PROMOTE SUICIDE CONSPIRACY	D+	9A36060	PROSUICIDE
PROMOTE SUICIDE SOLICITATION	D+	9A36060	PROSUICIDE
PROMOTING COMMERCIAL SEXUAL ABUSE OF A MINOR	A	968A101	PRSEXABSMI
PROMOTING COMMERCIAL SEXUAL ABUSE OF A MINOR ATTEMPTED	B	968A101	PRSEXABSMI

OFFENSE TITLE	CATEGORY	RCW	JRA CODE
PROMOTING COMMERCIAL SEXUAL ABUSE OF A MINOR CONSPIRACY	B	968A101	PRSEXABSMI
PROMOTING COMMERCIAL SEXUAL ABUSE OF A MINOR SOLICITATION	B	968A101	PRSEXABSMI
PROMOTING PROSTITUTION 1	B+	9A88070	PROPROST1
PROMOTING PROSTITUTION 1 ATTEMPT	C+	9A88070	PROPROST1
PROMOTING PROSTITUTION 1 CONSPIRACY	C+	9A88070	PROPROST1
PROMOTING PROSTITUTION 1 SOLICITATION	C+	9A88070	PROPROST1
PROMOTING PROSTITUTION 2	C+	9A88080	PROPROST2
PROMOTING PROSTITUTION 2 ATTEMPT	D+	9A88080	PROPROST2
PROMOTING PROSTITUTION 2 CONSPIRACY	D+	9A88080	PROPROST2
PROMOTING PROSTITUTION 2 SOLICITATION	D+	9A88080	PROPROST2
RAPE 1	A	9A44040	RAPE1
RAPE 1 ATTEMPT	B+	9A44040	RAPE1
RAPE 1 CONSPIRACY	B+	9A44040	RAPE1
RAPE 1 SOLICITATION	B+	9A44040	RAPE1
RAPE 2	A-	9A44050	RAPE2
RAPE 2 ATTEMPT	B+	9A44050	RAPE2
RAPE 2 CONSPIRACY	B+	9A44050	RAPE2
RAPE 2 SOLICITATION	B+	9A44050	RAPE2
RAPE 3	C+	9A44060	RAPE3
RAPE 3 ATTEMPT	D+	9A44060	RAPE3
RAPE 3 CONSPIRACY	D+	9A44060	RAPE3
RAPE 3 SOLICITATION	D+	9A44060	RAPE3
RAPE OF A CHILD 1	A-	9A44073	RAPECHILD1
RAPE OF A CHILD 1 ATTEMPT	B+	9A44073	RAPECHILD1
RAPE OF A CHILD 1 CONSPIRACY	B+	9A44073	RAPECHILD1
RAPE OF A CHILD 1 SOLICITATION	B+	9A44073	RAPECHILD1
RAPE OF A CHILD 2	B+	9A44076	RAPECHILD2
RAPE OF A CHILD 2 ATTEMPT	C+	9A44076	RAPECHILD2
RAPE OF A CHILD 2 CONSPIRACY	C+	9A44076	RAPECHILD2
RAPE OF A CHILD 2 SOLICITATION	C+	NULL	RAPECHILC2
RAPE OF A CHILD 3	C	9A44079	RAPECHILD3
RAPE OF A CHILD 3 ATTEMPT	D	9A44079	RAPECHILD3
RAPE OF A CHILD 3 CONSPIRACY	D	9A44079	RAPECHILD3
RAPE OF A CHILD 3 SOLICITATION	D	9A44079	RAPECHILD3
RECKLESS BURNING 1	C	9A48040	RECKBURN1
RECKLESS BURNING 1 ATTEMPT	D	9A48040	RECKBURN1
RECKLESS BURNING 1 CONSPIRACY	D	9A48040	RECKBURN1
RECKLESS BURNING 1 SOLICITATION	D	9A48040	RECKBURN1
RECKLESS BURNING 2	D	9A48050	RECKBURN2
RECKLESS BURNING 2 ATTEMPT	E	9A48050	RECKBURN2
RECKLESS BURNING 2 CONSPIRACY	E	9A48050	RECKBURN2
RECKLESS BURNING 2 SOLICITATION	E	9A48050	RECKBURN2
RECKLESS DRIVING	E	4661500	RECKDRIV
RECKLESS ENDANGER	D+	9A36050	RECKEND
RECKLESS ENDANGER ATTEMPT	E	9A36050	RECKEND

The Caseload Forecast Council is not liable for errors or omissions in the manual, for sentences that may be inappropriately calculated as a result of a practitioner's or court's reliance on the manual, or for any other written or verbal information related to adult or juvenile sentencing. The scoring sheets are intended to provide assistance in most cases but does not cover all permutations of the scoring rules. If you find any errors or omissions, we encourage you to report them to the Caseload Forecast Council.

OFFENSE TITLE	CATEGORY	RCW	JRA CODE
RECKLESS ENDANGER CONSPIRACY	E	9A36050	RECKEND
RECKLESS ENDANGER SOLICITATION	E	9A36050	RECKEND
REFUSING TO LEAVE PUBLIC PROPERTY	D	28A6350	REFLEAVE
RENDERING CRIMINAL ASSISTANCE 1	B	9A76070	RENDCRIM
RENDERING CRIMINAL ASSISTANCE 1 ATTEMPT	C	9A76070	RENDCRIM
RENDERING CRIMINAL ASSISTANCE 1 CONSPIRACY	C	9A76070	RENDCRIM
RENDERING CRIMINAL ASSISTANCE 1 SOLICITATION	C	9A76070	RENDCRIM
RENDERING CRIMINAL ASSISTANCE 2	D+	9A76080	RENDCRIM2
RENDERING CRIMINAL ASSISTANCE 2 ATTEMPT	E	9A76080	RENDCRIM2
RENDERING CRIMINAL ASSISTANCE 2 CONSPIRACY	E	9A76080	RENDCRIM2
RENDERING CRIMINAL ASSISTANCE 2 SOLICITATION	E	9A76080	RENDCRIM2
RESIDENTIAL BURGLARY	B	9A52025	BURGRES
RESIDENTIAL BURGLARY ATTEMPT	C	9A52025	BURGRES
RESIDENTIAL BURGLARY CONSPIRACY	C	9A52025	BURGRES
RESIDENTIAL BURGLARY SOLICITATION	C	9A52025	BURGRES
RESISTING ARREST	E	9A76040	RESARREST
RETAIL THEFT WITH EXTENUATING CIRCUMSTANCES 1	B	9A56360	THEFT1RET
RETAIL THEFT WITH EXTENUATING CIRCUMSTANCES 1 ATTEMPTED	C	9A56360	THEFT1RET
RETAIL THEFT WITH EXTENUATING CIRCUMSTANCES 1 CONSPIRACY	C	9A56360	THEFT1RET
RETAIL THEFT WITH EXTENUATING CIRCUMSTANCES 1 SOLICIATION	C	9A56360	THEFT1RET
RETAIL THEFT WITH EXTENUATING CIRCUMSTANCES 2	C	9A56360	THEFT2RET
RETAIL THEFT WITH EXTENUATING CIRCUMSTANCES 2 ATTEMPTED	D	9A56360	THEFT2RET
RETAIL THEFT WITH EXTENUATING CIRCUMSTANCES 2 CONSPIRACY	D	9A56360	THEFT2RET
RETAIL THEFT WITH EXTENUATING CIRCUMSTANCES 2 SOLICITATION	D	9A56360	THEFT2RET
RETAIL THEFT WITH EXTENUATING CIRCUMSTANCES 3	C	9A56360	THEFT3RET
RETAIL THEFT WITH EXTENUATING CIRCUMSTANCES 3 ATTEMPTED	D	9A56360	THEFT3RET
RETAIL THEFT WITH EXTENUATING CIRCUMSTANCES 3 CONSPIRACY	D	9A56360	THEFT3RET
RETAIL THEFT WITH EXTENUATING CIRCUMSTANCES 3 SOLICITATION	D	9A56360	THEFT3RET
RIOT WITH WEAPON	C+	9A8401W	RIOTWWEAP
RIOT WITH WEAPON ATTEMPT	D+	9A8401W	RIOTWWEAP
RIOT WITH WEAPON CONSPIRACY	D+	9A8401W	RIOTWWEAP
RIOT WITH WEAPON SOLICITATION	D+	9A8401W	RIOTWWEAP
RIOT WITHOUT WEAPON	D+	9A8401U	RIOTWOWEAP
RIOT WITHOUT WEAPON ATTEMPT	E	9A8401U	RIOTWOWEAP
RIOT WITHOUT WEAPON CONSPIRACY	E	9A8401U	RIOTWOWEAP

OFFENSE TITLE	CATEGORY	RCW	JRA CODE
RIOT WITHOUT WEAPON SOLICITATION	E	9A8401U	RIOTWOWEAP
ROBBERY 1	A	9A56200	ROBBERY1
ROBBERY 1 ACCOMPLICE	A	9A08020	ROB1ACC
ROBBERY 1 ATTEMPT	B+	9A56200	ROBBERY1
ROBBERY 1 CONSPIRACY	B+	9A56200	ROBBERY1
ROBBERY 1 SOLICITATION	B+	9A56200	ROBBERY1
ROBBERY 2	B+	9A56210	ROBBERY2
ROBBERY 2 ATTEMPT	C+	9A56210	ROBBERY2
ROBBERY 2 CONSPIRACY	C+	9A56210	ROBBERY2
ROBBERY 2 SOLICITATION	C+	9A56210	ROBBERY2
SALE OF CONTROL SUBSTANCE FOR PROFIT	C+	6950410	SALECONSUB
SENDING, BRINGING INTO STATE DEPICTIONS OF MINOR ENGAGED IN SEXUALLY EXPLICIT CONDUCT 1	B	968A060	SBCHPORN1
SENDING, BRINGING INTO STATE DEPICTIONS OF MINOR ENGAGED IN SEXUALLY EXPLICIT CONDUCT 1 ATTEMPT	C	968A060	SBCHPORN1
SENDING, BRINGING INTO STATE DEPICTIONS OF MINOR ENGAGED IN SEXUALLY EXPLICIT CONDUCT 1 CONSPIRACY	C	968A060	SBCHPORN1
SENDING, BRINGING INTO STATE DEPICTIONS OF MINOR ENGAGED IN SEXUALLY EXPLICIT CONDUCT 1 SOLICITATION	C	968A060	SBCHPORN1
SENDING, BRINGING INTO STATE DEPICTIONS OF MINOR ENGAGED IN SEXUALLY EXPLICIT CONDUCT 2	C	968A060	SBCHPORN2
SENDING, BRINGING INTO STATE DEPICTIONS OF MINOR ENGAGED IN SEXUALLY EXPLICIT CONDUCT 2 ATTEMPT	D	968A060	SBCHPORN2
SENDING, BRINGING INTO STATE DEPICTIONS OF MINOR ENGAGED IN SEXUALLY EXPLICIT CONDUCT 2 CONSPIRACY	D	968A060	SBCHPORN2
SENDING, BRINGING INTO STATE DEPICTIONS OF MINOR ENGAGED IN SEXUALLY EXPLICIT CONDUCT 2 SOLICITATION	D	968A060	SBCHPORN2
SENTENCE RESCINDED	UK	9975	SENRESCIND
SENTENCE REVERSED AND REMANDED	X	NULL	SENTREVERS
SEX OFFENDER PAROLE REVOKE	V	9976	SOPARREV
SEXUAL EXPLOITATION OF A MINOR	B	968A040	SEXEXPLMNR
SEXUAL EXPLOITATION OF A MINOR ATTEMPT	C	968A040	SEXEXPLMNR
SEXUAL EXPLOITATION OF A MINOR CONSPIRACY	C	968A040	SEXEXPLMNR
SEXUAL EXPLOITATION OF A MINOR SOLICITATION	C	968A040	SEXEXPLMNR
SEXUAL VIOLATION OF HUMAN REMAINS	C	9A44105	SEXVIOLREM
SEXUAL VIOLATION OF HUMAN REMAINS ATTEMPT	D	9A44105	SEXVIOLREM
SEXUAL VIOLATION OF HUMAN REMAINS CONSPIRACY	D	9A44105	SEXVIOLREM
SEXUAL VIOLATION OF HUMAN REMAINS SOLICITATION	D	9A44105	SEXVIOLREM
STALKING (1 TIME)	D	9A46110	STALK
STALKING (1 TIME) ATTEMPT	E	9A46110	STALK

The Caseload Forecast Council is not liable for errors or omissions in the manual, for sentences that may be inappropriately calculated as a result of a practitioner's or court's reliance on the manual, or for any other written or verbal information related to adult or juvenile sentencing. The scoring sheets are intended to provide assistance in most cases but does not cover all permutations of the scoring rules. If you find any errors or omissions, we encourage you to report them to the Caseload Forecast Council.

OFFENSE TITLE	CATEGORY	RCW	JRA CODE
STALKING (1 TIME) CONSPIRACY	E	9A46110	STALK
STALKING (1 TIME) SOLICITATION	E	9A46110	STALK
STALKING (REPEAT)	C	9A46111	STALKREP
STALKING (REPEAT) ATTEMPT	D	9A46111	STALKREP
STALKING (REPEAT) CONSPIRACY	D	9A46111	STALKREP
STALKING (REPEAT) SOLICITATION	D	9A46111	STALKREP
TAKING MOTOR VEHICLE WITHOUT OWNERS PERMISSION	B	9A56070	TAMVWOOP1
TAKING MOTOR VEHICLE WITHOUT OWNERS PERMISSION ATTEMPTED	C	9A56070	TAMVWOOP1
TAKING MOTOR VEHICLE WITHOUT OWNERS PERMISSION CONSPIRACY	C	9A56070	TAMVWOOP1
TAKING MOTOR VEHICLE WITHOUT OWNERS PERMISSON SOLICITATION	C	9A56070	TAMVWOOP1
TAKING MOTOR VEHICLE WITHOUT PERMISSION 2	C	9A56070	TAMVWOOP2
TAKING MOTOR VEHICLE WITHOUT PERMISSION 2 ATTEMPT	D	9A56070	TAMVWOOP2
TAKING MOTOR VEHICLE WITHOUT PERMISSION 2 CONSPIRACY	D	9A56070	TAMVWOOP2
TAKING MOTOR VEHICLE WITHOUT PERMISSION 2 SOLICITATION	D	9A56070	TAMVWOOP2
TAMPERING WITH A WITNESS	C	9A72120	TAMPWITN
TAMPERING WITH A WITNESS ATTEMPT	D	9A72120	TAMPWITN
TAMPERING WITH A WITNESS CONSPIRACY	D	9A72120	TAMPWITN
TAMPERING WITH A WITNESS SOLICITATION	D	9A72120	TAMPWITN
TAMPERING WITH FIRE ALARM APPARATUS	E	940100	TAMPFIREAL
TAMPERING WITH PHYSICAL EVIDENCE	D	9A72150	TAMPEVID
TAMPERING WITH PHYSICAL EVIDENCE ATTEMPT	D	9A72150	TAMPEVID
TAMPERING WITH PHYSICAL EVIDENCE CONSPIRACY	D	9A72150	TAMPEVID
TAMPERING WITH PHYSICAL EVIDENCE SOCLICITATION	D	9A72150	TAMPEVID
THEFT 1	B	9A56030	THEFT1
THEFT 1 ATTEMPT	C	9A56030	THEFT1
THEFT 1 CONSPIRACY	C	9A56030	THEFT1
THEFT 1 SOLICITATION	C	9A56030	THEFT1
THEFT 2	C	9A56040	THEFT2
THEFT 2 ATTEMPT	D	9A56040	THEFT2
THEFT 2 CONSPIRACY	D	9A56040	THEFT2
THEFT 2 SOLICITATION	D	9A56040	THEFT2
THEFT 3	D	9A56050	THEFT3
THEFT 3 ATTEMPT	E	9A56050	THEFT3
THEFT 3 CONSPIRACY	E	9A56050	THEFT3
THEFT 3 SOLICITATION	E	9A56050	THEFT3
THEFT OF A MOTOR VEHICLE	B	9A56030	THEFTVEH
THEFT OF A MOTOR VEHICLE ATTEMPTED	C	9A56030	THEFTVEH
THEFT OF A MOTOR VEHICLE CONSPIRACY	C	9A56030	THEFTVEH
THEFT OF A MOTOR VEHICLE SOLICITATION	C	9A56030	THEFTVEH

The Caseload Forecast Council is not liable for errors or omissions in the manual, for sentences that may be inappropriately calculated as a result of a practitioner's or court's reliance on the manual, or for any other written or verbal information related to adult or juvenile sentencing. The scoring sheets are intended to provide assistance in most cases but does not cover all permutations of the scoring rules. If you find any errors or omissions, we encourage you to report them to the Caseload Forecast Council.

OFFENSE TITLE	CATEGORY	RCW	JRA CODE
THEFT OF FIREARM	B	9A56300	THEFTFIREA
THEFT OF FIREARM ATTEMPT	C	9A56300	THEFTFIREA
THEFT OF FIREARM CONSPIRACY	C	9A56300	THEFTFIREA
THEFT OF FIREARM SOLICITATION	C	9A56300	THEFTFIREA
THEFT OF LIVESTOCK	B	9A56080	THEFTLIVES
THEFT OF LIVESTOCK ATTEMPT	C	9A56080	THEFTLIVES
THEFT OF LIVESTOCK CONSPIRACY	C	9A56080	THEFTLIVES
THEFT OF LIVESTOCK SOLICITATION	C	9A56080	THEFTLIVES
THEFT OF STOLEN FIREARM	B	9A56300	THEFTSTFIR
THEFT OF STOLEN FIREARM ATTEMPT	C	9A56300	THEFTSTFIR
THEFT OF STOLEN FIREARM CONSPIRACY	C	9A56300	THEFTSTFIR
THEFT OF STOLEN FIREARM SOLICITATION	C	9A56300	THEFTSTFIR
TRAFFICKING (HUMAN) 2 DEGREE	A	9A40100	TRAFFIKNG2
TRAFFICKING (HUMAN) 2 DEGREE ATTEMPT	B	9A40100	TRAFFIKNG2
TRAFFICKING (HUMAN) 2 DEGREE CONSPIRACY	B	9A40100	TRAFFIKNG2
TRAFFICKING (HUMAN) 2 DEGREE SOLICITATION	B	9A40100	TRAFFIKNG2
TRAFFICKING IN STOLEN PROPERTY 1 DEGREE	B	9A82050	TRAFSTPRO1
TRAFFICKING IN STOLEN PROPERTY 1 DEGREE ATTEM	C	9A82050	TRAFSTPRO1
TRAFFICKING IN STOLEN PROPERTY 1 DEGREE CONSP	C	9A82050	TRAFSTPRO1
TRAFFICKING IN STOLEN PROPERTY 1 DEGREE SOLIC	C	9A82050	TRAFSTPRO1
TRAFFICKING IN STOLEN PROPERTY 2 DEGREE	C	9A82055	TRAFSTPRO2
TRAFFICKING IN STOLEN PROPERTY 2 DEGREE ATTEMPT	D	9A82055	TRAFSTPRO2
TRAFFICKING IN STOLEN PROPERTY 2 DEGREE CONSPIRACY	D	9A82055	TRAFSTPRO2
TRAFFICKING IN STOLEN PROPERTY 2 DEGREE SOLICITATION	D	9A82055	TRAFSTPRO2
UNKNOWN OFFENSE	UK	9999998	UNKNOWNOFF
UNLAWFUL IMPRISONMENT	C+	9A40040	UNLAWIMPRI
UNLAWFUL IMPRISONMENT ATTEMPT	D+	9A40040	UNLAWIMPRI
UNLAWFUL IMPRISONMENT CONSPIRACY	D+	9A40040	UNLAWIMPRI
UNLAWFUL IMPRISONMENT SOLICITATION	D+	9A40040	UNLAWIMPRI
UNLAWFUL INHALATION	E	947A020	UNLAWINHAL
UNLAWFUL POSSESSION OF FIREARM 1	B	941041	PFIREARM1
UNLAWFUL POSSESSION OF FIREARM 1 ATTEMPT	C	941041	PFIREARM1
UNLAWFUL POSSESSION OF FIREARM 1 CONSPIRACY	C	941041	PFIREARM1
UNLAWFUL POSSESSION OF FIREARM 1 SOLICITATION	C	941041	PFIREARM1
UNLAWFUL POSSESSION OF FIREARM 2	C	941042	PFIREARM2
UNLAWFUL POSSESSION OF FIREARM 2 ATTEMPT	D	941042	PFIREARM2
UNLAWFUL POSSESSION OF FIREARM 2 CONSPIRACY	D	941042	PFIREARM2
UNLAWFUL POSSESSION OF FIREARM 2 SOLICITATION	D	941042	PFIREARM2
UNLAWFUL POSSESSION, PRODUCTION OF INSTRUMENT OF FINANCIAL FRAUD	C	9A56320	FRAUDFIN
UNLAWFUL POSSESSION, PRODUCTION OF INSTRUMENT OF FINANCIAL FRAUD	D	9A56320	FRAUDFIN

OFFENSE TITLE	CATEGORY	RCW	JRA CODE
UNLAWFUL POSSESSION, PRODUCTION OF INSTRUMENT OF FINANCIAL FRAUD	D	9A56320	FRAUDFIN
UNLAWFUL POSSESSION, PRODUCTION OF INSTRUMENT OF FINANCIAL FRAUD	D	9A56320	FRAUDFIN
VEHICLE PROWLING 1	C	9A52095	VEHPROWL1
VEHICLE PROWLING 1 ATTEMPT	D	9A52095	VEHPROWL1
VEHICLE PROWLING 1 CONSPIRACY	D	9A52095	VEHPROWL1
VEHICLE PROWLING 1 SOLICITATION	D	9A52095	VEHPROWL1
VEHICLE PROWLING 2	D	9A52100	VEHPROWL2
VEHICLE PROWLING 2 ATTEMPT	E	9A52100	VEHPROWL2
VEHICLE PROWLING 2 CONSPIRACY	E	9A52100	VEHPROWL2
VEHICLE PROWLING 2 SOLICITATION	E	9A52100	VEHPROWL2
VEHICULAR ASSAULT	C	4661522	VEHASSAULT
VEHICULAR ASSAULT ATTEMPT	D	4661522	VEHASSAULT
VEHICULAR ASSAULT CONSPIRACY	D	4661522	VEHASSAULT
VEHICULAR ASSAULT SOLICITATION	D	4661522	VEHASSAULT
VEHICULAR HOMICDE NOT VIOLENT (Must be on Court Order)	B+	4661520	VEHHOMICNV
VEHICULAR HOMICDE NOT VIOLENT ATTEMPT	C+	4661520	VEHHOMICNV
VEHICULAR HOMICDE NOT VIOLENT CONSPIRACY	C+	4661520	VEHHOMICNV
VEHICULAR HOMICDE NOT VIOLENT SOLICITATION	C+	4661520	VEHHOMICNV
VEHICULAR HOMICDE SOLICITATION	C+	4661520	VEHHOMICID
VEHICULAR HOMICIDE	B+	4661520	VEHHOMICID
VEHICULAR HOMICIDE ATTEMPT	C+	4661520	VEHHOMICID
VEHICULAR HOMICIDE CONSPIRACY	C+	4661520	VEHHOMICID
VIEWING DEPICTIONS OF MINOR ENGAGED IN SEXUALLY EXPLICIT CONDUCT 1	B	968A075	VIEWCHPRN1
VIEWING DEPICTIONS OF MINOR ENGAGED IN SEXUALLY EXPLICIT CONDUCT 1 ATTEMPTED	C	968A075	VIEWCHPRN1
VIEWING DEPICTIONS OF MINOR ENGAGED IN SEXUALLY EXPLICIT CONDUCT 1 CONSIRACY	C	968A075	VIEWCHPRN1
VIEWING DEPICTIONS OF MINOR ENGAGED IN SEXUALLY EXPLICIT CONDUCT 1 SOLICITATION	C	968A075	VIEWCHPRN1
VIEWING DEPICTIONS OF MINOR ENGAGED IN SEXUALLY EXPLICIT CONDUCT 2	C	968A075	VIEWCHPRN2
VIEWING DEPICTIONS OF MINOR ENGAGED IN SEXUALLY EXPLICIT CONDUCT 2 ATTEMPTED	D	968A075	VIEWCHPRN2
VIEWING DEPICTIONS OF MINOR ENGAGED IN SEXUALLY EXPLICIT CONDUCT 2 CONSIRACY	D	968A075	VIEWCHPRN2
VIEWING DEPICTIONS OF MINOR ENGAGED IN SEXUALLY EXPLICIT CONDUCT 2 SOLICITATION	D	968A075	VIEWCHPRN2
VIOLATION OF COURT ORDER	V	9980	VIOLCO
VIOLATION OF PROTECTION ORDER	C	2650110	VIOLPO
VIOLATION OF PROTECTION ORDER ATTEMPT	D+	2650110	VIOLPO
VIOLATION OF PROTECTION ORDER CONSPIRACY	D+	2650110	VIOLPO
VIOLATION OF PROTECTION ORDER SOLICITATION	D+	2650110	VIOLPO
VIOLATION OF SEXUAL ASSAULT PROTECTION	C	2650110	VIOLSEXAO

OFFENSE TITLE	CATEGORY	RCW	JRA CODE
ORDER			
VIOLATION OF SSODA ORDER	V	9979	VIOLSSODA
VIOLATION OF UNIFORM CONTROLLED SUBSTANCES ACT POSS WITH INTENT TO DELIVER MARIJUANA or OTHER NONNARCOTIC Sch I, II, III	C	6950401	POSINTDNON
VIOLATION OF UNIFORM CONTROLLED SUBSTANCES ACT POSS WITH INTENT TO DELIVER MARIJUANA or OTHER NONNARCOTIC Sch I, II, III	D	6950401	POSINTDNON
VIOLATION OF UNIFORM CONTROLLED SUBSTANCES ACT POSS WITH INTENT TO DELIVER MARIJUANA or OTHER NONNARCOTIC Sch I, II, III	D	6950401	POSINTDNON
VIOLATION OF UNIFORM CONTROLLED SUBSTANCES ACT POSS WITH INTENT TO DELIVER MARIJUANA or OTHER NONNARCOTIC Sch I, II, III	D	6950401	POSINTDNON
VIOLATION OF UNIFORM CONTROLLED SUBSTANCES ACT- NARCOTIC, METHAMPHETAMINE OR FLUNITRAZEPAM SALE ATTEMPTED	B+	695040A	SALENARC
VIOLATION OF UNIFORM CONTROLLED SUBSTANCES ACT- NARCOTIC, METHAMPHETAMINE OR FLUNITRAZEPAM SALE CONSPIRACY	B+	695040A	SALENARC
VIOLATION OF UNIFORM CONTROLLED SUBSTANCES ACT- NARCOTIC, METHAMPHETAMINE OR FLUNITRAZEPAM SALE SOLICITATION	B+	695040A	SALENARC
VIOLATION OF UNIFORM CONTROLLED SUBSTANCES ACT--NARCOTIC, METHAMPHETAMINE OR FLUNITRAZEPAM SALE	B+	695040A	SALENARC
VIOLATION OF UNIFORM CONTROLLED SUBSTANCES ACT--NARCOTIC, METHAMPHETAMINE, OR FLUNITRAZEPAM COUNTERFEIT SUBSTANCE	B	695040C	COUNTNARC
VIOLATION OF UNIFORM CONTROLLED SUBSTANCES ACT--NARCOTIC, METHAMPHETAMINE, OR FLUNITRAZEPAM POSS WITH INTENT TO DELIVER	B+	695040A	POSINTDEL
VIOLATION OF UNIFORM CONTROLLED SUBSTANCES ACT--NONNARCOTIC COUNTERFEIT SUBSTANCE	C	695040D	COUNTNNARC
VIOLATION OF UNIFORM CONTROLLED SUBSTANCES ACT--NONNARCOTIC COUNTERFEIT SUBSTANCE ATTEMPT	D	695040D	COUNTNNARC
VIOLATION OF UNIFORM CONTROLLED SUBSTANCES ACT--NONNARCOTIC COUNTERFEIT SUBSTANCE CONSPIRACY	D	695040D	COUNTNNARC
VIOLATION OF UNIFORM CONTROLLED SUBSTANCES ACT--NONNARCOTIC COUNTERFEIT SUBSTANCE SOLICITATION	D	695040D	COUNTNNARC
VIOLATION OF UNIFORM CONTROLLED SUBSTANCES ACT--NONNARCOTIC SALE	C	695040B	SALENNARC
VIOLATION OF UNIFORM CONTROLLED SUBSTANCES ACT--POSSESSION OF A CONTROLLED SUBSTANCE	C	6950401	POSCONTSUB

OFFENSE TITLE	CATEGORY	RCW	JRA CODE
VIOLATION OF UNIFORM CONTROLLED SUBSTANCES ACT--POSSESSION OF A CONTROLLED SUBSTANCE ATTEMPT	C	6950401	POSCONTSUB
VIOLATION OF UNIFORM CONTROLLED SUBSTANCES ACT--POSSESSION OF A CONTROLLED SUBSTANCE CONSPIRACY	C	6950401	POSCONTSUB
VIOLATION OF UNIFORM CONTROLLED SUBSTANCES ACT--POSSESSION OF A CONTROLLED SUBSTANCE SOLICITATION	C	6950401	POSCONTSUB
VIOLATION OF UNIFORM CONTROLLED SUBSTANCES ACT--SALE OF SUBSTITUTE SUBSTANCE	C	695040E	SALESUBSUB
VOYEURISM	C	9A44115	VOYEURISM
VOYEURISM ATTEMPT	D	9A44115	VOYEURISM
VOYEURISM CONSPIRACY	D	9A44115	VOYEURISM
VOYEURISM SOLICTATION	D	9A44115	VOYEURISM
WEAPON WITHOUT A PERMIT	E	941050	WEAPONWOP
WEAPONS APPARENTLY CAPABLE OF PRODUCING BODILY HARM	D	941270	WEAPONCBH
WEAPONS APPARENTLY CAPABLE OF PRODUCING BODILY HARM ATTEMPTED	E	941270	WEAPONCBH
WEAPONS APPARENTLY CAPABLE OF PRODUCING BODILY HARM CONSPIRACY	E	941270	WEAPONCBH
WEAPONS APPARENTLY CAPABLE OF PRODUCING BODILY HARM SOLICITATION	E	941270	WEAPONCBH

APPENDIX C

Note: Appendix C provides a list of JRA offenses code as a courtesy. These codes are used by JRA in its client tracking system. New codes are added as needed by JRA.

APPENDIX C: JRA OFFENSE CODES BY OFFENSE CATEGORY

OFFENSE TITLE	CATEGORY	RCW	JRA CODE
CATEGORY A+			
MURDER 1	A+	9A32030	MURDER1
MURDER 2	A+	9A32050	MURDER2
CATEGORY A			
ARSON 1	A	9A48020	ARSON1
ASSAULT 1	A	9A36011	ASSAULT1
ASSAULT 2 WITH SM	A	9A36021	ASSAULT2SM
ASSAULT OF CHILD 1	A	9A36120	ASSAULTCH1
HOMICIDE BY WATERCRAFT, BY DISREGARD FOR THE SAFETY OF OTHERS	A	79A6050	HOMICIDEWD
HOMICIDE BY WATERCRAFT, OPERATING ANY VESSEL IN A RECKLESS MANNER	A	79A605A	HOMICIDEWR
HOMICIDE BY WATERCRAFT, WHILE UNDER THE INFLUENCE OF INTOXICATING LIQUOR OR ANY DRUG	A	79A605B	HOMICIDEWI
KIDNAP 1	A	9A40020	KIDNAP1
MURDER 1 ATTEMPT	A	9A32030	MURDER1
MURDER 1 CONSPIRACY	A	9A32030	MURDER1
MURDER 1 SOLICITATION	A	9A32030	MURDER1
OTHER A OFFENSE	A	1340357	OTHERAOFF
POSSESSION OF EXPLOSIVE DEVICES	A	7074180	POSEXPDEV
POSSESSION OF INCENDIARY DEVICE	A	940120	POSINCEND
PROMOTING COMMERCIAL SEXUAL ABUSE OF A MINOR	A	968A101	PRSEXABSMI
RAPE 1	A	9A44040	RAPE1
ROBBERY 1	A	9A56200	ROBBERY1
ROBBERY 1 ACCOMPLICE	A	9A08020	ROB1ACC
TRAFFICKING (HUMAN) 2 DEGREE	A	9A40100	TRAFFIKNG2
CATEGORY A-			
CHILD MOLESTATION 1	A-	9A44083	CHILDMOL1
RAPE 2	A-	9A44050	RAPE2
RAPE OF A CHILD 1	A-	9A44073	RAPECHILD1
CATEGORY B+			
ARSON 1 ATTEMPT	B+	9A48020	ARSON1
ARSON 1 CONSPIRACY	B+	9A48020	ARSON1
ARSON 1 SOLICITATION	B+	9A48020	ARSON1
ASSAULT 1 ATTEMPT	B+	9A36011	ASSAULT1
ASSAULT 1 CONSPIRACY	B+	9A36011	ASSAULT1
ASSAULT 1 SOLICITATION	B+	9A36011	ASSAULT1

OFFENSE TITLE	CATEGORY	RCW	JRA CODE
ASSAULT 2	B+	9A36021	ASSAULT2
ASSAULT 2 ACCOMPLICE	B+	9A36021	ASSAULT2AC
ASSAULT 2 WITH SM ATTEMPT	B+	9A36021	ASSAULT2SM
ASSAULT 2 WITH SM CONSPIRACY	B+	9A36021	ASSAULT2SM
ASSAULT 2 WITH SM SOLICITATION	B+	9A36021	ASSAULT2SM
BURGLARY 1	B+	9A52020	BURG1
CHILD MOLESTATION 1 ATTEMPT	B+	9A44083	CHILDMOL1
CHILD MOLESTATION 1 CONSPIRACY	B+	9A44083	CHILDMOL1
CHILD MOLESTATION 1 SOLICITATION	B+	9A44083	CHILDMOL1
DRIVE BY SHOOTING	B+	9A36045	DBSHOOTING
DUTY TO ATTENDED VEHICLE OR OTHER PROPERTY IN CASE OF DEATH	B+	4652020	DUTYDEATH
EXTORTION 1	B+	9A56120	EXTORTION1
HIT-RUN DEATH	B+	4652022	HITRUNDE
INDECENT LIBERTIES WITH FORCIBLE COMPULSION	B+	9A44100	INDLIBFC
INDECENT LIBERTIES WITHOUT FORCIBLE COMPULSION	B+	9A44100	INDLIB
INTIMIDATING A PUBLIC SERVANT	B+	9A76180	INTPUBSERV
INTIMIDATING WITNESS	B+	9A72110	INTWITNESS
KIDNAP 1 ATTEMPT	B+	9A40020	KIDNAP1
KIDNAP 1 CONSPIRACY	B+	9A40020	KIDNAP1
KIDNAP 1 SOLICITATION	B+	9A40020	KIDNAP1
KIDNAP 2	B+	9A40030	KIDNAP2
MANSLAUGHTER 1	B+	9A32060	MANSL1
MURDER 2 ATTEMPT	B+	9A32050	MURDER2
MURDER 2 CONSPIRACY	B+	9A32050	MURDER2
MURDER 2 SOLICITATION	B+	9A32050	MURDER2
OTHER A OFFENSE ATTEMPT	B+	1340357	OTHERAOFF
OTHER A OFFENSE CONSPIRACY	B+	1340357	OTHERAOFF
OTHER A OFFENSE SOLICITATION	B+	1340357	OTHERAOFF
OTHER B+OFFENSE	B+	1340357	OTHERB+OFF
POSSESSION OF EXPLOSIVE DEVICES ATTEMPT	B+	7074180	POSEXPDEV
POSSESSION OF EXPLOSIVE DEVICES CONSPIRACY	B+	7074180	POSEXPDEV
POSSESSION OF EXPLOSIVE DEVICES SOLICITATION	B+	7074180	POSEXPDEV
POSSESSION OF INCENDIARY DEVICE ATTEMPT	B+	940120	POSINCEND
POSSESSION OF INCENDIARY DEVICE CONSPIRACY	B+	940120	POSINCEND
POSSESSION OF INCENDIARY SOLICITATION	B+	940120	POSINCEND
PROMOTING PROSTITUTION 1	B+	9A88070	PROPROST1
RAPE 1 ATTEMPT	B+	9A44040	RAPE1
RAPE 1 CONSPIRACY	B+	9A44040	RAPE1
RAPE 1 SOLICITATION	B+	9A44040	RAPE1
RAPE 2 ATTEMPT	B+	9A44050	RAPE2
RAPE 2 CONSPIRACY	B+	9A44050	RAPE2
RAPE 2 SOLICITATION	B+	9A44050	RAPE2
RAPE OF A CHILD 1 ATTEMPT	B+	9A44073	RAPECHILD1
RAPE OF A CHILD 1 CONSPIRACY	B+	9A44073	RAPECHILD1
RAPE OF A CHILD 1 SOLICITATION	B+	9A44073	RAPECHILD1

OFFENSE TITLE	CATEGORY	RCW	JRA CODE
RAPE OF A CHILD 2	B+	9A44076	RAPECHILD2
ROBBERY 1 ATTEMPT	B+	9A56200	ROBBERY1
ROBBERY 1 CONSPIRACY	B+	9A56200	ROBBERY1
ROBBERY 1 SOLICITATION	B+	9A56200	ROBBERY1
ROBBERY 2	B+	9A56210	ROBBERY2
VEHICULAR HOMICDE NOT VIOLENT (Must be on Court Order)	B+	4661520	VEHHOMICNV
VEHICULAR HOMICIDE	B+	4661520	VEHHOMICID
VIOLATION OF UNIFORM CONTROLLED SUBSTANCES ACT- NARCOTIC, METHAMPHETAMINE OR FLUNITRAZEPAM SALE ATTEMPTED	B+	695040A	SALENARC
VIOLATION OF UNIFORM CONTROLLED SUBSTANCES ACT- NARCOTIC, METHAMPHETAMINE OR FLUNITRAZEPAM SALE CONSPIRACY	B+	695040A	SALENARC
VIOLATION OF UNIFORM CONTROLLED SUBSTANCES ACT- NARCOTIC, METHAMPHETAMINE OR FLUNITRAZEPAM SALE SOLICITATION	B+	695040A	SALENARC
VIOLATION OF UNIFORM CONTROLLED SUBSTANCES ACT--NARCOTIC, METHAMPHETAMINE OR FLUNITRAZEPAM SALE	B+	695040A	SALENARC
VIOLATION OF UNIFORM CONTROLLED SUBSTANCES ACT--NARCOTIC, METHAMPHETAMINE, OR FLUNITRAZEPAM POSS WITH INTENT TO DELIVER	B+	695040A	POSINTDEL
CATEGORY B			
ANIMAL CRUELTY 1	B	1652205	ANIMCRUEL1
ARSON 2	B	9A48030	ARSON2
ASSAULT BY WATERCRAFT	B	79A6060	ASSAULTWC
ASSAULT OF CHILD 1 ATTEMPT	B	9A36120	ASSAULTCH1
ASSAULT OF CHILD 1 CONSPIRACY	B	9A36120	ASSAULTCH1
ASSAULT OF CHILD 1 SOLICITATION	B	9A36120	ASSAULTCH1
ASSAULT OF CHILD 2	B	9A36130	ASSAULTCH2
BOMB THREAT	B	961160	BOMBTHREAT
BURGLARY 2	B	9A52030	BURG2
CHILD MOLESTATION 2	B	9A44086	CHILDMOL2
COMMERCIAL SEXUAL ABUSE OF A MINOR	B	968A100	SEXABUSEMI
CONTROLLED SUBSTANCES HOMICIDE	B	6950415	HOMICIDECS
DEALING IN DEPICTIONS OF MINOR ENGAGED IN SEXUALLY EXPLICIT CONDUCT 1	B	968A050	DELCHPORN1
FAIL TO REGISTER AS A SEX OFFENDER TWO OR MORE PRIOR OCCASIONS	B	9A44132	FAILREGSx3
HOMICIDE BY WATERCRAFT, BY DISREGARD FOR THE SAFETY OF OTHERS ATTEMPT	B	79A6050	HOMICIDEWD
HOMICIDE BY WATERCRAFT, BY DISREGARD FOR THE SAFETY OF OTHERS CONSPIRACY	B	79A6050	HOMICIDEWD
HOMICIDE BY WATERCRAFT, BY DISREGARD FOR THE SAFETY OF OTHERS SOLICITATION	B	79A6050	HOMICIDEWD

OFFENSE TITLE	CATEGORY	RCW	JRA CODE
HOMICIDE BY WATERCRAFT, OPERATING ANY VESSEL IN A RECKLESS MANNER ATTEMPT	B	79A605A	HOMICIDEWR
HOMICIDE BY WATERCRAFT, OPERATING ANY VESSEL IN A RECKLESS MANNER CONSPIRACY	B	79A605A	HOMICIDEWR
HOMICIDE BY WATERCRAFT, OPERATING ANY VESSEL IN A RECKLESS MANNER SOLICITATION	B	79A605A	HOMICIDEWR
HOMICIDE BY WATERCRAFT, WHILE UNDER THE INFLUENCE OF INTOXICATING LIQUOR OR ANY DRUG ATTEMPT	B	79A605B	HOMICIDEWI
HOMICIDE BY WATERCRAFT, WHILE UNDER THE INFLUENCE OF INTOXICATING LIQUOR OR ANY DRUG CONSPIRACY	B	79A605B	HOMICIDEWI
HOMICIDE BY WATERCRAFT, WHILE UNDER THE INFLUENCE OF INTOXICATING LIQUOR OR ANY DRUG SOLICITATION	B	79A605B	HOMICIDEWI
INCEST 1	B	9A64020	INCEST1
INTRODUCING CONTRABAND 1	B	9A76140	INTCONT1
MALICIOUS MISCHIEF 1	B	9A48070	MALMIS1
ORGANIZED RETAIL THEFT 1	B	9A56350	THEFT1ORG
OTHER B OFFENSE	B	1340357	OTHERBOFF
POSSESSION OF A STOLEN VEHICLE	B	9A56068	POSSTOLVEH
POSSESSION OF DEPICTIONS OF MINOR ENGAGED IN SEXUALLY EXPLICIT CONDUCT 1	B	968A070	POSCHPORN1
POSSESSION OF STOLEN FIREARM	B	9A56310	PSFIREARM
POSSESSION OF STOLEN PROPERTY 1	B	9A56150	PSP1
POSSESSION OF WEAPONS BY PRISONER STATE FACILITY	B	994040	POSWEAPONB
PROMOTING COMMERCIAL SEXUAL ABUSE OF A MINOR ATTEMPTED	B	968A101	PRSEXABSMI
PROMOTING COMMERCIAL SEXUAL ABUSE OF A MINOR CONSPIRACY	B	968A101	PRSEXABSMI
PROMOTING COMMERCIAL SEXUAL ABUSE OF A MINOR SOLICITATION	B	968A101	PRSEXABSMI
RENDERING CRIMINAL ASSISTANCE 1	B	9A76070	RENDCRIM
RESIDENTIAL BURGLARY	B	9A52025	BURGRES
RETAIL THEFT WITH EXTENUATING CIRCUMSTANCES 1	B	9A56360	THEFT1RET
SENDING, BRINGING INTO STATE DEPICTIONS OF MINOR ENGAGED IN SEXUALLY EXPLICIT CONDUCT 1	B	968A060	SBCHPORN1
SEXUAL EXPLOITATION OF A MINOR	B	968A040	SEXEXPLMNR
TAKING MOTOR VEHICLE WITHOUT OWNERS PERMISSION	B	9A56070	TAMVWOOP1
THEFT 1	B	9A56030	THEFT1
THEFT OF A MOTOR VEHICLE	B	9A56030	THEFTVEH
THEFT OF FIREARM	B	9A56300	THEFTFIREA
THEFT OF LIVESTOCK	B	9A56080	THEFTLIVES
THEFT OF STOLEN FIREARM	B	9A56300	THEFTSTFIR

OFFENSE TITLE	CATEGORY	RCW	JRA CODE
TRAFFICKING (HUMAN) 2 DEGREE ATTEMPT	B	9A40100	TRAFFIKNG2
TRAFFICKING (HUMAN) 2 DEGREE CONSPIRACY	B	9A40100	TRAFFIKNG2
TRAFFICKING (HUMAN) 2 DEGREE SOLICITATION	B	9A40100	TRAFFIKNG2
TRAFFICKING IN STOLEN PROPERTY 1 DEGREE	B	9A82050	TRAFSTPRO1
UNLAWFUL POSSESSION OF FIREARM 1	B	941041	PFIREARM1
VIEWING DEPICTIONS OF MINOR ENGAGED IN SEXUALLY EXPLICIT CONDUCT 1	B	968A075	VIEWCHPRN1
VIOLATION OF UNIFORM CONTROLLED SUBSTANCES ACT--NARCOTIC, METHAMPHETAMINE, OR FLUNITRAZEPAM COUNTERFEIT SUBSTANCE	B	695040C	COUNTNARC
CATEGORY C+			
ASSAULT 2 ACCOMPLICE ATTEMPTED	C+	9A36021	ASSAULT2AC
ASSAULT 2 ACCOMPLICE CONSPIRACY	C+	9A36021	ASSAULT2AC
ASSAULT 2 ACCOMPLICE SOLICITATION	C+	9A36021	ASSAULT2AC
ASSAULT 2 ATTEMPT	C+	9A36021	ASSAULT2
ASSAULT 2 CONSPIRACY	C+	9A36021	ASSAULT2
ASSAULT 2 SOLICITATION	C+	9A36021	ASSAULT2
ASSAULT 3	C+	9A36031	ASSAULT3
BURGLARY 1 ATTEMPT	C+	9A52020	BURG1
BURGLARY 1 CONSPIRACY	C+	9A52020	BURG1
BURGLARY 1 SOLICITATION	C+	9A52020	BURG1
CHILD MOLESTATION 2 ATTEMPT	C+	9A44086	CHILDMOL2
CHILD MOLESTATION 2 CONSPIRACY	C+	9A44086	CHILDMOL2
CHILD MOLESTATION 2 SOLICITATION	C+	9A44086	CHILDMOL2
CUSTODIAL ASSAULT	C+	9A36100	CUSASSAULT
DRIVE BY SHOOTING ATTEMPT	C+	9A36045	DBSHOOTING
DRIVE BY SHOOTING CONSPIRACY	C+	9A36045	DBSHOOTING
DRIVE BY SHOOTING SOLICITATION	C+	9A36045	DBSHOOTING
EXTORTION 1 ATTEMPT	C+	9A56120	EXTORTION1
EXTORTION 1 CONSPIRACY	C+	9A56120	EXTORTION1
EXTORTION 1 SOLICITATION	C+	9A56120	EXTORTION1
EXTORTION 2	C+	9A56130	EXTORTION2
HIT-RUN DEATH ATTEMPT	C+	4652022	HITRUNDE
HIT-RUN DEATH CONSPIRACY	C+	4652022	HITRUNDE
HIT-RUN DEATH SOLICITATION	C+	4652022	HITRUNDE
INDECENT LIBERTIES WITH FORCIBLE COMPULSION ATTEMPT	C+	9A44100	INDLIBFC
INDECENT LIBERTIES WITH FORCIBLE COMPULSION CONSPIRACY	C+	9A44100	INDLIBFC
INDECENT LIBERTIES WITH FORCIBLE COMPULSION SOLICITATION	C+	9A44100	INDLIBFC
INDECENT LIBERTIES WITHOUT FORCIBLE COMPULSION ATTEMPT	C+	9A44100	INDLIB
INDECENT LIBERTIES WITHOUT FORCIBLE COMPULSION CONSPIRACY	C+	9A44100	INDLIB
INDECENT LIBERTIES WITHOUT FORCIBLE COMPULSION SOLICITATION	C+	NULL	INDLIBWOC

OFFENSE TITLE	CATEGORY	RCW	JRA CODE
INTIMIDATING A PUBLIC SERVANT ATTEMPT	C+	9A76180	INTPUBSERV
INTIMIDATING A PUBLIC SERVANT CONSPIRACY	C+	9A76180	INTPUBSERV
INTIMIDATING A PUBLIC SERVANT SOLICITATION	C+	9A76180	INTPUBSERV
INTIMIDATING WITNESS ATTEMPT	C+	9A72110	INTWITNESS
INTIMIDATING WITNESS CONSPIRACY	C+	9A72110	INTWITNESS
INTIMIDATING WITNESS SOLICITATION	C+	9A72110	INTWITNESS
KIDNAP 2 ATTEMPT	C+	9A40030	KIDNAP2
KIDNAP 2 CONSPIRACY	C+	9A40030	KIDNAP2
KIDNAP 2 SOLICITATION	C+	9A40030	KIDNAP2
LEGEND DRUG WITH INTENT TO DELIVER	C+	694103A	LEGDRUGSAL
MANSLAUGHTER 1 ATTEMPT	C+	9A32060	MANSL1
MANSLAUGHTER 1 CONSPIRACY	C+	9A32060	MANSL1
MANSLAUGHTER 1 SOLICITATION	C+	9A32060	MANSL1
MANSLAUGHTER 2	C+	9A32070	MANSL2
OTHER B+OFFENSE ATTEMPT	C+	1340357	OTHERB+OFF
OTHER B+OFFENSE CONSPIRACY	C+	1340357	OTHERB+OFF
OTHER B+OFFENSE SOLICITATION	C+	1340357	OTHERB+OFF
OTHER C+OFFENSE	C+	1340357	OTHERC+OFF
PROMOTE SUICIDE	C+	9A36060	PROSUICIDE
PROMOTING PROSTITUTION 1 ATTEMPT	C+	9A88070	PROPROST1
PROMOTING PROSTITUTION 1 CONSPIRACY	C+	9A88070	PROPROST1
PROMOTING PROSTITUTION 1 SOLICITATION	C+	9A88070	PROPROST1
PROMOTING PROSTITUTION 2	C+	9A88080	PROPROST2
RAPE 3	C+	9A44060	RAPE3
RAPE OF A CHILD 2 ATTEMPT	C+	9A44076	RAPECHILD2
RAPE OF A CHILD 2 CONSPIRACY	C+	9A44076	RAPECHILD2
RAPE OF A CHILD 2 SOLICITATION	C+	NULL	RAPECHILC2
RIOT WITH WEAPON	C+	9A8401W	RIOTWWEAP
ROBBERY 2 ATTEMPT	C+	9A56210	ROBBERY2
ROBBERY 2 CONSPIRACY	C+	9A56210	ROBBERY2
ROBBERY 2 SOLICITATION	C+	9A56210	ROBBERY2
SALE OF CONTROL SUBSTANCE FOR PROFIT	C+	6950410	SALECONSUB
UNLAWFUL IMPRISONMENT	C+	9A40040	UNLAWIMPRI
VEHICULAR HOMICDE NOT VIOLENT ATTEMPT	C+	4661520	VEHHOMICNV
VEHICULAR HOMICDE NOT VIOLENT CONSPIRACY	C+	4661520	VEHHOMICNV
VEHICULAR HOMICDE NOT VIOLENT SOLICITATION	C+	4661520	VEHHOMICNV
VEHICULAR HOMICDE SOLICITATION	C+	4661520	VEHHOMICID
VEHICULAR HOMICIDE ATTEMPT	C+	4661520	VEHHOMICID
VEHICULAR HOMICIDE CONSPIRACY	C+	4661520	VEHHOMICID
CATEGORY C			
ALIEN POSSESSION OF FIREARMS	C	941171	POSFIRARMA
ARSON 2 ATTEMPT	C	9A48030	ARSON2
ARSON 2 CONSPIRACY	C	9A48030	ARSON2
ARSON 2 SOLICITATION	C	9A48030	ARSON2
ASSAULT BY WATERCRAFT ATTEMPT	C	79A6060	ASSAULTWC
ASSAULT BY WATERCRAFT CONSPIRACY	C	79A6060	ASSAULTWC
ASSAULT BY WATERCRAFT SOLICITATION	C	79A6060	ASSAULTWC

The Caseload Forecast Council is not liable for errors or omissions in the manual, for sentences that may be inappropriately calculated as a result of a practitioner's or court's reliance on the manual, or for any other written or verbal information related to adult or juvenile sentencing. The scoring sheets are intended to provide assistance in most cases but does not cover all permutations of the scoring rules. If you find any errors or omissions, we encourage you to report them to the Caseload Forecast Council.

OFFENSE TITLE	CATEGORY	RCW	JRA CODE
ASSAULT OF CHILD 2 ATTEMPT	C	9A36130	ASSAULTCH2
ASSAULT OF CHILD 2 CONSPIRACY	C	9A36130	ASSAULTCH2
ASSAULT OF CHILD 2 SOLICITATION	C	9A36130	ASSAULTCH2
ATTEMPTING TO ELUDE A POLICE VEHICLE	C	4661024	ELUDEPV
BOMB THREAT ATTEMPT	C	961160	BOMBTHREAT
BOMB THREAT CONSPIRACY	C	961160	BOMBTHREAT
BOMB THREAT SOLICITATION	C	961160	BOMBTHREAT
BURGLARY 2 ATTEMPT	C	9A52030	BURG2
BURGLARY 2 CONSPIRACY	C	9A52030	BURG2
BURGLARY 2 SOLICITATION	C	9A52030	BURG2
CHILD MOLESTATION 3	C	9A44089	CHILDMOL3
COMMERCIAL SEXUAL ABUSE OF A MINOR ATTEMPTED	C	968A100	SEXABUSEMI
COMMERCIAL SEXUAL ABUSE OF A MINOR CONSPIRACY	C	968A100	SEXABUSEMI
COMMERCIAL SEXUAL ABUSE OF A MINOR SOLICITATION	C	968A100	SEXABUSEMI
COMMUNICATING WITH A MINOR FOR IMMORAL PURPOSE - SUBSEQUENT SEX OFFENSE	C	968A090	COMMINORSS
CONTROLLED SUBSTANCES HOMICIDE ATTEMPT	C	6950415	HOMICIDECS
CONTROLLED SUBSTANCES HOMICIDE CONSPIRACY	C	6950415	HOMICIDECS
CONTROLLED SUBSTANCES HOMICIDE SOLICITATION	C	6950415	HOMICIDECS
CRIMINAL IMPERSONATION 1	C	9A60040	IMPERSON1
CUSTODIAL INTERFERENCE 1	C	9A40060	CUSINTER1
CUSTODIAL INTERFERENCE 2 SUBSEQUENT	C	9A40070	CUSINTER2S
CYBERSTALKING C FELONY W PREVIOUS HARASSMENT	C	961260	CYBSTALKC
DEALING IN DEPICTIONS OF MINOR ENGAGED IN SEXUALLY EXPLICIT CONDUCT 1 ATTEMPT	C	968A050	DELCHPORN1
DEALING IN DEPICTIONS OF MINOR ENGAGED IN SEXUALLY EXPLICIT CONDUCT 1 CONSPIRACY	C	968A050	DELCHPORN1
DEALING IN DEPICTIONS OF MINOR ENGAGED IN SEXUALLY EXPLICIT CONDUCT 1 SOLICITATION	C	968A050	DELCHPORN1
DEALING IN DEPICTIONS OF MINOR ENGAGED IN SEXUALLY EXPLICIT CONDUCT 2	C	968A050	DELCHPORN2
DISARMING LAW ENFORCEMENT OFFICER	C	9A76023	DISLAWOFF
DUTY TO ATTENDED VEHICLE OR OTHER PROPERTY IN CASE OF DEATH ATTEMPT	C	4652020	DUTYDEATH
DUTY TO ATTENDED VEHICLE OR OTHER PROPERTY IN CASE OF DEATH CONSPIRACY	C	4652020	DUTYDEATH
DUTY TO ATTENDED VEHICLE OR OTHER PROPERTY IN CASE OF DEATH SOLICITATION	C	4652020	DUTYDEATH
DUTY TO ATTENDED VEHICLE OR OTHER PROPERTY IN CASE OF INJURY	C	4652020	DUTYINJ
ESCAPE 1	C	9A76110	ESCAPE1
ESCAPE 1 ATTEMPT	C	9A76110	ESCAPE1
ESCAPE 1 CONSPIRACY	C	9A76110	ESCAPE1

OFFENSE TITLE	CATEGORY	RCW	JRA CODE
ESCAPE 1 SOLICITATION	C	9A76110	ESCAPE1
ESCAPE 2	C	9A76120	ESCAPE2
ESCAPE 2 ATTEMPT	C	9A76120	ESCAPE2
ESCAPE 2 CONSPIRACY	C	9A76120	ESCAPE2
ESCAPE 2 SOLICITATION	C	9A76120	ESCAPE2
FAIL TO REGISTER AS A KIDNAPPER	C	9A44132	FAILREGK
FAIL TO REGISTER AS A SEX OFFENDER	C	9A44132	FAILREGS
FORGERY	C	9A60020	FORGERY
FRAUDULENTLY OBTAINING CONTROLLED SUBSTANCE	C	6950401	FRAUDOBTCS
HARASSMENT - MALICIOUS Disc against race,color,relig,ance,nat.origin,gender,sexualorient,ment,phys,or sensory handicap	C	9A36080	HARASSMAL
HARASSMENT - WITH THREAT TO KILL	C	9A46020	HARASTHRTC
HARASSMENT SAME VICTIM OR VICTIMS FAMILY	C	9A46020	HARASSC
HIT-RUN INJURY	C	4652021	HITRUNIN
IDENTITY THEFT 1	C	9350200	IDENTITY1
INCEST 1 ATTEMPT	C	9A64020	INCEST1
INCEST 1 CONSPIRACY	C	9A64020	INCEST1
INCEST 1 SOLICITATION	C	9A64020	INCEST1
INCEST 2	C	9A64020	INCEST2
INDECENT EXPOSURE (VICTIM <14) REPEAT	C	9A8801D	INDEXP<14R
INDECENT EXPOSURE (VICTIM 14+) REPEAT	C	9A88010	INDEXP14+R
INTRODUCING CONTRABAND 1 ATTEMPT	C	9A76140	INTCONT1
INTRODUCING CONTRABAND 1 CONSPIRACY	C	9A76140	INTCONT1
INTRODUCING CONTRABAND 1 SOLICITATION	C	9A76140	INTCONT1
INTRODUCING CONTRABAND 2	C	9A76150	INTCONT2
LICENSE REQUIRED TO MANUFACTURE, PURCHASE, SELL, USE, POSSESS, TRANSPORT, OR STORE EXPLOSIVES	C	7074022	EXPLLICREQ
MAINTAIN A DWELLING OR PLACE FOR CONTROLLED SUBSTANCE	C	6950402	MDCONTSUB
MALICIOUS MISCHIEF 1 ATTEMPT	C	9A48070	MALMIS1
MALICIOUS MISCHIEF 1 CONSPIRACY	C	9A48070	MALMIS1
MALICIOUS MISCHIEF 1 SOLICITATION	C	9A48070	MALMIS1
MALICIOUS MISCHIEF 2	C	9A48080	MALMIS2
OBTAIN LEGEND DRUG	C	6941020	OBTLEGDRUG
ORGANIZED RETAIL THEFT 1 ATTEMPTED	C	9A56350	THEFT1ORG
ORGANIZED RETAIL THEFT 1 CONSPIRACY	C	9A56350	THEFT1ORG
ORGANIZED RETAIL THEFT 1 SOLICITATION	C	9A56350	THEFT1ORG
ORGANIZED RETAIL THEFT 2	C	9A56350	THEFT2ORG
OTHER B OFFENSE ATTEMPT	C	1340357	OTHERBOFF
OTHER B OFFENSE CONSPIRACY	C	1340357	OTHERBOFF
OTHER B OFFENSE SOLICITATION	C	1340357	OTHERBOFF
OTHER C OFFENSE	C	1340357	OTHERCOFF
POSSESSION OF A STOLEN VEHICLE ATTEMPTED	C	9A56068	POSSTOLVEH

The Caseload Forecast Council is not liable for errors or omissions in the manual, for sentences that may be inappropriately calculated as a result of a practitioner's or court's reliance on the manual, or for any other written or verbal information related to adult or juvenile sentencing. The scoring sheets are intended to provide assistance in most cases but does not cover all permutations of the scoring rules. If you find any errors or omissions, we encourage you to report them to the Caseload Forecast Council.

OFFENSE TITLE	CATEGORY	RCW	JRA CODE
POSSESSION OF A STOLEN VEHICLE ATTEMPTED CONSPIRACY	C	9A56068	POSSTOLVEH
POSSESSION OF A STOLEN VEHICLE SOLICITATION	C	9A56068	POSSTOLVEH
POSSESSION OF DEPICTIONS OF MINOR ENGAGED IN SEXUALLY EXPLICIT CONDUCT	C	968A070	POSCHPORN2
POSSESSION OF DEPICTIONS OF MINOR ENGAGED IN SEXUALLY EXPLICIT CONDUCT 1 ATTEMPT	C	968A070	POSCHPORN1
POSSESSION OF DEPICTIONS OF MINOR ENGAGED IN SEXUALLY EXPLICIT CONDUCT 1 CONSPIRACY	C	968A070	POSCHPORN1
POSSESSION OF DEPICTIONS OF MINOR ENGAGED IN SEXUALLY EXPLICIT CONDUCT 1 SOLICITATION	C	968A070	POSCHPORN1
POSSESSION OF FIREARM BY MINOR (<18 YEARS)	C	941040	PFIREARMM
POSSESSION OF FIREARM BY MINOR (<18 YEARS) ATTEMPT	C	941040	PFIREARMM
POSSESSION OF FIREARM BY MINOR (<18 YEARS) CONSPIRACY	C	941040	PFIREARMM
POSSESSION OF FIREARM BY MINOR (<18 YEARS) SOLICITATION	C	941040	PFIREARMM
POSSESSION OF MACHINE GUN OR SHORT-BARRELED SHOTGUN OR RIFLE	C	941190	POSMACHGUN
POSSESSION OF STOLEN FIREARM ATTEMPT	C	9A56310	PSFIREARM
POSSESSION OF STOLEN FIREARM CONSPIRACY	C	9A56310	PSFIREARM
POSSESSION OF STOLEN FIREARM SOLICITATION	C	9A56310	PSFIREARM
POSSESSION OF STOLEN PROPERTY 1 ATTEMPT	C	9A56150	PSP1
POSSESSION OF STOLEN PROPERTY 1 CONSPIRACY	C	9A56150	PSP1
POSSESSION OF STOLEN PROPERTY 1 SOLICITATION	C	9A56150	PSP1
POSSESSION OF STOLEN PROPERTY 2	C	9A56160	PSP2
POSSESSION OF WEAPONS BY PRISONER COUNTY FACILITY	C	994040	POSWEAPONC
POSSESSION OF WEAPONS BY PRISONER STATE FACILITY ATTEMPTED	C	994040	POSWEAPONS
POSSESSION OF WEAPONS BY PRISONER STATE FACILITY CONSPIRACY	C	994040	POSWEAPONS
POSSESSION OF WEAPONS BY PRISONER STATE FACILITY SOLICITAITON	C	994040	POSWEAPONS
RAPE OF A CHILD 3	C	9A44079	RAPECHILD3
RECKLESS BURNING 1	C	9A48040	RECKBURN1
RENDERING CRIMINAL ASSISTANCE 1 ATTEMPT	C	9A76070	RENDCRIM
RENDERING CRIMINAL ASSISTANCE 1 CONSPIRACY	C	9A76070	RENDCRIM
RENDERING CRIMINAL ASSISTANCE 1 SOLICITATION	C	9A76070	RENDCRIM
RESIDENTIAL BURGLARY ATTEMPT	C	9A52025	BURGRES
RESIDENTIAL BURGLARY CONSPIRACY	C	9A52025	BURGRES
RESIDENTIAL BURGLARY SOLICITATION	C	9A52025	BURGRES
RETAIL THEFT WITH EXTENUATING CIRCUMSTANCES 1 ATTEMPTED	C	9A56360	THEFT1RET
RETAIL THEFT WITH EXTENUATING CIRCUMSTANCES 1 CONSPIRACY	C	9A56360	THEFT1RET

OFFENSE TITLE	CATEGORY	RCW	JRA CODE
RETAIL THEFT WITH EXTENUATING CIRCUMSTANCES 1 SOLICIATION	C	9A56360	THEFT1RET
RETAIL THEFT WITH EXTENUATING CIRCUMSTANCES 2	C	9A56360	THEFT2RET
RETAIL THEFT WITH EXTENUATING CIRCUMSTANCES 3	C	9A56360	THEFT3RET
SENDING, BRINGING INTO STATE DEPICTIONS OF MINOR ENGAGED IN SEXUALLY EXPLICIT CONDUCT 1 ATTEMPT	C	968A060	SBCHPORN1
SENDING, BRINGING INTO STATE DEPICTIONS OF MINOR ENGAGED IN SEXUALLY EXPLICIT CONDUCT 1 CONSPIRACY	C	968A060	SBCHPORN1
SENDING, BRINGING INTO STATE DEPICTIONS OF MINOR ENGAGED IN SEXUALLY EXPLICIT CONDUCT 1 SOLICITATION	C	968A060	SBCHPORN1
SENDING, BRINGING INTO STATE DEPICTIONS OF MINOR ENGAGED IN SEXUALLY EXPLICIT CONDUCT 2	C	968A060	SBCHPORN2
SEXUAL EXPLOITATION OF A MINOR ATTEMPT	C	968A040	SEXEXPLMNR
SEXUAL EXPLOITATION OF A MINOR CONSPIRACY	C	968A040	SEXEXPLMNR
SEXUAL EXPLOITATION OF A MINOR SOLICITATION	C	968A040	SEXEXPLMNR
SEXUAL VIOLATION OF HUMAN REMAINS	C	9A44105	SEXVIOLREM
STALKING (REPEAT)	C	9A46111	STALKREP
TAKING MOTOR VEHICLE WITHOUT OWNERS PERMISSION ATTEMPTED	C	9A56070	TAMVWOOP1
TAKING MOTOR VEHICLE WITHOUT OWNERS PERMISSION CONSPIRACY	C	9A56070	TAMVWOOP1
TAKING MOTOR VEHICLE WITHOUT OWNERS PERMISSON SOLICITATION	C	9A56070	TAMVWOOP1
TAKING MOTOR VEHICLE WITHOUT PERMISSION 2	C	9A56070	TAMVWOOP2
TAMPERING WITH A WITNESS	C	9A72120	TAMPWITN
THEFT 1 ATTEMPT	C	9A56030	THEFT1
THEFT 1 CONSPIRACY	C	9A56030	THEFT1
THEFT 1 SOLICITATION	C	9A56030	THEFT1
THEFT 2	C	9A56040	THEFT2
THEFT OF A MOTOR VEHICLE ATTEMPTED	C	9A56030	THEFTVEH
THEFT OF A MOTOR VEHICLE CONSPIRACY	C	9A56030	THEFTVEH
THEFT OF A MOTOR VEHICLE SOLICITATION	C	9A56030	THEFTVEH
THEFT OF FIREARM ATTEMPT	C	9A56300	THEFTFIREA
THEFT OF FIREARM CONSPIRACY	C	9A56300	THEFTFIREA
THEFT OF FIREARM SOLICITATION	C	9A56300	THEFTFIREA
THEFT OF LIVESTOCK ATTEMPT	C	9A56080	THEFTLIVES
THEFT OF LIVESTOCK CONSPIRACY	C	9A56080	THEFTLIVES
THEFT OF LIVESTOCK SOLICITATION	C	9A56080	THEFTLIVES
THEFT OF STOLEN FIREARM ATTEMPT	C	9A56300	THEFTSTFIR
THEFT OF STOLEN FIREARM CONSPIRACY	C	9A56300	THEFTSTFIR
THEFT OF STOLEN FIREARM SOLICITATION	C	9A56300	THEFTSTFIR
TRAFFICKING IN STOLEN PROPERTY 1 DEGREE ATTEM	C	9A82050	TRAFSTPRO1

OFFENSE TITLE	CATEGORY	RCW	JRA CODE
TRAFFICKING IN STOLEN PROPERTY 1 DEGREE CONSP	C	9A82050	TRAFSTPRO1
TRAFFICKING IN STOLEN PROPERTY 1 DEGREE SOLIC	C	9A82050	TRAFSTPRO1
TRAFFICKING IN STOLEN PROPERTY 2 DEGREE	C	9A82055	TRAFSTPRO2
UNLAWFUL POSSESSION OF FIREARM 1 ATTEMPT	C	941041	PFIREARM1
UNLAWFUL POSSESSION OF FIREARM 1 CONSPIRACY	C	941041	PFIREARM1
UNLAWFUL POSSESSION OF FIREARM 1 SOLICITATION	C	941041	PFIREARM1
UNLAWFUL POSSESSION OF FIREARM 2	C	941042	PFIREARM2
UNLAWFUL POSSESSION, PRODUCTION OF INSTRUMENT OF FINANCIAL FRAUD	C	9A56320	FRAUDFIN
VEHICLE PROWLING 1	C	9A52095	VEHPROWL1
VEHICULAR ASSAULT	C	4661522	VEHASSAULT
VIEWING DEPICTIONS OF MINOR ENGAGED IN SEXUALLY EXPLICIT CONDUCT 1 ATTEMPTED	C	968A075	VIEWCHPRN1
VIEWING DEPICTIONS OF MINOR ENGAGED IN SEXUALLY EXPLICIT CONDUCT 1 CONSIRACY	C	968A075	VIEWCHPRN1
VIEWING DEPICTIONS OF MINOR ENGAGED IN SEXUALLY EXPLICIT CONDUCT 1 SOLICITATION	C	968A075	VIEWCHPRN1
VIEWING DEPICTIONS OF MINOR ENGAGED IN SEXUALLY EXPLICIT CONDUCT 2	C	968A075	VIEWCHPRN2
VIOLATION OF PROTECTION ORDER	C	2650110	VIOLPO
VIOLATION OF SEXUAL ASSAULT PROTECTION ORDER	C	2650110	VIOLSEXAO
VIOLATION OF UNIFORM CONTROLLED SUBSTANCES ACT POSS WITH INTENT TO DELIVER MARIJUANA or OTHER NONNARCOTIC Sch I, II, III	C	6950401	POSINTDNON
VIOLATION OF UNIFORM CONTROLLED SUBSTANCES ACT--NONNARCOTIC COUNTERFEIT SUBSTANCE	C	695040D	COUNTNNARC
VIOLATION OF UNIFORM CONTROLLED SUBSTANCES ACT--NONNARCOTIC SALE	C	695040B	SALENNARC
VIOLATION OF UNIFORM CONTROLLED SUBSTANCES ACT--POSSESSION OF A CONTROLLED SUBSTANCE	C	6950401	POSCONTSUB
VIOLATION OF UNIFORM CONTROLLED SUBSTANCES ACT--POSSESSION OF A CONTROLLED SUBSTANCE ATTEMPT	C	6950401	POSCONTSUB
VIOLATION OF UNIFORM CONTROLLED SUBSTANCES ACT--POSSESSION OF A CONTROLLED SUBSTANCE CONSPIRACY	C	6950401	POSCONTSUB
VIOLATION OF UNIFORM CONTROLLED SUBSTANCES ACT--POSSESSION OF A CONTROLLED SUBSTANCE SOLICITATION	C	6950401	POSCONTSUB
VIOLATION OF UNIFORM CONTROLLED SUBSTANCES ACT--SALE OF SUBSTITUTE SUBSTANCE	C	695040E	SALESUBSUB
VOYEURISM	C	9A44115	VOYEURISM

OFFENSE TITLE	CATEGORY	RCW	JRA CODE
CATEGORY D+			
ASSAULT 3 ATTEMPT	D+	9A36031	ASSAULT3
ASSAULT 3 CONSPIRACY	D+	9A36031	ASSAULT3
ASSAULT 3 SOLICITATION	D+	9A36031	ASSAULT3
ASSAULT 4	D+	9A36041	ASSAULT4
COERCION	D+	9A36070	COERCION
CUSTODIAL ASSAULT ATTEMPT	D+	9A36100	CUSASSAULT
CUSTODIAL ASSAULT CONSPIRACY	D+	9A36100	CUSASSAULT
CUSTODIAL ASSAULT SOLICITATION	D+	9A36100	CUSASSAULT
DUTY TO ATTENDED VEHICLE OR OTHER PROPERTY IN CASE OF STRIKING BODY OF DECEASED	D+	4652020	DUTYBODY
EXTORTION 2 ATTEMPT	D+	9A56130	EXTORTION2
EXTORTION 2 CONSPIRACY	D+	9A56130	EXTORTION2
EXTORTION 2 SOLICITATION	D+	9A56130	EXTORTION2
INDECENT EXPOSURE (VICTIM <14)	D+	9A8801C	INDEXP<14
LEGEND DRUG WITH INTENET TO DELIVER SOLICITATION	D+	694103A	LEGDRUGSAL
LEGEND DRUG WITH INTENT TO DELIVER CONSPIRACY	D+	694103A	LEGDRUGSAL
LEGEND DRUG WITH INTENT TO DELLIVER ATTEMPT	D+	694103A	LEGDRUGSAL
MANSLAUGHTER 2 ATTEMPT	D+	9A32070	MANSL2
MANSLAUGHTER 2 CONSPIRACY	D+	9A32070	MANSL2
MANSLAUGHTER 2 SOLICITATION	D+	9A32070	MANSL2
OTHER C+OFFENSE ATTEMPT	D+	1340357	OTHERC+OFF
OTHER C+OFFENSE CONSPIRACY	D+	1340357	OTHERC+OFF
OTHER C+OFFENSE SOLICITATION	D+	1340357	OTHERC+OFF
OTHER D+OFFENSE	D+	1340357	OTHERD+OFF
POSSESSION OF DANGEROUS WEAPON	D+	941250	POSDANGW
PROMOTE SUICIDE ATTEMPT	D+	9A36060	PROSUICIDE
PROMOTE SUICIDE CONSPIRACY	D+	9A36060	PROSUICIDE
PROMOTE SUICIDE SOLICITATION	D+	9A36060	PROSUICIDE
PROMOTING PROSTITUTION 2 ATTEMPT	D+	9A88080	PROPROST2
PROMOTING PROSTITUTION 2 CONSPIRACY	D+	9A88080	PROPROST2
PROMOTING PROSTITUTION 2 SOLICITATION	D+	9A88080	PROPROST2
RAPE 3 ATTEMPT	D+	9A44060	RAPE3
RAPE 3 CONSPIRACY	D+	9A44060	RAPE3
RAPE 3 SOLICITATION	D+	9A44060	RAPE3
RECKLESS ENDANGER	D+	9A36050	RECKEND
RENDERING CRIMINAL ASSISTANCE 2	D+	9A76080	RENDCRIM2
RIOT WITH WEAPON ATTEMPT	D+	9A8401W	RIOTWWEAP
RIOT WITH WEAPON CONSPIRACY	D+	9A8401W	RIOTWWEAP
RIOT WITH WEAPON SOLICITATION	D+	9A8401W	RIOTWWEAP
RIOT WITHOUT WEAPON	D+	9A8401U	RIOTWOWEAP
UNLAWFUL IMPRISONMENT ATTEMPT	D+	9A40040	UNLAWIMPRI
UNLAWFUL IMPRISONMENT CONSPIRACY	D+	9A40040	UNLAWIMPRI
UNLAWFUL IMPRISONMENT SOLICITATION	D+	9A40040	UNLAWIMPRI
VIOLATION OF PROTECTION ORDER ATTEMPT	D+	2650110	VIOLPO

OFFENSE TITLE	CATEGORY	RCW	JRA CODE
VIOLATION OF PROTECTION ORDER CONSPIRACY	D+	2650110	VIOLPO
VIOLATION OF PROTECTION ORDER SOLICITATION	D+	2650110	VIOLPO
CATEGORY D			
AIMING OR DISCHARGING FIREARMS, DANGEROUS WEAPONS	D	941230	DANWEAPAD
ALIEN POSSESSION OF FIREARMS ATTEMPTED	D	941171	POSFIRARMA
ALIEN POSSESSION OF FIREARMS CONSPIRACY	D	941171	POSFIRARMA
ALIEN POSSESSION OF FIREARMS SOLICITATION	D	941171	POSFIRARMA
ANIMAL CRUELTY 1 ATTEMPT	D	1652205	ANIMCRUEL1
ANIMAL CRUELTY 1 CONSPIRACY	D	1652205	ANIMCRUEL1
ANIMAL CRUELTY 1 SOLICITATION	D	1652205	ANIMCRUEL1
ATTEMPTING TO ELUDE A POLICE VEHICLE ATTEMPT	D	4661024	ELUDEPV
ATTEMPTING TO ELUDE A POLICE VEHICLE CONSPIRACY	D	4661024	ELUDEPV
ATTEMPTING TO ELUDE A POLICE VEHICLE SOLICITATION	D	4661024	ELUDEPV
AUTO THEFT TOOLS (MAKING OR POSSESSING)	D	9A56063	AUTOTOOLS
BURG TOOLS (POSSESSION OF)	D	9A52060	BURGTOOLS
CARRY WEAPON TO SCHOOL	D	941280	CARWEAPSCH
CHILD MOLESTATION 3 ATTEMPTED	D	9A44089	CHILDMOL3
CHILD MOLESTATION 3 CONSPIRACY	D	9A44089	CHILDMOL3
CHILD MOLESTATION 3 SOLICITATION	D	9A44089	CHILDMOL3
COMMUNICATING WITH A MINOR FOR IMMORAL PURPOSE	D	968A090	COMMINOR
COMMUNICATING WITH A MINOR FOR IMMORAL PURPOSE - SUBSEQUENT SEX OFFENSE ATTEMPT	D	968A090	COMMINORSS
COMMUNICATING WITH A MINOR FOR IMMORAL PURPOSE - SUBSEQUENT SEX OFFENSE CONSPIRACY	D	968A090	COMMINORSS
COMMUNICATING WITH A MINOR FOR IMMORAL PURPOSE - SUBSEQUENT SEX OFFENSE SOLICITATION	D	968A090	COMMINORSS
CONTEMPT	D	721040	CONTEMPT
CRIMINAL IMPERSONATION 1 ATTEMPT	D	9A60040	IMPERSON1
CRIMINAL IMPERSONATION 1 CONSPIRACY	D	9A60040	IMPERSON1
CRIMINAL IMPERSONATION 1 SOLICITATION	D	9A60040	IMPERSON1
CRIMINAL IMPERSONATION 2	D+	9A60045	IMPERSON2
CRIMINAL TRESPASS 1	D	9A52070	CRIMTRES1
CUSTODIAL INTERFERENCE 1 ATTEMPT	D	9A40060	CUSINTER1
CUSTODIAL INTERFERENCE 1 CONSPIRACY	D	9A40060	CUSINTER1
CUSTODIAL INTERFERENCE 1 SOLICITATION	D	9A40060	CUSINTER1
CUSTODIAL INTERFERENCE 2	D	9A40070	CUSINTER2
CUSTODIAL INTERFERENCE 2 ATTEMPT	D	9A40070	CUSINTER2
CUSTODIAL INTERFERENCE 2 CONSPIRACY	D	9A40070	CUSINTER2
CUSTODIAL INTERFERENCE 2 SOLICITATION	D	9A40070	CUSINTER2
CUSTODIAL INTERFERENCE 2 SUBSEQUEENT SOLICITATION	D	9A40070	CUSINTER2S
CUSTODIAL INTERFERENCE 2 SUBSEQUENT ATTEMPT	D	9A40070	CUSINTER2S
CUSTODIAL INTERFERENCE 2 SUBSEQUENT	D	9A40070	CUSINTER2S

The Caseload Forecast Council is not liable for errors or omissions in the manual, for sentences that may be inappropriately calculated as a result of a practitioner's or court's reliance on the manual, or for any other written or verbal information related to adult or juvenile sentencing. The scoring sheets are intended to provide assistance in most cases but does not cover all permutations of the scoring rules. If you find any errors or omissions, we encourage you to report them to the Caseload Forecast Council.

OFFENSE TITLE	CATEGORY	RCW	JRA CODE
CONSPIRACY			
CYBERSTALKING	D	961260	CYBSTALK
CYBERSTALKING W PREVIOUS HARASSMENT ATTEMPTED	D	961260	CYBSTALK
CYBERSTALKING W PREVIOUS HARASSMENT CONSPIRACY	D	961260	CYBSTALK
CYBERSTALKING W PREVIOUS HARASSMENT SOLICITATION	D	961260	CYBSTALK
DEALING IN DEPICTIONS OF MINOR ENGAGED IN SEXUALLY EXPLICIT CONDUCT 2 ATTEMPT	D	968A050	DELCHPORN2
DEALING IN DEPICTIONS OF MINOR ENGAGED IN SEXUALLY EXPLICIT CONDUCT 2 CONSPIRACY	D	968A050	DELCHPORN2
DEALING IN DEPICTIONS OF MINOR ENGAGED IN SEXUALLY EXPLICIT CONDUCT 2 SOLICITATION	D	968A050	DELCHPORN2
DISARMING LAW ENFORCEMENT OFFICER ATTEMPTED	D	9A76023	DISLAWOFF
DISARMING LAW ENFORCEMENT OFFICER CONSPIRACY	D	9A76023	DISLAWOFF
DISARMING LAW ENFORCEMENT OFFICER SOLICITATION	D	9A76023	DISLAWOFF
DRIVING UNDER INFLUENCE	D	4661515	DUI
DRIVING WHILE LICENSE INVALIDATED	D	4620342	DWIL
DRIVING WHILE LICENSE INVALIDATED 2	D	4620342	DWIL2
DUTY TO ATTENDED VEHICLE OR OTHER PROPERTY IN CASE OF INJURY ATTEMPT	D	4652020	DUTYINJ
DUTY TO ATTENDED VEHICLE OR OTHER PROPERTY IN CASE OF INJURY CONSPIRACY	D	4652020	DUTYINJ
DUTY TO ATTENDED VEHICLE OR OTHER PROPERTY IN CASE OF INJURY SOLICITATION	D	4652020	DUTYINJ
ESCAPE 3	D	9A76130	ESCAPE3
FAIL TO REGISTER AS A KIDNAPPER ATTEMPT	D	9A44132	FAILREGK
FAIL TO REGISTER AS A KIDNAPPER CONSPIRACY	D	9A44132	FAILREGK
FAIL TO REGISTER AS A KIDNAPPER SOLICITATION	D	9A44132	FAILREGK
FAIL TO REGISTER AS A SEX OFFENDER ATTEMPT	D	9A44132	FAILREGS
FAIL TO REGISTER AS A SEX OFFENDER CONSPIRACY	D	9A44132	FAILREGS
FAIL TO REGISTER AS A SEX OFFENDER SOLICITATION	D	9A44132	FAILREGS
FALSE REPORTING	D	9A84040	FALSEREP
FORGERY ATTEMPT	D	9A60020	FORGERY
FORGERY CONSPIRACY	D	9A60020	FORGERY
FORGERY SOLICITATION	D	9A60020	FORGERY
HARASSMENT	D	9A46020	HARASSD
HARASSMENT - MALICIOUS Disc against race,color,relig,ance,nat.origin,gender,sexualorient,ment,phys,or sensory handicap	D	9A36080	HARASSMAL

OFFENSE TITLE	CATEGORY	RCW	JRA CODE
HARASSMENT - MALICIOUS Disc against race,color,relig,ance,nat.origin,gender,sexualorient,ment,phys,or sensory handicap	D	9A36080	HARASSMAL
HARASSMENT - MALICIOUS Disc against race,color,relig,ance,nat.origin,gender,sexualorient,ment,phys,or sensory handicap	D	9A36080	HARASSMAL
HARASSMENT SAME VICTIM OR VICTIMS FAMILY ATTEMPTED	D	9A46020	HARASSC
HARASSMENT SAME VICTIM OR VICTIMS FAMILY CONSPIRACY	D	9A46020	HARASSC
HARASSMENT SAME VICTIM OR VICTIMS FAMILY SOLICITATION	D	9A46020	HARASSC
HIT-RUN ATTENDED	D	4652022	HITRUNAT
HIT-RUN INJURY ATTEMPT	D	4652021	HITRUNIN
HIT-RUN INJURY CONSPIRACY	D	4652021	HITRUNIN
HIT-RUN INJURY SOLICITATION	D	4652021	HITRUNIN
IDENTITY THEFT 1 ATTEMPT	D	9350200	IDENTITY1
IDENTITY THEFT 1 CONSPIRACY	D	9350200	IDENTITY1
IDENTITY THEFT 1 SOLICITATION	D	9350200	IDENTITY1
IDENTITY THEFT 2	D	9350200	IDENTITY2
INCEST 2 ATTEMPT	D	9A64020	INCEST2
INCEST 2 CONSPIRACY	D	9A64020	INCEST2
INCEST 2 SOLICITATION	D	9A64020	INCEST2
INTERFERING WITH THE REPORTING OF DOMESTIC VIOLENCE	D	9A36150	DVREPINTER
INTIMIDATING ANOTHER PERSON BY USE OF A WEAPON	D	941270	INTWWEAPON
INTRODUCING CONTRABAND 2 ATTEMPT	D	9A76150	INTCONT2
INTRODUCING CONTRABAND 2 CONSPIRACY	D	9A76150	INTCONT2
INTRODUCING CONTRABAND 2 SOLICITATION	D	9A76150	INTCONT2
LICENSE REQUIRED TO MANUFACTURE, PURCHASE, SELL, USE, POSSESS, TRANSPORT, OR STORE EXPLOSIVES ATTEMPTED	D	7074022	EXPLLICREQ
LICENSE REQUIRED TO MANUFACTURE, PURCHASE, SELL, USE, POSSESS, TRANSPORT, OR STORE EXPLOSIVES CONSPIRACY	D	7074022	EXPLLICREQ
LICENSE REQUIRED TO MANUFACTURE, PURCHASE, SELL, USE, POSSESS, TRANSPORT, OR STORE EXPLOSIVES SOLICITATION	D	7074022	EXPLLICREQ
MAKING FALSE OR MISLEADING STATEMENTS TO A PUBLIC SERVANT	D	9A76175	FALSESTATE
MALICIOUS MISCHIEF 2 ATTEMPT	D	9A48080	MALMIS2
MALICIOUS MISCHIEF 2 CONSPIRACY	D	9A48080	MALMIS2
MALICIOUS MISCHIEF 2 SOLICITATION	D	9A48080	MALMIS2
MALICIOUS MISCHIEF 3	D	9A48090	MALMIS3
OBSTRUCTING A PUBLIC SERVANT	D	9A76020	OBSPUBSERV
OBSTRUCTING LAW ENFORCEMENT OFFICER	D	9A76020	OBSLAWOFF

OFFENSE TITLE	CATEGORY	RCW	JRA CODE
OBTAIN LEGEND DRUG ATTEMPT	D	6941020	OBTLEGDRUG
OBTAIN LEGEND DRUG CONSPIRACY	D	6941020	OBTLEGDRUG
OBTAIN LEGEND DRUG SOLICITATION	D	6941020	OBTLEGDRUG
ORGANIZED RETAIL THEFT 2 ATTEMPTED	D	9A56350	THEFT2ORG
ORGANIZED RETAIL THEFT 2 CONSPIRACY	D	9A56350	THEFT2ORG
ORGANIZED RETAIL THEFT 2 SOLICITATION	D	9A56350	THEFT2ORG
OTHER C OFFENSE ATTEMPT	D	1340357	OTHERCOFF
OTHER C OFFENSE CONSPIRACY	D	1340357	OTHERCOFF
OTHER C OFFENSE SOLICITATION	D	1340357	OTHERCOFF
OTHER OFFENSE EQUIVALENT TO ADULT GROSS MISDEMEANOR	D	1340357	OTHERDOFF
POSSESSION OF DANGEROUS WEAPON AT SCHOOL	D	941280	POSDANGWAS
POSSESSION OF DEPICTIONS OF MINOR ENGAGED IN SEXUALLY EXPLICIT CONDUCT ATTEMPT	D	968A070	POSCHPORN2
POSSESSION OF DEPICTIONS OF MINOR ENGAGED IN SEXUALLY EXPLICIT CONDUCT CONSPIRACY	D	968A070	POSCHPORN2
POSSESSION OF DEPICTIONS OF MINOR ENGAGED IN SEXUALLY EXPLICIT CONDUCT SOLICITATION	D	968A070	POSCHPORN2
POSSESSION OF MACHINE GUN OR SHORT-BARRELED SHOTGUN OR RIFLE ATTEMPT	D	941190	POSMACHGUN
POSSESSION OF MACHINE GUN OR SHORT-BARRELED SHOTGUN OR RIFLE CONSPIRACY	D	941190	POSMACHGUN
POSSESSION OF MACHINE GUN OR SHORT-BARRELED SHOTGUN OR RIFLE SOLICITATION	D	941190	POSMACHGUN
POSSESSION OF STOLEN PROPERTY 2 ATTEMPT	D	9A56160	PSP2
POSSESSION OF STOLEN PROPERTY 2 CONSPIRACY	D	9A56160	PSP2
POSSESSION OF STOLEN PROPERTY 2 SOLICITATION	D	9A56160	PSP2
POSSESSION OF STOLEN PROPERTY 3	D	9A56170	PSP3
POSSESSION OF WEAPONS BY PRISONER COUNTY FACILITY ATTEMPTED	D	994040	POSWEAPON
POSSESSION OF WEAPONS BY PRISONER COUNTY FACILITY CONSPIRACY	D	994040	POSWEAPON
POSSESSION OF WEAPONS BY PRISONER COUNTY FACILITY SOLICITATION	D	994040	POSWEAPON
RAPE OF A CHILD 3 ATTEMPT	D	9A44079	RAPECHILD3
RAPE OF A CHILD 3 CONSPIRACY	D	9A44079	RAPECHILD3
RAPE OF A CHILD 3 SOLICITATION	D	9A44079	RAPECHILD3
RECKLESS BURNING 1 ATTEMPT	D	9A48040	RECKBURN1
RECKLESS BURNING 1 CONSPIRACY	D	9A48040	RECKBURN1
RECKLESS BURNING 1 SOLICITATION	D	9A48040	RECKBURN1
RECKLESS BURNING 2	D	9A48050	RECKBURN2
REFUSING TO LEAVE PUBLIC PROPERTY	D	28A6350	REFLEAVE
RETAIL THEFT WITH EXTENUATING CIRCUMSTANCES 2 ATTEMPTED	D	9A56360	THEFT2RET
RETAIL THEFT WITH EXTENUATING CIRCUMSTANCES 2 CONSPIRACY	D	9A56360	THEFT2RET

OFFENSE TITLE	CATEGORY	RCW	JRA CODE
RETAIL THEFT WITH EXTENUATING CIRCUMSTANCES 2 SOLICITATION	D	9A56360	THEFT2RET
RETAIL THEFT WITH EXTENUATING CIRCUMSTANCES 3 ATTEMPTED	D	9A56360	THEFT3RET
RETAIL THEFT WITH EXTENUATING CIRCUMSTANCES 3 CONSPIRACY	D	9A56360	THEFT3RET
RETAIL THEFT WITH EXTENUATING CIRCUMSTANCES 3 SOLICITATION	D	9A56360	THEFT3RET
SENDING, BRINGING INTO STATE DEPICTIONS OF MINOR ENGAGED IN SEXUALLY EXPLICIT CONDUCT 2 ATTEMPT	D	968A060	SBCHPORN2
SENDING, BRINGING INTO STATE DEPICTIONS OF MINOR ENGAGED IN SEXUALLY EXPLICIT CONDUCT 2 CONSPIRACY	D	968A060	SBCHPORN2
SENDING, BRINGING INTO STATE DEPICTIONS OF MINOR ENGAGED IN SEXUALLY EXPLICIT CONDUCT 2 SOLICITATION	D	968A060	SBCHPORN2
SEXUAL VIOLATION OF HUMAN REMAINS ATTEMPT	D	9A44105	SEXVIOLREM
SEXUAL VIOLATION OF HUMAN REMAINS CONSPIRACY	D	9A44105	SEXVIOLREM
SEXUAL VIOLATION OF HUMAN REMAINS SOLICITATION	D	9A44105	SEXVIOLREM
STALKING (1 TIME)	D	9A46110	STALK
STALKING (REPEAT) ATTEMPT	D	9A46111	STALKREP
STALKING (REPEAT) CONSPIRACY	D	9A46111	STALKREP
STALKING (REPEAT) SOLICITATION	D	9A46111	STALKREP
TAKING MOTOR VEHICLE WITHOUT PERMISSION 2 ATTEMPT	D	9A56070	TAMVWOOP2
TAKING MOTOR VEHICLE WITHOUT PERMISSION 2 CONSPIRACY	D	9A56070	TAMVWOOP2
TAKING MOTOR VEHICLE WITHOUT PERMISSION 2 SOLICITATION	D	9A56070	TAMVWOOP2
TAMPERING WITH A WITNESS ATTEMPT	D	9A72120	TAMPWITN
TAMPERING WITH A WITNESS CONSPIRACY	D	9A72120	TAMPWITN
TAMPERING WITH A WITNESS SOLICITATION	D	9A72120	TAMPWITN
TAMPERING WITH PHYSICAL EVIDENCE	D	9A72150	TAMPEVID
TAMPERING WITH PHYSICAL EVIDENCE ATTEMPT	D	9A72150	TAMPEVID
TAMPERING WITH PHYSICAL EVIDENCE CONSPIRACY	D	9A72150	TAMPEVID
TAMPERING WITH PHYSICAL EVIDENCE SOCLICITATION	D	9A72150	TAMPEVID
THEFT 2 ATTEMPT	D	9A56040	THEFT2
THEFT 2 CONSPIRACY	D	9A56040	THEFT2
THEFT 2 SOLICITATION	D	9A56040	THEFT2
THEFT 3	D	9A56050	THEFT3
TRAFFICKING IN STOLEN PROPERTY 2 DEGREE ATTEMPT	D	9A82055	TRAFSTPRO2
TRAFFICKING IN STOLEN PROPERTY 2 DEGREE CONSPIRACY	D	9A82055	TRAFSTPRO2

OFFENSE TITLE	CATEGORY	RCW	JRA CODE
TRAFFICKING IN STOLEN PROPERTY 2 DEGREE SOLICITATION	D	9A82055	TRAFSTPRO2
UNLAWFUL POSSESSION OF FIREARM 2 ATTEMPT	D	941042	PFIREARM2
UNLAWFUL POSSESSION OF FIREARM 2 CONSPIRACY	D	941042	PFIREARM2
UNLAWFUL POSSESSION OF FIREARM 2 SOLICITATION	D	941042	PFIREARM2
UNLAWFUL POSSESSION, PRODUCTION OF INSTRUMENT OF FINANCIAL FRAUD	D	9A56320	FRAUDFIN
UNLAWFUL POSSESSION, PRODUCTION OF INSTRUMENT OF FINANCIAL FRAUD	D	9A56320	FRAUDFIN
UNLAWFUL POSSESSION, PRODUCTION OF INSTRUMENT OF FINANCIAL FRAUD	D	9A56320	FRAUDFIN
VEHICLE PROWLING 1 ATTEMPT	D	9A52095	VEHPROWL1
VEHICLE PROWLING 1 CONSPIRACY	D	9A52095	VEHPROWL1
VEHICLE PROWLING 1 SOLICITATION	D	9A52095	VEHPROWL1
VEHICLE PROWLING 2	D	9A52100	VEHPROWL2
VEHICULAR ASSAULT ATTEMPT	D	4661522	VEHASSAULT
VEHICULAR ASSAULT CONSPIRACY	D	4661522	VEHASSAULT
VEHICULAR ASSAULT SOLICITATION	D	4661522	VEHASSAULT
VIEWING DEPICTIONS OF MINOR ENGAGED IN SEXUALLY EXPLICIT CONDUCT 2 ATTEMPTED	D	968A075	VIEWCHPRN2
VIEWING DEPICTIONS OF MINOR ENGAGED IN SEXUALLY EXPLICIT CONDUCT 2 CONSIRACY	D	968A075	VIEWCHPRN2
VIEWING DEPICTIONS OF MINOR ENGAGED IN SEXUALLY EXPLICIT CONDUCT 2 SOLICITATION	D	968A075	VIEWCHPRN2
VIOLATION OF UNIFORM CONTROLLED SUBSTANCES ACT POSS WITH INTENT TO DELIVER MARIJUANA or OTHER NONNARCOTIC Sch I, II, III	D	6950401	POSINTDNON
VIOLATION OF UNIFORM CONTROLLED SUBSTANCES ACT POSS WITH INTENT TO DELIVER MARIJUANA or OTHER NONNARCOTIC Sch I, II, III	D	6950401	POSINTDNON
VIOLATION OF UNIFORM CONTROLLED SUBSTANCES ACT POSS WITH INTENT TO DELIVER MARIJUANA or OTHER NONNARCOTIC Sch I, II, III	D	6950401	POSINTDNON
VIOLATION OF UNIFORM CONTROLLED SUBSTANCES ACT--NONNARCOTIC COUNTERFEIT SUBSTANCE ATTEMPT	D	695040D	COUNTNNARC
VIOLATION OF UNIFORM CONTROLLED SUBSTANCES ACT--NONNARCOTIC COUNTERFEIT SUBSTANCE CONSPIRACY	D	695040D	COUNTNNARC
VIOLATION OF UNIFORM CONTROLLED SUBSTANCES ACT--NONNARCOTIC COUNTERFEIT SUBSTANCE SOLICITATION	D	695040D	COUNTNNARC
VOYEURISM ATTEMPT	D	9A44115	VOYEURISM
VOYEURISM CONSPIRACY	D	9A44115	VOYEURISM
VOYEURISM SOLICTATION	D	9A44115	VOYEURISM

OFFENSE TITLE	CATEGORY	RCW	JRA CODE
WEAPONS APPARENTLY CAPABLE OF PRODUCING BODILY HARM	D	941270	WEAPONCBH
CATEGORY E			
AIMING OR DISCHARGING FIREARMS, DANGEROUS WEAPONS ATTEMPTED	E	941230	DANWEAPAD
AIMING OR DISCHARGING FIREARMS, DANGEROUS WEAPONS CONSPIRACY	E	941230	DANWEAPAD
AIMING OR DISCHARGING FIREARMS, DANGEROUS WEAPONS SOLICITATION	E	941230	DANWEAPAD
ALTERATION OF IDENTIFYING MARKS ON FIREARM	E	941140	FIRARMALT
ALTERATION OF IDENTIFYING MARKS ON FIREARM ATTEMPTED	E	941140	FIRARMALT
ALTERATION OF IDENTIFYING MARKS ON FIREARM CONSPIRACY	E	941140	FIRARMALT
ALTERATION OF IDENTIFYING MARKS ON FIREARM SOLICITATION	E	941140	FIRARMALT
ANIMAL CRUELTY 2	E	1652207	ANIMCRUEL2
ASSAULT 4 ATTEMPT	E	9A36041	ASSAULT4
ASSAULT 4 CONSPIRACY	E	9A36041	ASSAULT4
ASSAULT 4 SOLICITATION	E	9A36041	ASSAULT4
AUTO THEFT TOOLS (MAKING OR POSSESSING) ATTEMPTED	E	9A56063	AUTOTOOLS
AUTO THEFT TOOLS (MAKING OR POSSESSING) CONSPIRACY	E	9A56063	AUTOTOOLS
AUTO THEFT TOOLS (MAKING OR POSSESSING) SOLICITATION	E	9A56063	AUTOTOOLS
BURG TOOLS (POSSESSION OF) ATTEMPT	E	9A52060	BURGTOOLS
BURG TOOLS (POSSESSION OF) CONSPIRACY	E	9A52060	BURGTOOLS
BURG TOOLS (POSSESSION OF) SOLICITIATION	E	9A52060	BURGTOOLS
CARRY WEAPON TO SCHOOL ATTEMPT	E	941280	CARWEAPSCH
CARRY WEAPON TO SCHOOL CONSPIRACY	E	941280	CARWEAPSCH
CARRY WEAPON TO SCHOOL SOLICITATION	E	941280	CARWEAPSCH
COERCION ATTEMPT	E	9A36070	COERCION
COERCION CONSPIRACY	E	9A36070	COERCION
COERCION SOLICITATION	E	9A36070	COERCION
COMMUNICATING WITH A MINOR FOR IMMORAL PURPOSE ATTEMPT	E	968A090	COMMINOR
COMMUNICATING WITH A MINOR FOR IMMORAL PURPOSE CONSPIRACY	E	968A090	COMMINOR
COMMUNICATING WITH A MINOR FOR IMMORAL PURPOSE SOLICITATION	E	968A090	COMMINOR
CRIMINAL IMPERSONATION 2 ATTEMPT	E	9A60045	IMPERSON2
CRIMINAL IMPERSONATION 2 CONSPIRACY	E	9A60045	IMPERSON2
CRIMINAL IMPERSONATION 2 SOLICITATION	E	9A60045	IMPERSON2
CRIMINAL TRESPASS 1 ATTEMPT	E	9A52070	CRIMTRES1
CRIMINAL TRESPASS 1 CONSPIRACY	E	9A52070	CRIMTRES1
CRIMINAL TRESPASS 1 SOLICITATION	E	9A52070	CRIMTRES1

The Caseload Forecast Council is not liable for errors or omissions in the manual, for sentences that may be inappropriately calculated as a result of a practitioner's or court's reliance on the manual, or for any other written or verbal information related to adult or juvenile sentencing. The scoring sheets are intended to provide assistance in most cases but does not cover all permutations of the scoring rules. If you find any errors or omissions, we encourage you to report them to the Caseload Forecast Council.

OFFENSE TITLE	CATEGORY	RCW	JRA CODE
CRIMINAL TRESPASS 2	E	9A52080	CRIMTRES2
CRIMINAL TRESPASS 2 ATTEMPT	E	9A52080	CRIMTRES2
CRIMINAL TRESPASS 2 CONSPIRACY	E	9A52080	CRIMTRES2
CRIMINAL TRESPASS 2 SOLICITATION	E	9A52080	CRIMTRES2
CYBERSTALKING ATTEMPTED	E	961260	CYBSTALK
CYBERSTALKING CONSPIRACY	E	961260	CYBSTALK
CYBERSTALKING SOLICITATION	E	961260	CYBSTALK
DISORDERLY CONDUCT	E	9A84030	DISCONDUCT
DISORDERLY CONDUCT ATTEMPT	E	9A84030	DISCONDUCT
DISORDERLY CONDUCT CONSPIRACY	E	9A84030	DISCONDUCT
DISORDERLY CONDUCT SOLICITATION	E	9A84030	DISCONDUCT
DISTURBING SCHOOL, SCHOOL ACTIVITIES OR MEETINGS	E	28A6350	DISTRBSCHL
DRIVER UNDER TWENTY-ONE CONSUMING ALCOHOL OR MARIJUANA	E	4661503	DUI_U21
DRIVER UNDER TWENTY-ONE CONSUMING ALCOHOL OR MARIJUANA ATTEMPTED	E	4661503	DUI_U21
DRIVER UNDER TWENTY-ONE CONSUMING ALCOHOL OR MARIJUANA CONSPIRACY	E	4661503	DUI_U21
DRIVER UNDER TWENTY-ONE CONSUMING ALCOHOL OR MARIJUANA SOLICITATION	E	4661503	DUI_U21
DRIVING UNDER INFLUENCE ATTEMPT	E	4661515	DUI
DRIVING UNDER INFLUENCE CONSPIRACY	E	4661515	DUI
DRIVING UNDER INFLUENCE SOLICITATION	E	4661515	DUI
DRIVING WITHOUT A LICENSE	E	4620021	DWOL
DRUG PARAPHERNALIA	E	6950412	DRUGPARA
DRVING WHILE LICENSE INVALIDATED 3	E	4620342	DWIL3
DUTY ON STRIKING UNATTENDED CAR OR OTHER PROPERTY	E	4652010	DUTYUNVEH
DUTY ON STRIKING UNATTENDED CAR OR OTHER PROPERTY ATTEMPT	E	4652010	DUTYUNVEH
DUTY ON STRIKING UNATTENDED CAR OR OTHER PROPERTY CONSPIRACY	E	4652010	DUTYUNVEH
DUTY ON STRIKING UNATTENDED CAR OR OTHER PROPERTY SOLICITATION	E	4652010	DUTYUNVEH
DUTY TO ATTENDED VEHICLE OR OTHER PROPERTY IN CASE OF STRIKING BODY OF DECEASED ATTEMPT	E	4652020	DUTYBODY
DUTY TO ATTENDED VEHICLE OR OTHER PROPERTY IN CASE OF STRIKING BODY OF DECEASED CONSPIRACY	E	4652020	DUTYBODY
DUTY TO ATTENDED VEHICLE OR OTHER PROPERTY IN CASE OF STRIKING BODY OF DECEASED SOLICITATION	E	4652020	DUTYBODY
ESCAPE 3 ATTEMPT	E	9A76130	ESCAPE3
ESCAPE 3 CONSPIRACY	E	9A76130	ESCAPE3
ESCAPE 3 SOLICITATION	E	9A76130	ESCAPE3
EXHIBITING EFFECTS/POSSESSION/CONSUMPTION OF ALCOHOL	E	6644270	POSCONSALC

The Caseload Forecast Council is not liable for errors or omissions in the manual, for sentences that may be inappropriately calculated as a result of a practitioner's or court's reliance on the manual, or for any other written or verbal information related to adult or juvenile sentencing. The scoring sheets are intended to provide assistance in most cases but does not cover all permutations of the scoring rules. If you find any errors or omissions, we encourage you to report them to the Caseload Forecast Council.

OFFENSE TITLE	CATEGORY	RCW	JRA CODE
FAILURE TO DISPERSE	E	9A84020	FAILDISP
FALSE REPORTING ATTEMPT	E	9A84040	FALSEREP
FALSE REPORTING CONSPIRACY	E	9A84040	FALSEREP
FALSE REPORTING SOLICITATION	E	9A84040	FALSEREP
HARASSMENT ATTEMPTED	E	9A46020	HARASSD
HARASSMENT CONSPIRACY	E	9A46020	HARASSD
HARASSMENT SOLICITATION	E	9A46020	HARASSD
HIT-RUN ATTENDED ATTEMPT	E	4652022	HITRUNAT
HIT-RUN ATTENDED CONSPIRACY	E	4652022	HITRUNAT
HIT-RUN ATTENDED SOLICITATION	E	4652022	HITRUNAT
HIT-RUN UNATTENDED	E	4652010	HITRUNUN
IDENTITY THEFT 2 ATTEMPT	E	9350200	IDENTITY2
IDENTITY THEFT 2 CONSPIRACY	E	9350200	IDENTITY2
IDENTITY THEFT 2 SOLICITATION	E	9350200	IDENTITY2
INDECENT EXPOSURE (VICTIM <14) ATTEMPT	E	9A8801C	INDEXP<14
INDECENT EXPOSURE (VICTIM <14) CONSPIRACY	E	9A8801C	INDEXP<14
INDECENT EXPOSURE (VICTIM <14) SOLICITATION	E	9A8801C	INDEXP<14
INDECENT EXPOSURE (VICTIM 14+)	E	9A8810A	INDEXP14+
INTERFERING WITH THE REPORTING OF DOMESTIC VIOLENCE ATTEMPTED	E	9A36150	DVREPINTER
INTERFERING WITH THE REPORTING OF DOMESTIC VIOLENCE CONSPIRACY	E	9A36150	DVREPINTER
INTERFERING WITH THE REPORTING OF DOMESTIC VIOLENCE SOLICITATION	E	9A36150	DVREPINTER
INTIMIDATING ANOTHER PERSON BY USE OF A WEAPON ATTEMPT	E	941270	INTWWEAPON
INTIMIDATING ANOTHER PERSON BY USE OF A WEAPON CONSPIRACY	E	941270	INTWWEAPON
INTIMIDATING ANOTHER PERSON BY USE OF A WEAPON SOLICITATION	E	941270	INTWWEAPON
INTRODUCING CONTRABAND 3	E	9A76160	INTCONT3
MAKING FALSE OR MISLEADING STATEMENT TO A PUBLIC SERVANT ATTEMPTED	E	9A76175	FALSESTATE
MAKING FALSE OR MISLEADING STATEMENT TO A PUBLIC SERVANT CONSPIRACY	E	9A76175	FALSESTATE
MAKING FALSE OR MISLEADING STATEMENT TO A PUBLIC SERVANT SOLICITATION	E	9A76175	FALSESTATE
MALICIOUS MISCHIEF 3 (<$50)	E	9A4809A	MALMIS3<50
MALICIOUS MISCHIEF 3 ATTEMPT	E	9A48090	MALMIS3
MALICIOUS MISCHIEF 3 CONSPIRACY	E	9A48090	MALMIS3
MALICIOUS MISCHIEF 3 SOLICITATION	E	9A48090	MALMIS3
OBSCENE PHONE CALLS	E	961230	OBSCENEPC
OBSTRUCTING A PUBLIC SERVANT ATTEMPT	E	9A76020	OBSPUBSERV
OBSTRUCTING A PUBLIC SERVANT CONSPIRACY	E	9A76020	OBSPUBSERV
OBSTRUCTING A PUBLIC SERVANT SOLICITATION	E	9A76020	OBSPUBSERV
OBSTRUCTING LAW ENFORCEMENT OFFICER ATTEMPT	E	9A76020	OBSLAWOFF

OFFENSE TITLE	CATEGORY	RCW	JRA CODE
OBSTRUCTING LAW ENFORCEMENT OFFICER CONSPIRACY	E	9A76020	OBSLAWOFF
OBSTRUCTING LAW ENFORCEMENT OFFICER SOLICITATION	E	9A76020	OBSLAWOFF
OFFERING AND AGREEING (PROSTITUTION)	E	9A88030	O&APROST
OTHER D+OFFENSE	E	1340357	OTHERD+OFF
OTHER D+OFFENSE	E	1340357	OTHERD+OFF
OTHER D+OFFENSE	E	1340357	OTHERD+OFF
OTHER OFFENSE EQUIVALENT TO ADULT GROSS MISDEMEANOR ATTEMPT	E	1340357	OTHERDOFF
OTHER OFFENSE EQUIVALENT TO ADULT GROSS MISDEMEANOR CONSPIRACY	E	1340357	OTHERDOFF
OTHER OFFENSE EQUIVALENT TO ADULT GROSS MISDEMEANOR SOLICITATION	E	1340357	OTHERDOFF
OTHER OFFENSE EQUIVALENT TO ADULT MISDEMEANOR	E	1340357	OTHEREOFF
PATRONIZING A PROSTITUTE	E	9A88110	PATPROSTI
PATRONIZING A PROSTITUTE ATTEMPTED	E	9A88110	PATPROSTI
PATRONIZING A PROSTITUTE CONSPIRACY	E	9A88110	PATPROSTI
PATRONIZING A PROSTITUTE SOLICITATION	E	9A88110	PATPROSTI
POSSESSION OF DANGEROUS WEAPON AT SCHOOL ATTEMPT	E	941280	POSDANGWAS
POSSESSION OF DANGEROUS WEAPON AT SCHOOL CONSPIRACY	E	941280	POSDANGWAS
POSSESSION OF DANGEROUS WEAPON AT SCHOOL SOLICITATION	E	941280	POSDANGWAS
POSSESSION OF DANGEROUS WEAPON ATTEMPT	E	941250	POSDANGW
POSSESSION OF DANGEROUS WEAPON CONSPIRACY	E	941250	POSDANGW
POSSESSION OF DANGEROUS WEAPON SOLICITATION	E	941250	POSDANGW
POSSESSION OF ILLEGAL FWRKS	E	7077255	POSILLFWKS
POSSESSION OF LEGEND DRUG	E	694103B	POSLEGDRUG
POSSESSION OF MARIJUANA <40 GRAMS	E	695040J	POSPOT<40
POSSESSION OF STOLEN PROPERTY 3 ATTEMPT	E	9A56170	PSP3
POSSESSION OF STOLEN PROPERTY 3 CONSPIRACY	E	9A56170	PSP3
POSSESSION OF STOLEN PROPERTY 3 SOLICITATION	E	9A56170	PSP3
RECKLESS BURNING 2 ATTEMPT	E	9A48050	RECKBURN2
RECKLESS BURNING 2 CONSPIRACY	E	9A48050	RECKBURN2
RECKLESS BURNING 2 SOLICITATION	E	9A48050	RECKBURN2
RECKLESS DRIVING	E	4661500	RECKDRIV
RECKLESS ENDANGER ATTEMPT	E	9A36050	RECKEND
RECKLESS ENDANGER CONSPIRACY	E	9A36050	RECKEND
RECKLESS ENDANGER SOLICITATION	E	9A36050	RECKEND
RENDERING CRIMINAL ASSISTANCE 2 ATTEMPT	E	9A76080	RENDCRIM2
RENDERING CRIMINAL ASSISTANCE 2 CONSPIRACY	E	9A76080	RENDCRIM2
RENDERING CRIMINAL ASSISTANCE 2 SOLICITATION	E	9A76080	RENDCRIM2
RESISTING ARREST	E	9A76040	RESARREST
RIOT WITHOUT WEAPON ATTEMPT	E	9A8401U	RIOTWOWEAP

The Caseload Forecast Council is not liable for errors or omissions in the manual, for sentences that may be inappropriately calculated as a result of a practitioner's or court's reliance on the manual, or for any other written or verbal information related to adult or juvenile sentencing. The scoring sheets are intended to provide assistance in most cases but does not cover all permutations of the scoring rules. If you find any errors or omissions, we encourage you to report them to the Caseload Forecast Council.

OFFENSE TITLE	CATEGORY	RCW	JRA CODE
RIOT WITHOUT WEAPON CONSPIRACY	E	9A8401U	RIOTWOWEAP
RIOT WITHOUT WEAPON SOLICITATION	E	9A8401U	RIOTWOWEAP
STALKING (1 TIME) ATTEMPT	E	9A46110	STALK
STALKING (1 TIME) CONSPIRACY	E	9A46110	STALK
STALKING (1 TIME) SOLICITATION	E	9A46110	STALK
TAMPERING WITH FIRE ALARM APPARATUS	E	940100	TAMPFIREAL
THEFT 3 ATTEMPT	E	9A56050	THEFT3
THEFT 3 CONSPIRACY	E	9A56050	THEFT3
THEFT 3 SOLICITATION	E	9A56050	THEFT3
UNLAWFUL INHALATION	E	947A020	UNLAWINHAL
VEHICLE PROWLING 2 ATTEMPT	E	9A52100	VEHPROWL2
VEHICLE PROWLING 2 CONSPIRACY	E	9A52100	VEHPROWL2
VEHICLE PROWLING 2 SOLICITATION	E	9A52100	VEHPROWL2
WEAPON WITHOUT A PERMIT	E	941050	WEAPONWOP
WEAPONS APPARENTLY CAPABLE OF PRODUCING BODILY HARM ATTEMPTED	E	941270	WEAPONCBH
WEAPONS APPARENTLY CAPABLE OF PRODUCING BODILY HARM CONSPIRACY	E	941270	WEAPONCBH
WEAPONS APPARENTLY CAPABLE OF PRODUCING BODILY HARM SOLICITATION	E	941270	WEAPONCBH
CATEGORY UNKNOWN			
DIAGNOSTIC ONLY	UK	9973	DIAGNOSTIC
SENTENCE RESCINDED	UK	9975	SENRESCIND
UNKNOWN OFFENSE	UK	9999998	UNKNOWNOFF
CATEGORY V			
GAME, TRAFFIC, TOBACCO AND OTHER VIOLATIONS	V	9972	VIOLATION
MULTIPLE DETENTION	V	9990000	MULTDET
SEX OFFENDER PAROLE REVOKE	V	9976	SOPARREV
VIOLATION OF COURT ORDER	V	9980	VIOLCO
VIOLATION OF SSODA ORDER	V	9979	VIOLSSODA
CATEGORY X			
SENTENCE REVERSED AND REMANDED	X	NULL	SENTREVERS